PAKISTAN'S BLASPHEMY LAWS

PAKISTAN'S BLASPHEMY LAWS

From Islamic Empires to the Taliban

BY SHEMEEM BURNEY ABBAS

UNIVERSITY OF TEXAS PRESS ◄►► *Austin*

First edition, 2013

Requests for permission to reproduce material from this work should be sent to:
Permissions
University of Texas Press
P.O. Box 7819
Austin, TX 78713-7819
utpress.utexas.edu/index.php/rp-form

⊗ The paper used in this book meets the minimum requirements of ANSI/NISO
Z39.48-1992 (R1997) (Permanence of Paper).

LIBRARY OF CONGRESS CATALOGING-IN-PUBLICATION DATA

Abbas, Shemeem Burney.
    Pakistan's blasphemy laws : from Islamic empires to the Taliban /
by Shemeem Burney Abbas. — First edition.
        p.   cm.
    Includes bibliographical references and index.
    ISBN 978-0-292-76212-1
    1. Blasphemy—Pakistan.   2. Blasphemy (Islam)   I. Title.
    KPL4172.A923   2013
    345.5491′0288—dc23   2012044362

doi:10.7560/745308

First paperback edition, 2014

CONTENTS

In the name of God, the Merciful.

Paradise is only at a place where no mulla lives,
Where no uproar and clamor from a mulla is heard.
May the world rid itself of the terror of a mulla,
May no one pay heed to his fatwas.
In a city where a mulla dwells,
No wise man is ever found.

DIWAN-E DARA SHIKOH

Dara Shikoh, a great Sufi mystic and intellectual (1615–1659), executed by his brother Aurengzeb for heresy in trying to create an interfaith dialogue with the Hindus.

I AM A WOMAN SCHOLAR OF SUFISM who was charged with blasphemy by state functionaries at a federal university in the capital of Islamabad in 1998 during the Nawaz Sharif government. This was six years after my return with a doctorate from the University of Texas at Austin.[1] My PhD dissertation was on "Speech Play and Verbal Art in the Indo-Pakistani Oral Sufi Tradition," an area toward which the faculty of clerics in my university were extremely hostile. The Sufis and clerics have never been friends, as much of Sufi poetry ridicules the clerics, the *sheikhs*, and the *mullas*. As a full professor and chair of the Department of English Language and Applied Linguistics at the Allama Iqbal Open University, I was accused of using "frequent, 'blasphemous' and derogatory remarks against Islam, the Holy Quran and the Prophet Muhammad (PBUH [peace be upon him])." A female junior faculty member in the department initiated the charge. A male junior colleague, an adjunct political appointee who was on contract and who could not get an appointment through the regular selection board, further backed the accusation. He corroborated that "Dr. Shemeem Abbas said, 'The Quran is an outdated book and should be put on the cupboard.'" For me, the female perpetrator recommended a fate like that of Salman Rushdie.

The accusation was encouraged by the vice chancellor whom the faculty of clerics had brought to the Allama Iqbal Open University from the International Islamic University in Islamabad. The clerics around the vice chancellor colluded in the charge, especially among them the dean of my faculty of humanities, who had a PhD in Islamic studies from a *madrassa* (religious seminary) in Lahore, the Jamia Ashrafia.[2] Many others like him had reached key positions within the university, such as deans of faculty and heads of departments, during General Muhammad Zia-ul-Haq's regime. These were individuals whose degrees were given "equivalence" through the rubber-stamping processes at the University Grants Commission in Islamabad in the 1980s at the height of Pakistan's "Islamization."[3] The late Dr. Muhammad Afzal, a close relative of General Zia-ul-Haq, in that period was the chairman of the University Grants Commission as well as the federal minister for education. Although a liberal intellectual with a graduate degree from the United States, he did uphold the rubber-stamping of the "mullaization" of the Pakistani academy. Consequently, the madrassa diplomas of the clerics were upgraded to doctorates; they were made scholars of Islam, or *'ulema*, to validate the Islamization of education in the region under General Zia-ul-Haq.

My instant action on being falsely charged with blasphemy was to seek an interview with the military secretary to the president of Pakistan, as the president is the chancellor of all the universities in the country. At that time it was Mr. Rafiq Tarar. Since I was a military war widow of the 1965 war with India, I got the interview immediately over the telephone with the military secretary, who asked me to also petition the president. I personally delivered my petition at the presidency, where the military personnel on the staff treated me with the utmost respect.

A few days before I went to meet with the president, I met with the chief justice of the High Court of Panjab Province, who was a family friend. The chief justice cautioned me not to mention anything about my work in Sufism to the president, Rafiq Tarar, as he was an *ahl-e hadith*, in other words, of the sect whose members practice conservative, orthodox Islam based largely on a textual reading of the Qur'an and *hadith* (sayings of the Prophet and his Companions).[4] The ahl-e hadith do not approve of the Sufis. However, with my petition as an army war widow whose husband had gone missing in a commando mission called Operation Gibraltar in 1965 in Srinagar (Indian-held Kashmir), the state had to take action. The state had to uphold the *jihad* rhetoric. The Qur'an promises unlimited rewards in paradise to those who die in jihad.

While I petitioned the president of Pakistan regarding the blasphemy accusation, I also responded to the charge through my immediate supervisor, a seminary cleric. In my response I said, "The procedure adopted in the instant case is unheard of under the E & D [Efficiency and Discipline] Rules. However, the counter allegations raised can be pleaded by Ms. X in defense during the inquiry."[5] I further affirmed in the response, "The charge of blasphemy is a serious matter. It is a cognizable offence. Ms. X may be advised to get an FIR [first investigation report] registered so that on the failure of the charge, its pushers and collaborators could be made answerable under the *qizaf* [slander or defamation] law and Section 211 of the Pakistan Penal Code (S211 of PPC)."

I copied my defense to the university's registrar and vice chancellor. Furthermore, I copied it to the university chancellor, who was President Tarar. In the defense I asserted, "For my own protection, I am forwarding a copy of this letter to the Chancellor, Allama Iqbal Open University." Consequently, the vice chancellor was summoned to the presidency and was told to apologize to me; other women faculty too were facing harassment in different ways, and thus with the plethora of complaints, the immediate directive to the vice chancellor was to put the house in order.[6] At the presidency, the matter was not just left at that. Within six months the president himself, his military secretary of the rank of brigadier general, the federal minister for education Syed Ghaus ʿAli Shah, and the entire ministry of education visited the university to verify the complaints and to correct the situation of the adverse soap-opera publicity that the university was getting in the tabloid Urdu press.

And although I was civil and dignified during the president's inspection, in order to preserve my integrity I eventually found a way to leave the university, where I knew I had no security. With my own limited funds I relocated to my alma mater, the University of Texas at Austin, in 1999 and wrote the manuscript of my first book, *The Female Voice in Sufi Ritual: Devotional Practices of Pakistan and India*, which the University of Texas Press published in 2002. I had some additional support from the United States Educational Foundation for a Fulbright travel grant. Furthermore, the American Institute for Pakistan Studies sponsored me for a lecture series in American universities.

However, after writing the book I went back to Pakistan, as I was on a sabbatical in Austin and had to report to my home-country university. Within a few months I returned to the University of Texas with admission into the creative writing program, and later I became a visiting faculty member. The tragedy of the Twin Towers in 2001 made it difficult for me to return to Pakistan. I applied for immigrant status to rebuild my life in the United States, where I am now on the faculty of the State University of New York at Purchase College. I had the support of the Scholars at Risk and the Institute of Education in New York in identifying this position, which made it possible for me to write this manuscript. I must make clear that while I create the contexts for Pakistan's blasphemy laws through my background as an educator, my arguments in this book are within the established frames of Islam. My credentials for engaging in such a discourse are that I am a practicing Muslim woman, a Hanafi Sunni adherent of Islam. My scholarship is informed matrilineally from a lineage of Islamic jurisconsults, distinguished scholars of Islamic law and *shariʿa*, well documented in Kanhyalal's *Tarikh-e Lahore* (a history of the city of Lahore).[7]

My mother was a writer who was additionally versed in the Qur'an and the shariʿa. My mother's ancestors had been the Muftis, Islamic jurisconsults of Lahore city since the time of Qutubdin Aibak, the slave sultan who founded the Delhi Sultanate, 1150–1210.[8] The family's scholars issued *fatwas* (scholarly opinions) on legal matters, and among those still living, many have distinguished themselves as writers, intellectuals, professionals, and military men, including my late husband, who was a recipient of one of the Pakistani army's highest gallantry awards, the *sitare-e jurat* (star of gal-

xiv PAKISTAN'S BLASPHEMY LAWS

lantry). It was my mother, herself a Mufti, who taught me to use the rhetoric of the mullas against them, and hence this manuscript.

Hanafi Sunni Islam of the kind in which I was raised is tolerant and accepting of other sects within Islam as well as the surrounding religious domains, such as Hinduism, Sikhism, Buddhism, Judaism, and Christianity. In my family, Sufi practices were common, such as going to the shrines of holy men, especially the Sufi *auliya* (wise men). In the faith that I follow, intermarriage between Hanafi Sunnis and Shiʿa is common, all integrated within the practice of Hanafi Islam. Hanafi Muslims share spiritual, intellectual, and social domains with the Shiʿa. My own maternal and paternal families represent these practices, as do most Muslims in the region. I have lived in Sunni and Shiʿa communities, and my experience of both Sunni and Shiʿa Islam informs my scholarship.[9] Furthermore, my scholarship is informed through training in comparative religions in academies in Pakistan, Saudi Arabia, the United States, and the United Kingdom.

ACKNOWLEDGMENTS

MANY INDIVIDUALS AND INSTITUTIONS have supported this research: At SUNY/Purchase College I acknowledge Thomas Schwartz, Elizabeth Langland, Suzanne Kessler, Peter Schwab, Nina Straus, Karen Kramer, Elise Lemire, Christina Williams, Karima Robinson, Nancy Kane, the librarians, and my students.

Rob Quinn of the Scholars at Risk Network, and Alan Goodman and Sarah Wilcox in the Institute of International Education, Scholar Rescue Fund found me the position at SUNY/Purchase.

The University of Texas at Austin, my alma mater, supported me for six years until I rebuilt my life. I thank Ernest Kaulbach, Hannah Wojciehowski, John Ruszkiewicz, Sue Heinzelman, Kamran Agahie, John Bordie, Joel Sherzer, Jim Magnuson, and Jacqui Thomas. Deane Willis and her female colleagues at the International Office sponsored my citizenship. The Pakistani community in Austin gave valuable input.

This book is the outcome of several public lectures that I gave. In Canada, I thank Richard Day at Queen's University in Kingston for hosting me, and Centennial College in Toronto hosted me on invitation from Eva Aboagoye. In America, I thank Purchase College, Columbia University, New York University, the New School, Manhattanville College, Stanford University, Emery-Riddle Aeronautical University, George P. Schultz National Foreign Affairs Training Center (through Anjum Khilji), the University of Texas at Austin, Duke University, University of Chicago, and Rice University.

In Pakistan, I am grateful to Akmal Wasim for facilitating the fieldwork at the Human Rights Commission and Shirkatgah Resource Center, which provided primary resources. Akmal's own input on the Objectives' Resolution was paramount.

Presses and individuals who gave copyrights for the digital material in the book are gratefully acknowledged.

Cynthia Nelson and Carolyn Russ were tireless in editing the book with me. At the University of Texas Press, Jim Burr had faith in the book, which was followed through by the Press's editors, designers, and marketing specialists.

The anonymous reviewers' critique was valuable in guiding major revisions. I value the reviewers' time.

Arlen Nydam was my continuous support in Austin where I wrote the book. His work drawing maps for me and downloading Internet images was my only assistance in the early, lonely stages of the manuscript. Until the very end, Arlen put the complex manuscript together, ready for the press. Arlen and I are alumni of the University of Texas and we were colleagues in the computer writing labs.

Others whom I thank are Pakistani colleagues, Fawzia Afzal-Khan and Pervez Hoodhboy for writing the blurbs in dangerous times.

All omissions and errors are entirely mine.

PAKISTAN'S BLASPHEMY LAWS

CHAPTER I

PAKISTAN'S MILITARY STATE
AND CIVIL SOCIETY

It was religion that facilitated whatever enterprise the senate and the
great men of Rome designed to undertake. —NICCOLO MACHIAVELLI

THE TRAGEDY OF THE TWIN TOWERS gave birth to this monograph.
Many lives were lost and loved ones disappeared before I ventured to write
accounts of what had been happening in the world outside the United
States for almost two decades. In countries where the CIA funded merce-
nary armies, the agency also colluded with seminary mullas to allow citizens
to be held hostage to state laws that truant regimes upheld in the name of
Islam. Among such state laws are the blasphemy laws in Pakistan and Hudood ordinances, laws to control women that included reducing the worth
of a woman's testimony to one-half of a man's and, in the case of rape,
having to produce four adult male Muslim witnesses to testify on her be-
half before rape could be proved.[1] In the absence of these witnesses she was
charged with *zina* (fornication).[2] The punishment ranged anywhere from
public stoning or lashing to execution.[3] Blasphemy laws are not subject to
bail, and the sentence is outright execution. These laws make a mockery of
the Prophet Muhammad's Islam and are a violation of social justice. The
"Islami" (Islamist) parties' slogan "Nizam-e Mustafa" (Muhammad's Islam) during Zulfiqar 'Ali Bhutto's regime of the 1970s was a full-blown larceny of Muhammad's Islam. Now the laws are also used to declare non-
Muslims as *kafirs* (infidels) and thus deserving extermination. These laws
currently affect international security and global terrorism since they have
become a tool in the arsenal of an extensive militant ideology. In early 2011
the bodyguard of Salman Taseer, the governor of Panjab Province, shot Taseer to death when the latter attempted to have these laws repealed.[4]

It was during Zulfiqar 'Ali Bhutto's regime that, under pressure from the
Islami parties and some Arab states, the Ahmediyya community was declared
non-Muslim; that is, the Ahmediyyas were excommunicated from the fold

of Islam. This marked the beginning of draconian laws being instituted in Islam's name that General Zia-ul-Haq imposed upon the citizenry after he declared martial law and overthrew the democratically elected government of Zulfiqar 'Ali Bhutto in order to become president of Pakistan in 1977. Bhutto was later executed after an "extrajudicial" trial on charges of causing the death of a political opponent, Nawab Muhammad Ahmed Khan Kasuri.

In this monograph I aim to put into perspective the Prophet Muhammad's Islam and his life as a lawgiver in Medina, where he governed his small community of Muslim followers. Illegitimate regimes like those of General Zia-ul-Haq have abused Muhammad's Islam to seek power in the name of Islamic law, or shari'a. This book explores how Islamic states since Muhammad's death have used blasphemy laws against citizens, claiming their origins from Muhammad's shari'a. These laws, in most cases, are in total violation of Muhammad's vision of social justice, or his shari'a. In fact, Muhammad himself never advocated a shari'a. He ruled through common sense on a day-to-day basis, many times applying the customary code of the region, or through the revelations that he received through ritual meditation. The shari'a is a creation of the Islamic states that arose after Muhammad's death.

In this book I will examine the historical contexts of blasphemy starting with the life of the Prophet Muhammad. The biographical data of the Prophet's life will be explored to contextualize the situations that perpetrators of blasphemy laws cite in order to validate truant regimes, political institutions, or the so-called Islamic organizations. Perpetrators in modern times include the states of Pakistan, Afghanistan, Egypt, Saudi Arabia, and Bangladesh, together with their cronies, the "Islamic" political parties. The virus is widespread.

As I write this book about Pakistan's blasphemy laws, I revisit the past. I see my own place in the politics of the region in Pakistan and Afghanistan as well as the manner in which events played out from 1980 to the present. I connect my work to the tragedy of the Twin Towers, the London and Madrid blasts, and global terrorism as well as the innumerable suicide bombings in which thousands of innocent citizens in my own country lost their lives and millions like the Swat refugees became homeless in their own motherland, living their lives in the excruciating heat of Peshawar and Islamabad refugee camps. This was as recent as the summer of 2009. No province in the country was willing to accept them.

The analysis in this book is primarily directed at exposing the questionable motives and rationale behind Pakistan's blasphemy laws that were resurrected during General Zia-ul-Haq's regime (1977–1988). However, to put the evolution of *kufr* (blasphemy) law in context, this work explores some major Islamic empires that appropriated prophetic authority from Muhammad to govern their vast lands. For instance, the 'Abbasid Empire claimed descent through the Prophet's uncle 'Abbas. Writing and codification of Islamic law started under the 'Abbasids (758–1258) in Iraq; under the Ommayads, generally referred to as the Moors (711–1492), in Spain; and among the Ottomans in Turkey (1299–1922).

I argue that the blasphemy laws were revived and made significantly more onerous under General Zia-ul-Haq for geopolitical control of the region that also included Afghanistan in order to bring down the Soviet Union, a defeat that finally ended the Cold War. Saudi Arabia dictated the template based on its own laws in the kingdom. Seeking validation in the name of the Nizam-e Mustafa, or Muhammad's Islam, these laws created a state-sponsored "infidel" ideology that not only has had an impact on citizens and led to social injustice but now affects international and global security as militant groups like the Taliban justify violence based on treating as infidels all Muslims and non-Muslims who do not subscribe to their militant interpretation of Islam.

I connect my writing to Arabia and the Arab Islamic empires including the one in Spain, al-Andalus, to be followed by the Ottomans. The Nizam-e Mustafa is the model the Pakistani state is following, adequately demonstrated through digital images in a poster that I use in the book. These images, which are the work of an anonymous artist, depict General Zia-ul-Haq's regime. Likewise, the caliphates that succeeded Muhammad turned to the Prophet's Arabia for validation, as did the Ottomans. The Ottoman caliphate and the earlier caliphates such as the Rashidun all sought validation from Muhammad in his Arabian community. That is the kind of "pristine" Islam to which countries like Pakistan are returning, backed by petrodollars from the Gulf Emirates. All these are creations resulting from the fall of the Ottoman Empire. I make connections between the present Pakistani state and the historical context of Muhammad's Islam in Arabia to give a fuller picture.

I am writing for multiple audiences in addition to the scholarly community. This book is directed to a wider readership encompassing policy makers, students in the academy such as those whom I teach in my many Islam classes at SUNY Purchase, and my peers. In general the book is also for informed readers in the west as well as in South Asia, the Middle East, and other global communities interested in present-day developments of international security emanating from Pakistan's blasphemy laws—the *takfiri* cult that the militants apply. The central discussion is about South Asia and the regions that are affected by these laws: Pakistan, Afghanistan, Bangladesh, and others, as well as India, which time and again receives the consequences.

Historical contexts covered in the book have evolved from my teaching and from interactions with liberal individuals in and outside the west who have desired a text on this subject: What is Islam about, what is the difference between the Sunni and the Shi'a, and why is blasphemy such an issue? I make these connections in the manuscript because it is also my own intellectual journey. Blasphemy, since international controversies erupted surrounding Salman Rushdie, Tasleema Nasreen, and others, has become a center-stage topic. I bring information on the subject into a single text that most readers will find handy. Apart from Karen Armstrong's book, most texts on Islam are lengthy or difficult to navigate on one's own.[5] And thus I have included a discussion on Muhammad's Arabia with the maps and charts in this book. These have been field-tested in the classroom for efficiency.

Multiple narratives run through the book; it is an interdisciplinary text. Additionally, because of my own interdisciplinary training and professional work I do use not only scholarly references but sources from literature, film, and digital media to demonstrate the complexity of the discourse as well as to make the narrative creatively engaging, especially for young readers who seek knowledge of world events that affect their lives. I focus on history to discuss the present blasphemy laws to argue that the Islamic world is complex, and therefore I create the multiple narratives around a discussion of Pakistan. The Talibanization of the Pakistani state based on its authoritarian regimes has led it to regress to medieval Arab tribal practices and thus calls for reopening some periods of Islamic history, particularly of its empires. I resurrect discussion of some of the empires here.

With Pakistan's recently acquired status as a nonmember NATO ally (March 2004) and a key player in the U.S.-led war against terrorism, the blasphemy laws are another arsenal in the stockpile of this nuclear-armed state. These laws drive the state's own authoritarianism and the militancy of its protégé, the Taliban, with whom the state and its various intelligence agencies have a bizarre relationship: sometimes affiliates but sometimes not affiliates. The Taliban are "jihadi proxies" of the Pakistani military. Born out of an illegitimate relationship with a military state that usurped the Nizam-e Mustafa through collusion with the religious parties, the blasphemy laws are indeed a sinister manifesto that are neither Islamic nor derived from the Prophet Muhammad.

PAKISTAN AND AFGHANISTAN

This work explores the text and context of Pakistan's blasphemy laws in the wider environment of Muhammad's life and his Islam in order to look at the dynamics of state, religion, and politics in the twenty-first century. The

MAP 1.1. Pakistan and Afghanistan. Arlen Nydam, 2009.

aim is to demystify the sanctity granted to these laws in Islam's name. Can a state like Pakistan, with sixty-five years of independence, of which thirty-four years have been dominated by the military, claim to deliver a secular democracy where Islam was to be used only for a moral and ethical code? Ironically, the very Islamic parties like the Jamaat-e Islami that opposed the creation of a Pakistani state, which promised a secular democracy, came to dominate the Pakistani state. A state that in India the Islamic parties unashamedly branded as "un-Islamic" is now the domain of these very Islamist parties and their associates, through which they have turned the state into a virtual theocracy.

Although never winning the elections—these parties could not muster even 5 percent of the vote—they threw their weight behind the military regime of Zia-ul-Haq, who needed validation in Islam's name. Later they threw their lot, with General Pervez Musharraf to ensure a theocratic state that was nowhere near the secular vision of the founding fathers, such as Muhammad ʿAli Jinnah and Muhammad Iqbal, who were a part of the Pakistan Movement that forced the British to leave India and give Muslims the separate homeland of Pakistan. India was thus partitioned in 1947. And although Pervez Musharraf professed secularism, he gave a new life to these parties following 9/11 because his own acceptance as the novel nonwestern ally in the NATO hierarchy depended on some measure of validation that he could only claim through the religious parties that were ever ready to sell themselves to a military regime. The Pakistani military state partnered with the religious parties for an "Islamic" cover as well as for the street power of these groups that could exploit Islam for political power.

However, to be fair to Ayub Khan and Yahya Khan, two earlier military dictators of the 1950s and '60s, they kept the Islamist parties in their place, where they belonged. Both these regimes were truly secular. They took no nonsense from the Islamist parties, as evidenced during the 1953 riots when Lahore was put under a curfew, and General Azam imposed martial law when the Jamaat-e Islami started a riot to declare the Qadianis and Ahmediyyas as non-Muslims. The movement was ignited from the Jamaat's headquarters in Mansura. The Jamaat-e Islami chief, Maulana Abul Aʿla Maududi, was arrested for sedition against the state. Under these military dictatorships, though, the loot and plunder of the land began that future politicians matched with equal spunk, with no exceptions: the Bhuttos, Zardaris, Sharifs, and Gujrat Chaudhrys, all of the same banditry.

Sadly, it was also the CIA that in 1978 sponsored and provided funds and weaponry to Zia-ul-Haq's military regime to confront the Soviets in Afghanistan. That weaponry Zia-ul-Haq bolstered with his so-called shariʿa laws in the name of Islam, among which were the blasphemy laws and the Hudood ordinances against women that enabled the general to proclaim himself Amir-ul Momineen, leader of the faithful, in the tradition of the caliphs who followed Muhammad. Mulla Omar later in Afghanistan assumed the same status. The dream of a caliphate was born of this adventure and was underwritten by the CIA. With a population bursting at close to 200 million, a literacy rate of 56 percent, and public expenditure on education as low as 2.6 to 1.8 percent of the gross domestic product in Pakistan, these laws have been used by the state against a virtually illiterate citizenry, minorities, and intellectuals who could question the state tyranny or its claims to being Islamic.[6] The state's enforcers of these laws, such as the Taliban were equally illiterate and thus delivered a shariʿa that was nothing but naked brutality, as seen in Afghanistan, Swat, and Waziristan. The male, mulla, and military collusion has been anything but democratic and in total violation of ethical or Islamic norms. Although in undivided India the Islamic parties opposed the creation of the Pakistani state, they moved to Pakistan and gave battle here.[7]

PAKISTAN'S WOMEN POLITICIANS

1.1. Fatima Jinnah (1893–1967), founding stateswoman of Pakistan (1940–1967), sister of Muhammad 'Ali Jinnah.

1.2. Benazir Bhutto (1953–2007), twice prime minister of Pakistan (1988–1990, 1993–1996), daughter of Z. A. Bhutto. Assassinated.

1.3. Begum Nusrat Bhutto (1929–2011), first chairwoman of Pakistan People's Party (1979–1983), wife of Z. A. Bhutto.

FOUNDING POLITICIANS

1.4. Muhammad 'Ali Jinnah (1876–1948), founder of Pakistan and All-India Muslim League, first governor-general of Pakistan (1947–1948).

1.5. Liaqat Ali Khan (1885–1951), first prime minister of Pakistan (1947–1951). Assassinated.

1.6. Zulfiqar 'Ali Bhutto (1928–1979), founder of Pakistan People's Party, president and prime minister of Pakistan (1971–1979). Executed.

1.7. Sheikh Mujibur Rahman (1920–1975), founder of Bangladesh, president and prime minister of Bangladesh (1971–1975). Assassinated.

MILITARY DICTATORS

1.8. Field Marshal Muhammad
Ayub Khan (1907–1974), president
of Pakistan (1958–1969).

1.9. General Agha Muhammad
Yahya Khan (1917–1980), president
of Pakistan (1969–1971).

1.10. General Muhammad Zia-
ul-Haq (1924–1988), president of
Pakistan (1977–1988). Killed in
plane crash.

1.11. General Pervez Musharraf
(1943–), president of Pakistan
(2001–2008).

This study is a qualitative, historical survey of *kufr*, or blasphemy, in some Islamic empires to demonstrate that laws on blasphemy or heresy were political creations of the state that derived authority from Muhammad's life or his example, *sunna*. The Pakistani state is no different. Muhammad's own life and his battles are central to the discussion here, together with excerpts from the Qur'an, to show that Muhammad was a man of peace who believed in social justice. His battles against his adversaries were short as they challenged his message in the same manner that Jesus or Moses was challenged. Muhammad was no empire builder, though his followers were, with the result that Islam has its own history of empire and imperialism.

Although in this book I argue for a secular Islamic state in the second millennium, it was necessary to bring in the Arab culture's strong oral traditions to help the audience understand the historical contexts in which Muhammad lived, the questions about his succession that led to the two *fitnas* (civil wars) in Islam, and the major differences between Sunni and Shi'a Islam that have formed the basis of blasphemy or heresy laws in Islamic empires.[8] Pakistan's blasphemy laws are no exception, as will be discussed in detail. Pakistan and the takfiri cult are further discussed together with the blasphemy laws to show that Pakistan's generals (serving and retired) had a dream of empire in Afghanistan, where they installed the Taliban as their proxies for "strategic depth," or what they have proudly called "strategic penetration." The Taliban ideology of the "other" who is the "infidel" and who, even if Muslim, is an apostate unless converted to its particular version of militant Islam is derived from Pakistan's carefully crafted blasphemy laws under Saudi supervision during the Afghan adventure of 1978. Other parties to the adventure, besides the CIA and the Pakistani military's Inter-Services Intelligence, were Saudi Arabia, the Afghan warlords, and the *mujahideen*, now the Taliban. The laws were superimposed on the existing blasphemy code that the British had put in place during their period as colonists in India to keep peace among the various ethnic and religious groups.[9]

Keeping in mind the audience for the book and the development of a blasphemy theme, historical contexts that followed the Prophet Muhammad are discussed through the *riddah*, Apostasy Wars in the caliph Abu Bekr's time. Other instances discussed in detail are those of Abu al-Mughis Husayn ibn Mansur al-Hallaj's trial and execution under the 'Abbasids, the Cordoba martyrs under the Ommayads or Moors in Spain, and the Neomartyrs under the Ottomans, as well as some details of the *fatwas* (scholarly opinions) that were compiled for blasphemy and heresy during the later Ottoman rule. Even states issued blasphemy and heresy fatwas against each other; for example, the Sunni Ottomans continuously issued heresy fatwas against the Shi'a Safavid state of Iran. These are highlighted in later materials. In all of this, the purpose is to demonstrate that the empires manipulated the shari'a, the law, for political agendas of control, thus underscoring the relationship of state, politics, and religion.

And though state politics in the second millennium need not be tied to religion, that being the citizens' private domain, modern Islamic states have upheld authority in Islam's name to bolster a regime's reputation and, by appropriating "sanctity," to make its actions acceptable to the citizens. Post-colonial Islamic states that won independence from the colonists had to do so in the name of Islam, and as such the quest for an Islamic identity haunts these states, resulting in skewed, *mala fide*, purportedly Islamic shari'a laws of the kind that Zia-ul-Haq perpetrated with collusion from western imperialists. Ahmed Ben Bella and Houari Boumedienne in Algeria and Zulfiqar 'Ali Bhutto in Pakistan were left-wing, partially socialist politicians who had to claim validation through Islam for their electorates to accept them and because an Islamic discourse was an effective tool against colonialism. It was the Islamic discourse that drove the French out of Algeria.[10] Z. A. Bhutto, in addition, used the slogan *roti, kapra, makan* (bread, clothes, housing)— none of which he took seriously except as rhetoric to feed his electorate for street power. Furthermore, Bhutto hosted the second Islamic Summit Conference in Lahore in 1974 to boost his credentials as leading Pakistan on the path to a truly Islamic state. Muhammad 'Ali Jinnah, too, had to use the discourse of a separate state for the Muslims in a united India, though Jinnah himself was secular. The same discourse was used to drive the Soviets out of Afghanistan and ultimately put an end to the Cold War. Ironically, it was the secular west that prompted an "Islamic discourse," and during that period 10,000 copies of the Qur'an were distributed in the southern Soviet republics that had large Muslim populations to incite opposition against the communist state.

We now have in Pakistan a military-mulla state (the democratically elected state can never win before the military that calls the shots even on foreign policy) that uses Islamic discourse against its own citizens. In retaliation, the illegitimate offspring that the military regimes sired and used as proxies— the Taliban and the militants—now challenge the military state itself; the takeover of the Pakistani army's general headquarters in Rawalpindi Cantonment in summer 2009 is an example. Taliban leaders announced that this takeover was a very small demonstration and they could take other, larger, valuable "assets" if need be. This was their message to a crony state of western imperialism, they affirmed. Again, in 2011 the Taliban takeover of Mehran, Pakistan's naval base in Karachi, in retaliation for Osama bin Laden's capture conveys a similar message.

What follows is a discussion of the ideology embedded in Pakistan's newfangled shari'a laws Zia-ul-Haq ordained that drives the present international militancy and that successive regimes, both military and civilian, have upheld for expedient agendas to serve their own purposes and in which Pakistani citizens are mere pawns and hostages. When these movements were afoot, the world did not care or perhaps even understand, but now these laws affect international security as they establish the divide between "believers" and "infidels," that being the driving force for the 9/11 perpetrators: attacking the United States for the militants was a jihad against the imperialist forces of Islam's enemies, whom they considered infidels.[11]

None of these laws or ideologies is Qur'anic or derived from the Prophet Muhammad's practices, which is the argument I make in this book.

IN 1998, WARNINGS OF 9/11

As I revisit that period of 1998 in which the blasphemy charge was brought against me and others, such as Dr. Younas Shaikh and a woman colleague, Dr. Surriya Shafi, who had a PhD in English from England and was teaching at the Government College University in Lahore, academics generally in the country were targets for the blasphemy charge (as detailed in back materials). Other world events were playing out, too, and such events were a warning of the 9/11 catastrophe. I connect the following events with the takfir ideology (in which one Muslim declares another Muslim a heretic) derived from Pakistan's blasphemy laws that were precursors of what was to come:

- the bombing of the American embassy in Nairobi,
- the bombing of the American embassy in Dar-es-Salaam, Tanzania,
- the killing of a faculty member in Kabul University, and
- state-supported terrorism in Pakistan as evidenced by the following six incidents:

    Mullas (clerics) of religious parties threatened to close women's NGOs in the northwestern parts of Pakistan. The Sharif government revoked the licenses of 2,000 NGOs.

    Mullas threatened to kidnap women of the NGOs and then forcibly marry them.

    Bishop Joseph committed suicide by shooting himself in Pakistan's Sahiwal Sessions Court because he was unable to get the release of a parishioner sentenced to death for blasphemy.

    A state confrontation arose between the Sharif government and the secular English press when Najam Sethi, editor of the *Friday Times*, and journalists A. Afridi of the *Frontier Post* and Hussain Haqqani were arrested.

Pakistan blasted its nuclear devices in the Chagi Hills of Balochistan in
response to India testing its nuclear arsenal at Pokharan.
The Taliban in Afghanistan blew up the Bamiyan Buddhas.

Within the same time frame as the above incidents and in fact taking their
cue from Pakistan and Afghanistan, as early as 1994 the mullas in Bangladesh
were issuing fatwas against NGOs that worked with women's education,
developmental programs, contraception, health, and income generation.
Fatwas were issued against the Grameen Bank and BRAC that supported
projects for women's income generation. In 1994 a fatwa was issued against
Tasleema Nasreen for her book *Lajja*, and secular presses were set on fire.
Bangladeshi mullas were pressing for blasphemy laws like those in Pakistan.[12]
The genesis of all these events can be traced back to the late 1970s and sub-
sequent years when General Zia-ul-Haq was installed in the region.

The 1980s were a crucial period for South Asia. The Soviets were already
in Afghanistan. The shah of Iran's regime had fallen, and the ayatollahs had
taken over in Iran. Jimmy Carter's government had dealt with the takeover
of the U.S. embassy in Tehran together with the hostage drama. The Reagan administration was concerned with the events in the region, and the
CIA became visibly engaged as the United States and its allies had to establish control over the territory as well as the Persian Gulf, with Soviet eyes
on a passage to its warm waters through Pakistan's Balochistan right into
the Arabian Sea (map 1.1). Pakistan and Afghanistan were the hub of activity between 1978 and 1988; multitudes of Afghan refugees flooded into Pakistan, and more than 3 million displaced Afghans have lived as refugees in
the country since then. On my daily commute from the Pakistan Ordnance
Factories area in Wah Cantonment, where I lived at that time, to my university, I saw an enormous number of Afghan refugees: women, children, and
old men traveling with their belongings on small, sturdy donkeys. The Afghan women, visible in their colored skirts and *chadors* (veils), were among
those who trekked into Pakistan. Besides the hardships of massive displace-
ment, 1.5 million Afghans lost their lives in the war.

Islamabad between 1980 and 1985 was among the world's ritziest capi-
tals. It was the Reagan era in the United States. In Islamabad "mujahideen"
leaders, dubbed as such by President Reagan, were fighting the infidel Rus-
sian communists who had occupied Afghanistan. Gulbadiyan Hikmatyar,
Burhanuddin Rabbani, Abdul Rashid Dostum, and many others were welcome guests in Islamabad, with photos flashed in the national press.[13] The
buzzword for General Zia-ul-Haq's administration became "Islamization."
Everything in Islamabad became "Islamization," and that cult dominated
the capital. Official orders were issued for prayers five times a day in all gov-

ernment offices, and workers were told to follow the Islamic injunction of prayers. Prayer breaks became mandatory in all government offices.

I had already experienced that in the Girls College of Education in Saudi Arabia, where I worked in 1978–1979. Everything closed down for prayer time in Riyadh by order of the state, and Saudi *mutaus* (religious police) made sure the edict was enforced. General Zia-ul-Haq was enforcing the Saudi Arabian Wahabi model of *sarkari* (colonial Islam) on Pakistan.

Wahabism is a form of Calvinism in Islam. Its founder, Muhammad bin 'Abd al-Wahab (1703–1792), who was from the Nejd in Arabia, believed that Muslims had gone astray from true Islam, which to him lay in following only the basic, literal text of the Qur'an. He was a follower of the conservative Hanbali school of Islam. 'Abd al-Wahab rejected the many schools of Islamic thought, jurisprudence, and mysticism, insisting that only his orthodox, tribal version was the authentic Islam. Modification of Islamic practices, according to 'Abd al-Wahab, was *bid'a*, or heresy. Muhammad bin Sa'ud of the al-Sa'ud family collaborated with 'Abd al-Wahab from 1745 to 1818, and thus the "first Saudi state" was born. Wahabism is now the dominant ideology of the Saudi state. The Taliban and al-Qaeda groups also uphold Wahabism to be the only Islam. South Asian Muslims had practiced Islam privately, without public display. Under Zia-ul-Haq, the catch phrase directed against women professionals and nonprofessionals was *chador aur char divari* (the veil and four walls).

Official orders were issued in 1981 at the federal universities as well as in all government education institutions, schools, colleges, and provincial universities making it mandatory for all women educators to cover themselves in the chador. Whether these orders were implemented is a different matter. Pakistan was becoming a theocracy.

Within the same period General Zia-ul-Haq enforced his draconian laws against women in the name of Islam: the Hudood ordinances, the *zina* (fornication) ordinance (1979), and the Law of Evidence (1983). Fragments of a Zia-ul-Haq–period poster are presented in figures 1.12–1.16. As if this were not enough, in 1986–1991 he issued the blasphemy laws, nowhere existent in the Holy Qur'an. These laws are used even now with impunity against intellectuals, minorities, and women; not even children are exempt (appendix 4). Before the cases of victims of the blasphemy laws can come up for judicial hearings, overzealous mobs or even the police have killed them. The practice continues. Obviously, state collusion is part of the extrajudicial killings. The state's role in such happenings is questionable.

The questions one asks here are these: Did the donor agencies that were involved in terminating the Cold War during the late 1970s collude in the imposition of such laws in the country, or did they simply not care? Was it

1.12. Untitled poster illustrating corporal punishments under the penal code in General Zia-ul-Haq's shariʿa. Date and artist unknown. From the collection of the late Professor George Rich of California State University, reproduced by Joanna Kirkpatrick in *Transports of Delight*, 2003, and online with her essay "Peaceable Kingdoms," revised 2012.

1.13. Detail of figure 1.12. At the top the Islamic Shahada is written: "There is no God but God and Muhammad is his Messenger." Below the Shahada is the slogan "Nizam-e Mustafa," which means "Muhammad's Islam." The Qur'an situated between the scales promises justice.

convenient for the donors to look the other way as long as agendas were implemented in the military and mulla collaboration? The generic CIA is well known as "a virtual government within the government." The State Department and the National Security Council, led by its adviser Zbigniew Brzezinski, also provided unlimited funds to the Pakistani military, especially to the Inter-Services Intelligence Agency, whose head at that time was General Gul Hamid. General Hamid had significant connections to the Saudis and the mujahideen. Thus, a powerful conglomerate of donor agencies was created, from the U.S. Agency for International Development (USAID) and its many affiliates to the jihadi madrassa organizations whose materials to indoctrinate the mujahideen were produced by the CIA and the University of Nebraska at an approximate cost of $50 million. The mujahideen, now the Taliban, still use the same manuals for their training.

To what extent did neocolonial collusion create the Taliban, which brought the unholiest laws to pass against women, minorities, intellectuals, and spiritual individuals in the name of Islam? Whose Islam was it that was imposed on the majority through an oppressive state machinery that foreign agencies like those the CIA funded? Was it even Islam? I shall explore these questions in this book. And although the people who lost their lives in Afghanistan, Pakistan, New York City, London, Madrid, and elsewhere as a result of this application of Islam cannot be brought back, at least the record can be documented.

My goal is to put political history in context as I have lived through it and become displaced. I am fully a participant of that catastrophe. Blasphemy, Nizam-e Mustafa, takfir, and kafir are part of a lexicon developed in the Zia-ul-Haq era. The details that are provided here are necessary to understand the contexts of the blasphemy laws, the institution of the laws, the circumstances in which the laws emerged, and how they are applied, not necessarily for Islam but for state control. According to these laws, it is the state's prerogative to designate any action of the citizen as non-Islamic or not in accordance with the shari'a.

The language of these laws is so nebulous and ill defined that any utterance can become blasphemy. These laws now affect international security, as militant groups use them to justify their extermination of non-Muslims whom they consider kafirs (infidels). Based on a *takfir* (infidel) ideology, such laws motivated the 9/11 perpetrators. It is essential for me to explore the social, administrative, and political contexts in which these Islamic laws operate. They affect citizens in Pakistan and citizens internationally. The investigations will shed light on issues of global security and of international terrorism and the ideology that drives it. As such it is also necessary to focus on the evolution of the blasphemy laws in the Islamic states after the death of Muhammad, the Prophet of Islam, as that is the source of the present-day militants' claim, the Nizam-e Mustafa (Muhammad's Islam). For sure Muhammad never advocated a militant ideology that violates human life or social justice within a state or internationally.

ALLAMA IQBAL OPEN UNIVERSITY IN ISLAMABAD

My role in this theater started in 1980 when I was selected to work for the Allama Iqbal Open University as an assistant professor of English. I had recently returned from working at the Girls College of Education in Riyadh; I had worked there for a year to assist the college in its graduate English program for teacher training. My appointment, on my return from Saudi Arabia, at the Allama Iqbal Open University in Islamabad was perhaps based on my Saudi credentials of having worked with women's education in Riyadh. I returned from Riyadh as a teacher-trainer. Maybe I was a suitable candidate, with Islamic credentials from Saudi Arabia as well as a graduate degree from secular England, thus qualified to deliver a contemporary "Islamic" educational package for the country.[14] The university appointed me to be the coordinator for an English-language program to retrain university and college teachers in Pakistan. Courses were created for master trainers in English at the university level who further trained other university and college teachers; the training eventually filtered down to the schools. Strong focus was put on women's training. With support from the British Council, British Overseas Development Agency, USAID, U.S. Information Service (USIS), and U.S. Educational Foundation in Pakistan (USEFP), seven major universities received resources including faculty training in Britain and the United States. Special English language centers were set up at Bahaudin Zakaria University in Multan, Peshawar University, Faisalabad, Karachi, and elsewhere. I took part in several training visits to Britain and Singapore and eventually went to the United States for a PhD at the University of Texas at Austin (1985–1992).

When I began working at the Allama Iqbal Open University, the process of implementing General Zia-ul-Haq's Islamic ordinances was in full swing. However, I was not aware of the sinister impact of these ordinances then, although when they were issued the texts of the ordinances were hair-raising for the twentieth century and for Islam, as there is always room for *ijtihad*, or independent reasoning, in Islam.

The Allama Iqbal Open University originated as a distance-education institution in 1974 with support from the British government. Today, we can see it as being the equivalent of the online teaching system, though in the early 1970s it was done through print materials, audio support, and weekly tutorials. This was during Zulfiqar 'Ali Bhutto's government. The object was to provide rapid grassroots education while at the same time to create an adult literacy system in the country. The method synchronized with Bhutto's liberal socialist approach. He also named the institution The People's Open University. In 1980, when I joined the university, it was in its infancy, with four student hostels that were acquired from an adjoining men's college. The model for the university was based on the British Open University. Hence, British consultants had a strong presence on campus, and they ensured faculty and staff training on the model of the British Open University. Briefly the setup was secular. However, according to General Zia-ul-Haq's particular Islamic agenda, the university was renamed the Allama Iqbal Open University after Pakistan's national poet who had put forth the idea of a separate homeland for the Muslims, which led to India's partitioning.[15]

The history of this university is essential to a discussion of a system that was set up for grassroots literacy but became the most coveted system in 1998 for the clerics. They disseminated their madrassa curriculum, or Dars-e

1.14. Detail of figure 1.12. Famous film star portrayed as a prostitute liable to punishment under Zia-ul-Haq's shariʿa.

Nizami (seminary system),[16] through the vast network of this national university, which had an enrollment of close to 80,000 students annually. The clerics knew the system's efficacy and over time viably hijacked that system for mass dissemination of the Dars-e Nizami; the state adequately supported the Dars-e Nizami through the distance-learning system of the university.[17] This very secular institution that the clerics hijacked became the microcosm for using Islamic blasphemy laws against secular academics, mainly those trained in the western academies of Britain and the United States. Similar practices were carried out in other state-owned universities, such as Government College University, Lahore. As stated earlier, a woman academic, Dr. Surriya Shafi, was charged with blasphemy as she made the mistake of using mermaids in the textbook design for an English course. She had to appear in endless hearings of the provincial assembly to defend herself; the conservative Urdu press in Lahore continuously harassed her through sensational publicity at the local parliament's hearings. Academics in English or those with secular ideas like Dr. Younas Shaikh were prime targets of the blasphemy laws. The female principal of a private secular English school in Islamabad was forced to flee the country for the same reasons.

Although Islam is not mutually exclusive with secularism or modernity, the clerics' version of Islam was orthodox, rigid, and exclusively text-based; that excluded the richness and diversity of Islamic culture and civilization.[18] Unfortunately, these were the people in power in 1998 when the blasphemy tool was applied extensively. At that time, most of the senior faculty, such as the deans, were madrassa clerics who colluded with the vice chancellor of the Allama Iqbal Open University. As stated earlier, the clerics had arranged for his appointment from the International Islamic University so that he would uphold their agendas.[19] The clerics virtually coerced the vice chancellor as a group; they would descend on his office and demand for him to appoint one of their colleagues to key positions. This malpractice continued to the extent that a male cleric got himself appointed as the head of the women's studies faculty. Out of disgust the government of the Netherlands withheld its funding of programs on women's issues; the administration had to correct the situation before the Netherlands resumed funding. Consequently, a female faculty was appointed to head the women's studies program. I observed these happenings as a faculty member at the time. During the day, the vice chancellor publicly professed secularism and ridiculed the clerics at academic meetings, but by night he secretly met with them in his home; by day he was a secular man and by night a Taliban.

The collusion between a state functionary like the vice chancellor and the clerics led to the repression of intellectuals, freethinkers, artists, and women in the university. Many women chairs of university departments and heads of programs were sent on forced leave because of one allegation or another, and although the women did put up a stiff resistance, some eventually left in order to preserve their integrity. One such woman was the chair of the zoology department. She resigned and opened her own private school. The Talibanization of the Pakistani academy was subtle but pernicious.[20] While the Afghan Taliban blatantly forbade women professionals such as doctors and educators to work, the Pakistani Taliban did it surreptitiously through harassment with complete state support. It eradicated many a fine intellect and visionary from the country's academy.

In the period when Zia-ul-Haq's so-called Islamic laws were devised and implemented (1978–2001), donor agencies like USAID and the British Overseas Development Agency in Islamabad as well as in the rest of the country looked the other way. Pakistani citizens cut each other's throats using laws like blasphemy; the covert civil war was contained in South Asia, in Afghanistan, Pakistan, and Bangladesh. I must admit that in 1998 as a woman professional I was naïve, unable to appreciate the warnings from male colleagues about the "agencies" and "agency wallas" operating in the country. They cautioned me several times about the horrendous things that could happen to me, but I failed to understand. It was much later, immediately after the Twin Towers fell, that I understood who the "agencies" were: Pakistan's Inter-Services Intelligence and the Federal Investigating Agency (FIA) in Islamabad and elsewhere.[21] But who were the agency donors in this part of the world?[22] What happened and what could have happened is a chilling story, even now as I revisit the past and see myself in context.[23]

1.15. Detail of figure 1.12. Famous film star shown as a drunkard, with others being executed or having hands chopped off as punishment for theft, bribery, and corruption under Zia-ul-Haq's shariʿa.

In 1998 the clerics in Pakistan and Afghanistan had a life of their own; they were heady and comfortable with their guaranteed support from the agencies; $60 billion had been poured into birthing them, nurturing them, and funding the Pakistani military. General Gul Hamid, the man who led the CIA-directed operation against the Soviets in Afghanistan in the late 1970s, was a regular state visitor at my university in 1998 talking about an Islamic revolution, this time a Wahabi one. He had retired from the military but was an ardent supporter of jihad against the infidels. As 9/11 revealed, the infidel was the west, most of all the United States.

Over time, General Zia-ul-Haq's other bits of Islamization policies became extremely bothersome: prior to the Zia-ul-Haq era, government-funded educational institutions focused on a broad range of curricula that looked upon the historical and social contexts of the Pakistan-India region as it had evolved over the centuries.[24] The pre-Islamic Buddhist and Hindu cultures were very much a part of the curriculum. Buddhist influence is still visible in the regions of Taxila and Swat in Pakistan, as it is in the Indus Valley civilization of the Sind. The history of the region encompasses vast Hindu and Buddhist cultures that flourished long before Islam's advent in the region in the eighth century CE. Muslim followers in the region take pride in this rich cultural heritage that is reflected in their tolerance and acceptance of other faith systems, as it is the history of their ancestors. The educational approach was holistic since the time of the partition. And this was the system in which I was fortunately educated.

Come General Zia-ul-Haq, everything had to be geared to a jihadist vision of Islam. The history of the region was rewritten to only cover the coming of Islam in India with Muhammad bin Qasim's invasion of Sind in 712 and Mahmud of Ghazni's raids on the Somnath Temple from 997 to 1030 as jihad against the kafirs, the non-Muslims of the Indian continent. All other histories of non-Muslim civilizations were dismissed as stories of infidels who only worshipped idols. The history now further emphasized the Islamic revivalist movements of the eighteenth century with Shah Waliullah's (1703–1762) discourse of jihad against infidel forces in India; the narratives glorified the martyrs Sayyid Ahmed Shaheed and Shah Ismail, both falling in jihad in Balakot on May 6, 1831. A shrine to the martyrs still stands in the region, in Mansehra, Pakistan.[25]

These were the centerpieces of an Islamic ideology for Pakistan as it led the CIA war against the Soviets in Afghanistan. During Zia-ul-Haq's regime the history of Pakistan's creation through the partition of India was part of the curriculum, too, minus the disintegration of the country through the breakaway of East Pakistan as the autonomous state of Bangladesh. Why? Because that would have resurrected the ugly role of the West Pakistani politicians in refusing to accept the results of the 1971 election under General Yahya Khan with the victory of Sheikh Mujibur Rahman's Awami League Party in East Pakistan. The seat of government would have been in Dacca, then East Pakistan, and that was not acceptable to the West Pakistani politicians, especially Zulfiqar ʿAli Bhutto. Bhutto threatened to break the legs of any West Pakistani politician who dared to go to the National Assembly session in Dacca. It would have further resurrected the atrocities of the Pakistani military in that part of the country, something that a fair majority of Pakistanis are in denial about to this day.[26]

The process of instituting an ostensibly Islamic curriculum had already started under Zulfiqar ʿAli Bhutto as the Arab states pressured him to Islamize the country, its constitution, and its social fabric. Bhutto complied in return for the bounty of the oil-rich states. All this will be discussed in detail in the succeeding chapters leading up to the manipulation of Islamic law, the shariʿa in the country.

ZIA-UL-HAQ'S PROSELYTIZING MISSION

Before the Zia-ul-Haq era, extracurricular activities in educational institutions were sports, drama, debate, and cultural shows. Now it was only *milads, naʿats,* and *dars,* learning the Holy Scripture and its basic interpretation. Dars under Saudi-trained women *muʿallimas* (proselytizers) meant evangelizing orthodox Wahabi Islam. I had never seen anything like this in Saudi Arabia. Saudi citizens entertained themselves with the finest Arabic music and high-quality secular television programs from the Arab world, mainly Egypt. Many of these programs dealt with radical gender issues. What I saw in Pakistan in that period in the female domain was a strange conglomeration of homegrown proselytizing through dars. The practice continues even now, much more acutely with massive funds thrown in from proselytizing states whose audiences and attendees are well-to-do urban housewives. Such congregations are now held in special women's enclaves of mosques in the Defense Housing Societies in Lahore and elsewhere.[27] Here, I want to make a distinction between pure canonical Islam and Islamic culture, its art, aesthetics, culture, and music. I grew up with the latter, although I was also trained to read the Qur'an and perform rituals such as prayer, fasting, and everything else that makes one a member of an Islamic community.[28]

One level of my own social life was linked with the Pakistani army circles—in which General Zia-ul-Haq's family and his network of army officers were major participants. As mentioned earlier, my husband, a commando officer of the Pakistani military, went missing in action during Operation Gibraltar in Indian-occupied Kashmir. In 1965 General Ayub Khan engaged in such adventurism purportedly on the wise counsel of his foreign minister Zulfiqar 'Ali Bhutto. Bhutto reportedly claimed that he advised such a move in order to humiliate the Pakistani generals. As a military widow I lived in Rawalpindi Cantonment, an exclusive military enclave created from Pakistan's and India's colonial history. My home in Rawalpindi was close to the Flashman's Hotel, the setting of some of Rudyard Kipling's works. Imported movies from India were entertainment for General Zia-ul-Haq's family and the network of his associates, mainly top-brass military sycophants. It was dars during the day while the men were at work and watching Bollywood movies in the evening with the family. Such was the mode of life among the wives of the officer cadre in Rawalpindi Cantonment.

Promotions and careers depended on attending dars parties catered with fancy cuisine serviced by efficient, uniformed orderlies. The wives were driven places like the military ordnance mess on the mall opposite the Pearl Continental Hotel in Rawalpindi in plush black cars that groomed military chauffeurs staffed.[29] Weekly, dars was part of social life usually headed by a corps commander's wife or a general's wife and sometimes even the military president's wife. This was the garrison culture started during Zia-ul-Haq's regime, and his legacy lives to this day. General Zia-ul-Haq's Islamization and militarization went hand in hand. His influence led to dars and milad sessions in women's domains. With the war in Afghanistan and the petrodollars flowing in from Arab states, Pakistanis were becoming born-again Muslims.[30]

1.16. Detail of figure 1.12. Fable of the lion and the lamb drinking from the same pond depicted with the lion representing the state and, in this scene, a goat as its citizens.

All this followed the 1974 events under Z. A. Bhutto, once he gave in to the pressure of the Saudi-backed Islamic parties to declare the Ahmediyya community as non-Muslims with the Khatam-e Nabuvat movement.[31] Later, Bhutto made the suicidal move to concede to a reelection in 1977, when a group of nine parties called the Pakistan National Alliance (PNA) accused him and his party members of rigging the national elections. Maulana Maududi and his Jamaat-e Islami were in the forefront of the PNA protests. They launched the notorious wheel-jam strike against Bhutto's government that revealed their street power to Bhutto. Bhutto's appeasement of the Islamic parties led to General Zia-ul-Haq heading a coup against him that eventually cost Bhutto his life: General Zia-ul-Haq supported a court case against Bhutto for the assassination of an opponent, Nawab Muhammad Ahmed Khan Kasuri. The courts, which Zia-ul-Haq supported, upheld the charge against Bhutto, and he was executed in 1979. The case is now being reopened. Incidentally and expediently, Bhutto superseded several senior army generals to make Zia-ul-Haq commander-in-chief of the Pakistani military, hoping that he would be a compliant general. Little did Bhutto know of General Zia-ul-Haq's secret militant-Islamic leanings. Zia-ul-Haq was the son of a mosque cleric who had made it into the officer cadre of the Pakistani military, which until Zia-ul-Haq's time was an extremely secular institution.

Despite his Islamization cult, General Zia-ul-Haq (contrary to Islamic shari'a and his own argument of chador aur char divari, veil and four walls for women) often went to the women's colleges for opening ceremonies and official visits. He was the most sought-after chief patron by the women's colleges, as a presidential visit meant generous funds for the institutions. At one point, out of sheer exasperation at the duplicity, I asked a surgeon general's wife who touted General Zia-ul-Haq's Islamization,

What's new about General Zia's Islam?

Are we not Muslims already?

Were our parents, their parents, and our grandparents not Muslims?

What's so new about this "Islam" that the general is trying to teach us?

And, by the way, what is he doing in women's colleges?

Is that Islamic?

The surgeon general's wife responded with total silence. She was among the chief ladies-in-waiting to Mrs. Zia-ul-Haq. I had personally seen some senior army officers' wives performing the *farshi salam* to Mrs. Zia-ul-Haq in the manner that this courtesy bow was offered to the empresses or Padshah Begum in Mughal India.[32] Usually, at social events an army chauffeur drove Mrs. Zia-ul-Haq in a plush black sedan, and she would wave to her audiences.

Under the influence of the chador aur char divari, a discourse for women was widely disseminated through Zia-ul-Haq's protégé Dr. Israrul Haq. In the 1980s Israrul Haq was the official state guest of Pakistani television and was a prime-time speaker. An entirely new cult of orthodoxy was taking over. Under the new dispensation, Islamic rituals like those for the celebration of Muharram and *rajab* that paid tribute to the family of the Prophet were becoming bid'a, or innovation, and hence heretical. These were rituals that were celebrated in women's networks for centuries. I had grown up with them, as had my mother and my father's mother. Dars parties became the substitutes under Zia-ul-Haq. Orthodox, Wahabi Islam was "correcting" the traditional South Asian eclectic Islam that was brought to the continent (via Iran and Afghanistan) through the Sufis and tolerant Muslim mentors and had been practiced since the ninth century. Pakistani South Asian Islam, liberal and integrated with surrounding cultural domains, was being pushed into a Saudiized, Wahabi version of Islam that was to be the canon of just that ideology. The primary proselytizing force was the military.

Why? Because this simplistic discourse was easy to disseminate among the grassroots populations; it appealed to the urban elites, especially the military. I saw the transition among my own family members in the Pakistani military who adopted the orthodox Islam. Official benefits were linked to it, in terms of remuneration and membership in elitist military clubs, promotions, and prized overseas appointments. The "jihadi Islamist" discourse was easy to use for dismantling the infidel, communist Soviet Union that had invaded Afghanistan and would soon be on Pakistan's borders. The CIA had outsourced that war to the Pakistani army for reportedly $60 billion over ten years. The Pakistani army further outsourced the war to the mullas, madrassas, and seminaries, a dime for each dollar received.[33] The Arab states made up for the rest on condition of the imposition of their Islamic laws and their Islamic franchise. This was the new country club. The military and mulla deal was total social and political control. Thus, the Islamist laws were enforced for hegemony, to prevent any disagreement or difference.[34]

Such were the blasphemy laws that a victim could be jailed without bail and charged with a crime punishable by death. The state was required to register the charge on a first investigation report (FIR) that a policeman with a fifth-grade education was empowered to register. Sometimes even that certificate was forged. Once the charge sheet was filed, the victim was considered guilty, without trial or further investigation. The Hudood ordinances, among them the zina ordinance and the law of evidence reducing women's voices to almost zero against a male voice, were an effective way to silence 50 percent of the population.[35] The laws were against women and were a potent tool to keep them out of politics. They were also intended to keep women out of the professions or from ever having a voice. Zia-ul-Haq's personal agenda in bringing about the laws against women was, perhaps, to keep Benazir Bhutto out of politics. After all, he had hanged her father, Prime Minister Zulfiqar 'Ali Bhutto. The Islamist laws in the region that include Pakistan, Afghanistan, and Bangladesh provide the perfect recipes to quell disagreement by creating horrendous consequences for anyone violating them. These laws have been used for a wide variety of tyrannical, authoritarian agendas, some of which will be investigated in this narrative.

Part of my objective in writing this book is to document, through personal experience and objective evidence, the context for the development of the blasphemy laws from the late 1970s to the present. Hence, this narrative is directed to my academic community as well as to informed individuals who would like to know more about the present contexts of the Pakistan-Afghanistan region that so profoundly affect the west. Because the west is very much a part of this narrative, perhaps this is also an exploration of American history overseas and at home and of British neocolonialism.

Individuals whose work and arguments form the basis for this book include the late-nineteenth- and early-twentieth-century Muslim scholars Moulavi Cheragh 'Ali, Syed Amir 'Ali, and 'Abdullah Yusuf 'Ali. Their work is significant as it represents a popular, tolerant Islamic scholarship generated from Hanafi Islam in India before the Arab tribal, Wahabi approach and the era of Saudi-trained 'ulema. Among recent scholars from whose work I draw are Fatima Mernissi, Wael Hallaq, Nazir Ahmad, Khaled Abou El Fadl, Osama Siddiqui and Zahra Hayat, 'Ali Eteraz, Ayesha Siddiqa, and Ahmed Rashid. I additionally refer to the activist input of Rashida Patel, Rubina

Saigol, Khawar Mumtaz, Farida Shaheed, Hina Gilana, and Asma Jenga-hir in challenging General Zia-ul-Haq's so-called Islamic laws. By integrat-ing these various perspectives, I present an indigenous, cross-cultural, secu-lar view of Islam and its scholarship over time. Asad 'Ali Ahmed's "Specters of Macaulay" (2009) focuses on Chapter 15, which this British colonial ad-ministrator put into India's blasphemy laws, that became the foundation for Zia-ul-Haq's Islamic ordinances. Although an excellent study of the colo-nial legal framework that has now become a postcolonial predicament, I find that the recent male scholarship including Asad 'Ali Ahmed's and Siddiqui's with input from Zahra Hayat, who is a female, is circumspect, remaining strictly within the legal frame that avoids activism. This is perhaps because of the threats from the Islamists.

Recent female scholarship on the subject of the Islamic ordinances, in-cluding Hudood and blasphemy, is proactive as discussed and documented here. Since Zia-ul-Haq's Islamic laws target women to eliminate them from public spaces as well as reduce their citizenship rights to zero, female schol-ars and activists are outspoken against these laws perpetrated in Muham-mad's name. These laws are no Nizam-e Mustafa, as the Qur'an speaks of women being equal to men, and Muhammad loved the women in his life: his consorts, his mother, and his wet nurse, Halima. Today's slogan of the Nizam-e Mustafa by the Islami parties in countries like Pakistan is to hi-jack Muhammad's name to simply wield hegemony over the resources of the land, and that includes the citizenry of the land, both men and women.

Intellectuals and activists will not use weapons to fight such orthodoxy, as they have the courage to think; they have the power of ideas, the power of the word, and the power of language to argue for secularism while they con-tinue to practice their faith privately. Twenty-first-century Islam will be one of reformation not dictated by gunpowder or terror but by peace and ratio-nality and most of all through discourse, which is the purpose of this book: to open a discussion for thought and the rights of citizenship in a twenty-first-century state like Pakistan where the majority of citizens are Muslims but where many forms of Islam exist—and where citizens are also Chris-tians, Hindus, Sikhs, Parsis, and Buddhists.

The Pakistani state needs to go to the Prophet Muhammad's Constitu-tion of Medina, the covenant the Prophet drew up with the Arab clans of his time and the Jewish and Christian tribes so that the groups could live in harmony. Are there any blasphemy laws in that covenant if one is to follow the Nizam-e Mustafa? The Medina Constitution is a prime example of the Nizam-e Mustafa. Let there be a study of the Medina Constitution and the compatibility of the blasphemy laws in accordance with that charter to ascertain the status of the minorities in Pakistan; until such time that a consensus is reached, Pakistan's blasphemy laws should be suspended. And since the Pakistani military calls the shots on any policy matter, let this institution spearhead the investigation of the blasphemy laws in accordance with the Medina Constitution. After all, these laws were promulgated through martial law. Let the Pakistani military show good faith that the Taliban jihadis are not its proxies and that it has the welfare of Pakistani citizens at heart. Then let the blasphemy laws be suspended, I ask the military.

If a study of the Medina Constitution does not uphold the blasphemy laws, then who is blaspheming by citing the Nizam-e Mustafa out of context? Who is committing kufr? The military state or its offspring the Taliban and the Islami jihadi parties quoting the Prophet falsely, *naooz-o billah*. I do not see any blasphemy reference in the Medina Constitution.[36]

CHAPTER 2

MUHAMMAD, THE MESSENGER

THE POLITICAL HISTORY OF ISLAM and the Prophet Muhammad's life is central to any discussion of blasphemy laws in an Islamic state. An accounting of the Prophet's biography and the early history of Islam will illuminate Muhammad's position on blasphemy, heresy, apostasy, and heterodoxy, especially as Muhammad never advocated blasphemy laws or a shari'a for blasphemy. I argue that Islamic states developed a shari'a (jurisprudence) using Muhammad's *hadith* (sayings) and his sunna (life examples) to strengthen their authority as divine representatives and interpreters of the Prophet's holy text. While authority is necessary to run the state machinery, manipulating the shari'a gave the state control over segments of the citizenry that it considered a threat.

I argue that blasphemy laws do not come from the Qur'an, nor are they derivable from the Prophet Muhammad's life and practice. These laws were created after Muhammad's death among the empires that arose outside Arabia, such as the 'Abbasids in Iraq, the Ommayads in al-Andalus (Spain), and the Ottomans in Turkey. Although shari'a developed from local laws and customs such as those that existed in the Byzantine and Persian Empires, as well as from Qur'anic applications, these earlier empires validated their laws through Muhammad's Islam.[1] They used stories from Muhammad's life and his hadith, and in evolving a shari'a, they justified incorporating local laws and customs, as something the Prophet also did, which was not untrue; sometimes the Prophet reasoned independently, from context, that a customary law made sense. Islamic law further evolved over centuries through different schools of thought, each of which emphasized a particular position on the shari'a as they followed the Prophet Muhammad's example or his Qur'an. Some followed the hadith more and others the Qur'an or a combination of both. There is no doubt that Islamic law evolved in a political domain to govern the vast Muslim empires, and blasphemy laws were established within that political context.

Barnaby Rogerson's 2003 biography of the Prophet Muhammad, among the many biographies, is the one that speaks most about Muhammad's life as a traveler in the regions of Arabia and the Levant and illuminates how his travels provided his oral and experiential education.[2] Rogerson's biography brings to the fore Arabia's rich oral and poetic heritage that forms the basis of the Qur'an and Muhammad's preparation for the ministry of Islam. The biography speaks of the Arab poets during Muhammad's time who relied on an oral tradition but who were not necessarily literate. Embedded deeply in the Qur'an are the oral poetic traditions of Arabia that the Prophet absorbed through his intelligence and sensitivity until he was ready to transmit a divine message, unique unto itself. Rogerson's narratives on Arabia's oral cultures during Muhammad's time offer insight into the richness of the Qur'an's linguistics, its metaphorical and symbolic content, and the Prophet's preparedness to receive the oral message. Despite being *ummi* (not literate), Muhammad was neither ignorant nor lacking in worldly experience, as he had a deep understanding of human nature and the nature of the spiritual world. All along he was being prepared for the message: he was a *rasul*, which in Arabic means "messenger."

'Abdullah Yusuf 'Ali's rendering of the Arabic Holy Qur'an and its English translation together with that of Maulana Abul A'la Maududi's translations are the sources for the translations and interpretations of the Qur'an that are discussed in this book.[3] Both scholars are read widely in the Muslim world and the non-Muslim world for their insights into the Arabic text of the Holy Qur'an and their erudite commentary and historical knowledge as well as their English translations. These are some of the best and most popular translations of original Arabic texts. Maududi's English translation goes into extensive detail correlating the *suras* (sections or verses) with the existing practices of Arabic oral poetry. Arab poets initiated their poems with sounds such as *alif, lam, mim, sa, ya,* and *sin* that included various consonants; this is how several of the suras in the Qur'an also begin. The practice was based on the belief that particular consonants have a *batin* (covert) meaning and a *zahir* (overt) meaning, nuanced by the manner in which they are recited. Thus, by extension, words have power both covert and overt. The practice found greater significance among the Sufi poets in the succeeding centuries. Panjabi Sufi poets called this practice the *siharifi*.

'Abdullah Yusuf 'Ali employs deep cross-referencing to the Prophet's education in an oral culture, all documented in the Qur'an. Thus, the Qur'anic text, though fixed in its original Arabic rendering, is open to semantic and contextual interpretation. That is why different suras of the Qur'an speak to different situations even if the situations seem similar. Minor contextual changes can bring about the difference. As a lawgiver, the Prophet spoke ac-

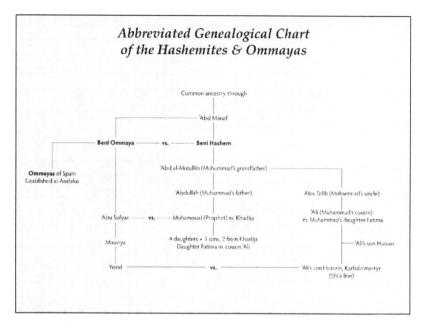

*Abbreviated Genealogical Chart
of the Hashemites & Ommayas*

Common ancestry through

'Abd Manaf

Beni Ommaya — vs. — Beni Hashem

Ommayas of Spain
Established al-Andalus

'Abd al-Mutallib (Muhammad's grandfather)

'Abdullah (Muhammad's father)   Abu Talib (Muhammad's uncle)

Abu Sufyan — vs. — Muhammad (Prophet) m. Khadija   'Ali (Muhammad's cousin)
                                                            m. Muhammad's daughter Fatima

Mauviya   4 daughters • 3 sons, 2 from Khadija
                  Daughter Fatima m. cousin 'Ali   'Ali's son Hassan

Yezid ——————————— vs. ——————————— 'Ali's son Hussein, Karbala martyr
                                                            (Shi'a line)

2.1. Genealogy improvised from Syed Amir 'Ali, *A Short History of the Saracens*,
originally published 1926.

cording to the context. The Qur'an is a rich text layered in meanings that
make a wide range of interpretations possible, hence the many schools of
fiqh (Islamic jurisprudence) and shari'a in Islamic law. The discussion that
follows connects the Qur'anic text to the context, especially as it pertains to
blasphemy. Qur'anic contexts will be explored, and examples from 'Abdullah
Yusuf 'Ali's *Meaning of the Holy Qur'an* shall be used to counter blasphemy
claims that zealots make.[4] Additionally, the Arab poets of the time and their
oral traditions will be discussed to demonstrate the blasphemy schema and
the poets' role in it.

The Prophet never created any blasphemy laws, nor did he condone
them. Based on social context theory, derived from sociolinguistics, speech
develops in a social context between speakers and listeners who interact
with each other in a particular social environment. The Prophet's life and
the context in which he operated are all about orality; disputes were set-
tled orally. Written citations attributing blasphemy laws to the Prophet are
presented out of context and are not valid. For instance, Muhammad, as
did the earlier prophet Moses, had to wield arms against his adversaries.
He fought many battles against other Arab tribes (jointly referred to as the
Quraysh). His own tribe within the Quraysh conglomerate was called the
Beni Hashem. His chief opponent was Abu Sufyan (figure 2.1), leader of

the Beni Ommaya tribe, also within the Quraysh conglomerate. The Beni Hashem and Beni Ommaya had a common ancestor, 'Abd Manaf. It must be understood that many of the battles the Prophet fought were between Arab tribes, not necessarily against some foreign invader. Some sections of the Qur'an record Muhammad's anguish against his enemies, but his quotations are frequently taken out of context in blasphemy literature, as will be documented later in this text.

MUHAMMAD'S EARLY YEARS

The Prophet Muhammad was born in Arabia in 570 CE to Aminah, a young widow. His father, 'Abdullah, who belonged to the influential Beni Hashem tribe of Mecca, died before the Prophet's birth (figure 2.1). With his father's death, Muhammad lost his inheritance. According to Arab custom Muhammad could not inherit directly from his paternal grandfather, 'Abd al-Mutallib. However, also according to tribal customs, Muhammad's grandfather, an influential patriarch of the Beni Hashem tribe, took over Muhammad's care and guardianship. As mentioned, at the time of Muhammad's birth the two most influential tribes among the Quraysh were the Beni Hashem, led by his grandfather, 'Abd al-Mutallib, and the Beni Ommaya, led by Abu Sufyan. These were rival clans that vied for the role of "caretakers of Mecca," or guardians of the Ka'aba, a cubical structure that embodies Islam's holiest shrine in the Grand Mosque of Mecca, where the annual *hajj* (pilgrimage) took place and where the powerful Bedouin tribes met annually.[5] The hajj is an ancient, pre-Islamic practice. When Muhammad began to advocate his message, close to 300 icons of idols, gods, and goddesses were housed in the Ka'aba to whom blood sacrifices were made. His message of one God was a threat to the wealthy tribes of Arabia, especially the Quraysh.

In 578, on the death of his grandfather, Muhammad's care passed to his uncle Abu Talib, the only blood brother of his father, 'Abdullah (figure 2.1). Until the very end of his life Abu Talib never converted to Islam, though when Muhammad received his first revelation at the age of forty, he continued to provide support to his nephew Muhammad and his mission to establish Islam.[6] Between the ages of nine and twelve Muhammad made his first commercial trip, with his uncle Abu Talib in a caravan going to Syria. From this period onward Muhammad traveled extensively in the Arab regions, to the Levant—Syria, Iraq, and the present Lebanon and Jordan; his travels in Petra and Palmyra are documented. He is also reported to have traveled to Yemen and along the trade route of the Red Sea, a favorite route of Arab merchants at the time. It is still a popular route, with Jeddah as a main port.

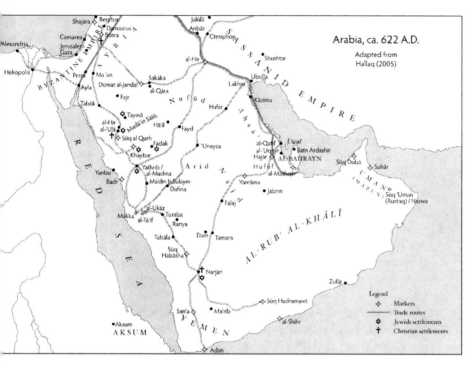

MAP 2.1. Muhammad's Arabia. Adapted from Hallaq, *Origins and Evolution of Islamic Law*, 2005, with permission of Cambridge University Press.

His travels with his uncle on business trips were the major source of Muhammad's education. On these journeys Muhammad absorbed much of the oral poetic traditions of the spoken Arabic language. He sat in the company of erudite rabbis and Christian priests. The trade caravans with which he traveled stopped in towns where Muhammad interacted with people in the inns, rabbis in synagogues, and priests in monasteries. Oral wisdom was everywhere, even in the markets. Muhammad traveled among the diverse communities of Manicheans, Zoroastrians, and Jewish people. He traveled among Christians. He traveled on the outskirts of the Byzantine Empire and right into Jerusalem.[7] Muhammad's education was derived from experience and listening to the sages of his time.

MUHAMMAD'S PROPHETHOOD

By the age of twenty-five Muhammad was a widely traveled businessman who had matured in the art of negotiating, knew the art of commerce, and was deeply steeped in the religious knowledge of the Abrahamic faiths, that is to say, Judaism and Christianity. In those times, Arab citizens like Muhammad were knowledgeable about the scriptures through oral culture. He was aware of the Hebrew and Aramaic texts. He was definitely steeped in the sophisticated oral poetic traditions of the Arab region. The sensuous imagery of the Qur'an and the poetry of the suras are proof of this.[8] Muhammad had experienced all the above as a prelude to the revelation.

When the message came, his major opponents were his own people, the Quraysh tribes and their influential members, other pagan tribes, and Jewish and Christian tribes. This was the context of his life at the time he received the message. In the beginning it was mostly the marginalized citizens who looked toward Islam (the word meaning "submission" or "peace") for social justice: slaves, the poor, orphans, children, exiles, persecuted minorities, widows, and people of color. Muhammad's reaching out to the underclasses with his message was threatening to the wealthy clans.

Muhammad fought battles, made alliances, and negotiated peace deals with the different tribes and married into some after the death of his first wife, Khadija, during whose lifetime he remained monogamous. However, instances linking his battles against the Quraysh or the Jewish and Christian tribes to the Prophet issuing blasphemy injunctions misrepresent the facts.

At the age of twenty-five, after Muhammad had successfully traded Khadija's goods on one of his travel itineraries, she, twice widowed and independently wealthy, proposed marriage to Muhammad through a matchmaker, Nufaysah.[9] Khadija was fifteen years older than Muhammad; she bore Muhammad six children—four daughters and two sons. Some say the Prophet buried three sons. Since the Prophet did not have sons to succeed him, his enemies called him *al-abtar*, a person without a tail, or someone without a successor.[10] Muhammad and Khadija were great partners. She was the first one to accept Islam.

Muhammad was inducted into the spiritual practices of his times through what he absorbed from other faiths, mainly Judaism and Christianity. During a meditation in the fasting month of Ramadan, the archangel Gabriel appeared to Muhammad. He received his first revelation, a short verse compiled in the last sections of the Qur'an. Muhammad was terrified, but Khadija counseled him. She consulted her cousin Waraqa bin Nofal, a Christian priest, who confirmed that indeed Muhammad was the prophet who was expected and whom the Judaic and Christian scriptures had predicted. Only, the Jews and Christians had anticipated that prophet would be of their own faith and not a new one.

At the time of Muhammad's birth, polytheism was common. Muhammad's Qur'anic revelations pertaining to one God were a threat to the social order. Though he was well versed in Arabic oral poetry, the tribes questioned his credentials because he was ummi, not literate. Muhammad held nocturnal meetings with his followers in which the verses of the Qur'anic revelations were recited, collectively chanted, repeated, and preserved mnemonically.[11]

In the beginning, opposition to Islam as a new faith stemmed from Muhammad's ummi status. His credentials were questioned because the faiths around him had highly developed literate scriptures. The following suras from the Qur'an refer to the Prophet's unlettered status:[12]

So believe
In Allah and His Messenger
The unlettered Prophet
Who believeth in Allah
And His Words: follow him
That ye may be guided
. . .

Those who follow the Messenger,
The unlettered Prophet,
Whom they find mentioned
In their own [Scriptures][13]
. . .

Help him, and follow the Light

Muhammad's conflicts with the Quraysh and some of the Christian and Jewish tribes and the consequent battles, negotiations, renegotiations, and uncertainties, which provide the so-called blasphemy contexts, derive from opposition to the Prophet's ministry and his ummi, illiterate status. It was also significant that he was not on the same economic footing with his oppressors.

THE GROWTH OF ISLAM

With the coming of Muhammad, a new order emerged that disrupted the tribal mores and wealth and most of all challenged formal education. In Arabia of the seventh century, Muhammad's message of social justice, economic equality, and regard for the oppressed—the poor, orphaned, and downtrodden—was revolutionary. It challenged the Arabian tribal hierarchy. The Prophet had experienced poverty, and he was an orphan who lived on the periphery of his Beni Hashem tribe. He herded his uncle Abu Talib's camels and livestock, as after the death of 'Abd al-Mutallib, his grandfather, there was not much in terms of resources. Muhammad inherited nothing and had to earn his keep. The wealthy Beni Ommaya and the tribes of Quraysh saw Muhammad as a nuisance. What was this poor, uneducated person trying to do?

The powerful Quraysh were against Muhammad's message of social and economic justice. So were some of the Jewish and Christian tribes who were allies of the Quraysh. As Muhammad received the revelation in short verses and spread his message of one God, his enemies in Mecca multiplied. This was especially true after his three main patrons died: his grandfather 'Abd al-Mutallib, his beloved wife Khadija, and a few years later his uncle Abu Talib. With all Muhammad's patrons in Mecca gone, the Quraysh launched a vile attack against him, so concerted that even his uncle Abu Lahab turned against him.[14] Muhammad's followers were relegated to a tiny corner of Mecca. A trade ban was imposed on him and his followers; they were starving, as no one would buy from them or sell to them. Tradition has it that it was during this period that the Prophet's paternal uncle Abu Lahab and his wife threw trash at him. These verses from the Qur'an are narratives of Muhammad expressing his anguish for his persecution at the hands of Abu Lahab and his wife. In his anguish Muhammad cries:[15]

Perish the hands
Of the Father of Flames
Perish he!

. . .

No profit to him
From all his wealth
And all his gains!

. . .

Burnt soon he will be
In a Fire
Of blazing flame!

. . .

His wife shall carry
The crackling wood—
As fuel!

. . .

A twisted rope
Of palm and leaf fibre
Round her neck[16]

Supporters of blasphemy laws quote verses such as these to justify retaliation, but Muhammad does not call for retaliation, as the verses illustrate.[17] These Qur'anic verses do not invoke personal retaliation from the Prophet on his uncle or his uncle's wife. At worst it could be interpreted to refer to the comeuppance that followed soon for Abu Lahab. He died in painful defeat. In the historical memory of Muslims both husband and wife go down as Islam's enemies. However, there is no justification for zealots to pull out references to this text to support their actions, and yet they do; they use these verses to justify their actions against those who do not subscribe to orthodox or militant Islam.

BLASPHEMY AND THE ARAB POETS

Poets had been part of the Arabian landscape for centuries. While often illiterate, they were eloquent in Arabic poetry and the colloquial idiom. The wealthy and the influential commissioned these poets to laud their ancestry, proclaim a victory, or taunt an enemy. Abu Sufyan, a wealthy nobleman and chief of the Beni Ommaya tribe, was an astute politician and one of Muhammad's enemies.[18] After the Battle of Badr and the defeat of the Beni Ommayas he commissioned the poet K'ab al-Ashraf to compose verses that satirized the Prophet.

In particular, K'ab satirized the Prophet's marriage to Hafsah, whose husband was killed in the Battle of Badr. She was the daughter of Omar al-Khattab, who was to become the second caliph after Muhammad. K'ab drew an analogy between Muhammad and King David, who married Bathsheba after her husband was slain in a battle fighting for King David. K'ab was eventually assassinated. It is claimed that the assassination was a response to the Prophet's prayer, quoted here in Rogerson:

"O Lord, deliver me from the son of al-Ashraf [K'ab] however thou wilt, for the evil he declareth and the poems he declaimeth." He is then reported to have said to his people, "Who is for me is against the son, of al-Ashraf, for he hath done me great injury . . . he wrote poetry against us and none of you shall do this but he shall be put to the sword."[19]

In later years, the Prophet's son-in-law 'Ali ibn Abi Talib threatened 160 lashes for anyone who brought up such comparisons. Once again, however, it is clear that the Prophet did not order an execution. Though the appeal is open to interpretation, proponents of blasphemy laws cite this incident as a call to militancy.

MUHAMMAD'S MESSAGE OF TOLERANCE

Proponents of the blasphemy laws cite verses from the Qur'an to justify capital punishment, but I have not found a single reference to this in 'Abdullah Yusuf 'Ali's translation or for that matter in Maududi's translation. In fact, "punishment for blasphemy" does not even appear in the index of 'Abdullah Yusuf 'Ali's translation except in reference to the "begotten son of Allah."[20] But ideological differences with Christians on the issue of the Trinity were a cause of animosity toward the Prophet and his message. Islam recognizes neither a Trinity nor Jesus as the son of God. That is discussed in extensive detail in Maududi's translation of the Holy Qur'an, where he asserts that Islam does not subscribe to the Trinity.[21] The Prophet's messages in Sura al-Ma'idah and Sura al-An'am speak clearly of Jesus as a messenger (like himself), Jesus's abilities to heal lepers, that he was the son of Mary, that he was strengthened by the Holy Spirit, that he talked to people even when he was a baby in the cradle, and that when he grew up he spoke with wisdom from the Torah. Jesus created the Gospel, but he was not the son of God; this is what Muslims believe. This is a major point of difference between Islam and some Christian sects; Islam does not accept the Trinity or the belief that Mary is the mother of God as Catholic doctrine teaches. Such a belief constitutes blasphemy in the Islamic faith. This may perhaps be the cause of the militant attacks against the Christian communities in Pakistan. Quoting from the Qur'an, Maududi translates lines of Sura al-An'am about God in this respect: "He is the Originator of the heavens and the earth: how shall He have a son, when he has no consort?" (243). Practices and belief systems are different. However, never once did the Prophet invoke retribution toward other creeds, even those that believed in the Trinity.

Other poets cited for insulting the Prophet through satirical poetry were 'Abdullah bin Ibn Zib'ari and two brothers, K'ab bin Zubair and Bujair bin Zubair.[22] However, over the course of time, these poets succumbed to Islam's appeal; they either converted to Islam or gave up the opposition. Women, too, were among the poets who wrote verses against the Prophet or spoke out against him. One such poet was 'Asma bin Merwan. A zealot assassinated her. Hind bint 'Utba, Abu Sufyan's wife, was a bitter opponent of the Prophet. Hind participated in the Battle of Badr and incited the Quraysh to fight against Muhammad. She did likewise in the Battle of Ohud and was one of the women who was outspoken against the Prophet and his message. However, after the conquest of Mecca, she converted to Islam. One does not know what the motives for conversion were, as the Beni Ommayas remained sworn enemies of Muhammad's Hashemite lineage for centuries.

From the instances given here, no evidence exists to pro
Prophet instituted punishments in the garb of blasphemy laws ag
women, or citizens who reviled him. He forgave his opponent;
ments such as executions for blasphemy in the Prophet's times
on different hadith, or sayings, of either the Prophet or his Companions.
They are not documented in the Qur'an. How the hadith evolved as part of
Islamic law or shari'a is controversial. This is a complex domain.

Seventh-century Arabia, as is still true, had a rich heritage of poetry and
song.[24] How could it be that the Prophet was not in tune with the mood
of his people and their cultural expressions of satire, ridicule, and revelry in
poetry? Painful as the poetry was, he endured his opponents. Current supporters of the blasphemy laws remove the Prophet's sayings and the sayings
of others from the social context of the time; his life and his sayings are reported out of context. The verses in the Qur'an have no relevance to blasphemy being punishable with death by human agency.

At times the Prophet's adversaries compared him to the poets of the desert as if he were a man possessed or mad and his Qur'anic revelations mad-
ness. His anguish emanated from the ridicule cast on him, aggravated by
his unlettered status, the denying of his message of social justice and human rights, his wisdom, and his sensitivity. Some examples of the Prophet's
anguish are quoted here.[25] In these verses Muhammad received solace
from God:[26]

Nun. By the Pen
And by the Record
Which men write
Thy art not
By the grace of thy Lord
Mad or possessed

The Qur'an is rich in examples like the above in which Muhammad receives
comfort for the message he brought for social justice. Sometimes the comfort Muhammad received was about retribution in the hereafter:

That House of the Hereafter
We shall give to those
Who intended not high-handedness
Or mischief on earth
And the End is (best)
For the righteous

The Qur'anic evidence indicates that Muhammad was counseled to leave justice to the Almighty. He was never commanded to bring blasphemy punishments against his perpetrators; he was to seek only mercy and forgiveness for them.

MUHAMMAD'S BATTLES

After his migration from Mecca to Medina in 622 Muhammad was firm in his belief that the economic power of the Quraysh, the merchant tribes, had to be squashed. They threatened his message too much. He began making preparations to attack the caravans—the Quraysh's source of wealth. One such battle was in March 624 at the Wells of Badr when a Quraysh caravan returning from Syria along the Red Sea route was intercepted (map 2.1). The Quraysh were 1,000 strong, while the Prophet and his followers amounted to 313 men, all poorly equipped. Nevertheless, the Muslims were passionate in their battle, and they defeated the Quraysh.[27] After this loss, the Quraysh paid poets like K'ab al-Ashraf to recite insulting poetry against Muhammad, an instance quoted profusely in blasphemy literature.[28]

The next battle the Prophet fought was in 625 at Ohud, outside Medina. Muhammad and his followers lost this battle largely due to the strength his enemies built through the work of the poets and rhapsodists who held significant influence in Arabia.[29] One such poet was Abu Uzza, who went among the tribes to excite them with his songs and poetry against the Muslims to persuade them to join the Quraysh confederacy in order to destroy Muhammad and his followers. Muhammad's followers executed Abu Uzza once he was captured. As such, a lot of blasphemy literature is based on narratives like Abu Azza's capture and execution. It further led to the creation of hate literature against poets; these are the unofficial origins of blasphemy laws in Islamic domains. Subsequently, the material was written down and documented in the Islamic empires. Poets and intellectuals became the prime suspects of blasphemy, as will be discussed later.

MUHAMMAD'S RELATIONS WITH JEWISH TRIBES AND OTHER NON-MUSLIMS

On the Arabian scene, in his struggles against his adversaries the Prophet's relationship with the Jewish tribes was complex. The major tribes were the Beni Nadir, Beni Qurayzah, and Beni Qaynuqa. They questioned the Prophet's authority, themselves coming from a literate tradition with highly developed scriptures. They questioned Muhammad's unlettered status and

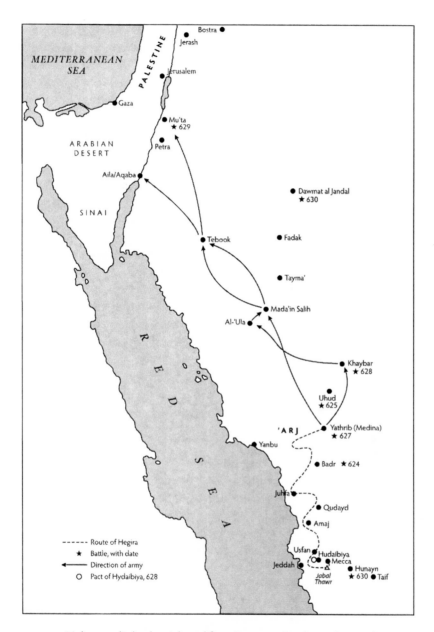

MAP 2.2. Muhammad's battles. Adapted from Rogerson, *Prophet Muhammad*, 2003, with permission from Barnaby Rogerson.

his revelations. They questioned him as a prophet. Additionally, they were wealthy, were a military threat, and were independent in their thinking and beliefs. They lived in fortified villages where they had a communal identity in the desert, and they were a formidable force to be dealt with. Moreover, they had strong political and economic alliances with Arabian tribes, especially the Beni Ommaya, who were Muhammad's adversaries.

Many times the Jewish tribes made alliances with Muhammad through other Arabian tribes but reneged on those treaties. Thus, these Arabian tribes are called the *munafikin* (traitors), and an entire heresiology literature emerged based on events in Muhammad's time that referred to Islam's enemies as the *munafikin*, or turncoats against Islam. This happened particularly during the Battle of the Trench in 627, when some communities that had alliances with Muhammad broke their treaties. Muhammad's victory in the Battle of the Trench resulted in the Jews of Medina being banished from the city. Later the Jewish tribes were banished from Khaybar, too, after Muhammad conquered their fortress. Much of the heresiology literature emanates from Muhammad's battles that he fought against his adversaries among the Arabian and Jewish tribes.[30] The events following the Battle of the Trench and the continuous animosity with Abu Sufyan and the Quraysh may have added to the sources of the blasphemy laws.

As a counterargument to those attributing blasphemy laws to the Prophet Muhammad, one can cite the charter the Prophet gave to Christians in the sixth year of the Hijra (the time of Muhammad's migration from Mecca), summarized here:[31]

The Prophet reached an understanding with the monks of the monastery of St. Catherine near Mt. Sinai and to all Christians, that secured significant privileges and immunities for the Christians. Severe penalties were assigned for Muslims violating this charter. Through this charter the Prophet took upon himself and his followers to protect all Christians, guard them from injuries, to defend their churches and the residences of their priests. They were not to be taxed unfairly. No bishop was to be driven out of his bishopric. No Christian was to be forced to give up his religion. No monk was to be expelled from his monastery. No pilgrim was to be detained from his pilgrimage. Nor were the Christian churches to be pulled down for the sake of building mosques or houses for Muslims. Christian women married to Muslim men were to enjoy their own religion and were not to be subjected to compulsion. If the Christians should stand in need of assistance for the repair of their churches or monasteries or other matters related to their religion, the Muslims were to assist them.

Muhammad's charter specifically affirms that "severe penalties were to be assigned for Muslims violating this charter." In the seventh year of the Hijra, when a rebellion of the Jews in Khaybar was suppressed, the Jews were allowed to keep their lands and property with the freedom to practice their religion. However, they had to pay a fixed land tax that was half the produce of their lands.[32] Would the Prophet have given such a charter for the Christians or allowed the Jews in Khaybar to retain their lands if he supported the contentious blasphemy laws?

Blasphemy laws in the Islamic state are contrary to the Prophet's sunna, his example. Before his death in Medina in 632, the Prophet made a farewell pilgrimage to Mecca. On the eighth day of Zil-Hajj, March 7, 632, he addressed his followers from the top of Jabal-ul Arafat, Mount Arafat. In his last sermon to his people, he said,

> Ye people! Listen to my words, for I know not whether another year will be vouchsafed to me after this year to find myself amongst you . . . Henceforth the vengeance of blood practiced in the days of paganism (Jahilyat) is prohibited; and all blood feud abolished . . . And your slaves! See that you feed them with such food as ye eat yourselves, and clothe them with the stuff that ye wear; and if they commit a fault which ye are not inclined to forgive, then part from them, for they are the servants of the Lord, and are not to be treated harshly. . . . All mankind is from Adam and Eve, an Arab has no superiority over a non-Arab nor has a non-Arab any superiority over an Arab: also a white has no superiority over a black nor a black has any superiority over white except by piety and good action.[33]

Having said these words, how then could the Prophet or the Qur'an approve the linguistic content of blasphemy laws in any Islamic state?

THE SEEDS OF BLASPHEMY LAWS AFTER MUHAMMAD'S DEATH

A possible source of the blasphemy laws that forbid the claim that there can be a prophet after Muhammad could be that immediately following Muhammad's demise, Abu Bekr became the caliph (632–634) and some of the tribal chiefs revolted. It was a significant rebellion against Islam. Many false prophets proclaimed ministries. This is known as the Apostasy Movement or the riddah wars (politico-religious uprisings); Caliph Abu Bekr had to fight to crush the rebellion. The claim of the riddah tribes was that their treaty was with Muhammad, and now that he was no longer alive, they were not

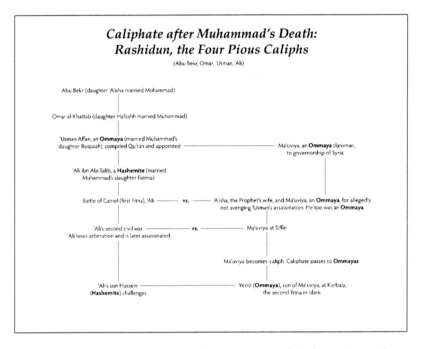

Caliphate after Muhammad's Death:
Rashidun, the Four Pious Caliphs
(Abu Bekr, Omar, 'Usman, 'Ali)

Abu Bekr (daughter 'A'isha married Muhammad)

Omar al-Khattab (daughter Hafsahh married Muhammad)

'Usman Affan, an **Ommaya** (married Muhammad's daughter Ruquiah), compiled Qu'ran and appointed ——————— Ma'uviya, an **Ommaya** clansman, to governorship of Syria

'Ali ibn Abi Talib, a **Hashemite** (married Muhammad's daughter Fatima)

Battle of Camel (first fitna), 'Ali ——— **vs.** ——— 'A'isha, the Prophet's wife, and Ma'uviya, an **Ommaya**, for allegedly not avenging 'Usman's assassination. He too was an **Ommaya**

'Ali's second civil war. ——— **vs.** ——— Ma'uviya at Siffin
'Ali loses arbitration and is later assassinated.

Ma'uviya becomes caliph. Caliphate passes to **Ommayas**.

'Ali's son Hussein ——————— Yezid (**Ommaya**), son of Ma'uviya, at Karbala,
(**Hashemite**) challenges   the second fitna in Islam

2.2. Shemeem Abbas, 2009. At the end of this succession of caliphs, Muhammad's grandson Hussein and his supporters are massacred in Karbala, establishing the S̲h̲i'a line through Hussein's son Zeinul 'Abideen, born from Hussein's Iranian wife. The Battle of Karbala establishes the Hashemite-Ommaya rift. S̲h̲i'ism gains roots in Iran, Iraq, Syria, Egypt, and India. The S̲h̲i'a imams trace descent from 'Ali, a Hashemite. This chart summarizes the contexts in which S̲h̲i'a and Sunni have charged each other with apostasy, heresy, blasphemy, and heterodoxy.

obliged to abide by the pact through his successor. They claimed that they could raid other tribes in the Muslim *ummah* (community). Abu Bekr had to put down these tribes. It was perhaps during the riddah wars that Muslims began to assert that Muhammad was the last and greatest of all prophets as Muslims challenged the riddah prophets.[34]

Apostasy, therefore, needs to be understood within the context of what Caliph Abu Bekr had to contend with in the post-Muhammad era: a revolt against the fledgling Islamic theology. At times, later Islamic leaders appropriated Qur'anic or prophetic authority by invoking broad definitions of and severe punishments for blasphemy, heresy, apostasy, or heterodoxy to legitimize political and ideological control. The schisms in Islam that arose after the time of Muhammad play into the blasphemy laws.

It was during 'Ali ibn Abi Talib's caliphate, the fourth in succession to Muhammad, that the first *fitna* (schism) happened in Islam (figure 2.2). It was a war between 'Ali and Muhammad's consort, 'A'isha bint-e Abu Bekr, whom Ma'uviya, the son of Abu Sufyan, supported. 'A'isha at that time was in her forties. When the Prophet died, 'A'isha was a childless widow of eighteen.[35] 'A'isha's kinsmen Talha and Zubair also supported 'A'isha, as each wanted the government of Qufa and Basra. Ma'uviya, who was a Beni Ommaya, had already been appointed to the governorship of Syria through his clansman Caliph 'Usman Affan. Fought in 656 near Basra, the conflict was called the Battle of Camel. 'A'isha directed the forces riding in a palanquin on the back of a camel. The palanquin was covered in veils. 'A'isha lost the battle, which was supposedly about 'Ali, the caliph, not having done enough to discover and punish the perpetrators of Caliph 'Usman's assassination. Spellberg affirms that it was a war of succession in which perhaps 'A'isha herself had a stake. 'Usman, too, was of the Beni Ommaya, and although he was a pious caliph, his reign is said to have been weak—showering favors on his clanspeople from the Beni Ommaya. It was during 'Usman's reign that Ma'uviya established himself as the governor of Syria, from which he reconquered Muhammad's Arabian empire. Later, it was the Beni Ommayas, his clansmen, who established the Muslim empire of al-Andalus in Spain.

Although 'A'isha lost the Battle of Camel to 'Ali and was imprisoned, she was later sent with dignity back to Medina, where she spent the rest of her life narrating the Prophet's hadith (some of which even the Shi'a acknowledge despite ideological difference with this consort of the Prophet). Later in life, she is said to have deeply regretted her opposition to 'Ali ibn Abi Talib in the Battle of Camel.

The conflicts after the Prophet did not stop there. Now Ma'uviya came out in the open, and a confrontation took place between him and 'Ali ibn Abi Talib at Siffin.[36] The matter was put up for arbitration. The results were not favorable for 'Ali, who was never really able to subjugate Ma'uviya until the end of his caliphate. After Siffin, 'Ali retreated in disappointment to Qufa, where he was assassinated in 661.

Some of the tribes were intensely disgusted with this post-Muhammad internecine warfare, that is to say, between his consort 'A'isha and his son-in-law 'Ali and then between 'Ali and Ma'uviya. These tribes asserted that only the Qur'an was the true Islam. All else was carved up, they claimed. They called themselves the Kharjis (exclusionists) and retreated to the southern Arabian Peninsula in areas around Yemen and Oman.[37]

Following the two civil wars after Muhammad's death, first between 'A'isha and 'Ali and then between Ma'uviya and 'Ali, the mutual practice of calling other groups of Muhammad's descendants "infidels" continued. Among Shi'a circles, *la'an* (condemnation) of the first three caliphs continued. The second fitna, at Karbala, perpetuated the practice among the Shi'a.

The third civil war (second fitna) in Islam was the Battle of Karbala. Here the Beni Hashem and Beni Ommaya conflict came to a head.[38] On becoming caliph in Damascus, Yezid demanded the allegiance of Muhammad's grandson Hussein, which Hussein refused on the grounds that Yezid did not represent Islam, for he was a debaucher and his ways were not Islamic but, rather, went back to the *jahilliya*, the pre-Islam, pre-Muhammad ways. Hussein lived in the Medina sanctuary, but instigated by the people of Qufa in Iraq who indicated that they would support him against Yezid, Hussein headed to Qufa—against the best advice of Muhammad's Companions (now extremely old), well-wishers, and politically astute Medinites. Hussein went to Qufa with close to 300 followers including his wives and children. At Karbala in Iraq, Yezid's forces intercepted Hussein and his followers. In the battle that followed, Hussein and his followers were massacred. Only one son, Zeinul 'Abideen, was spared, as he was too sick for the battlefield. Historically, he is known as 'Abid the Sick. The women and children were marched off to Yezid's capital in Damascus.

During Muharram, the Karbala tragedy is reenacted annually among Shi'a communities with passion and pageantry the world over and especially in Iran, as the Shi'a claim that one of Hussein's wives, Shahr Bano, was an Iranian princess and Zeinul 'Abideen was her son. South Asian Shi'a claim that as a prisoner of war in the Arab-Iranian conflicts, Shahr Bano chose to marry Hussein for his prestigious Hashemite heritage. (However, when I brought up this conversation with an Iranian colleague at the University of Texas, the colleague said that Iranians look upon Shahr Bano as a victim, if anything, of the Arabs.) The Shi'a *imams* are traced to Imam Zeinul 'Abideen and his Irani connection through Shahr Bano. The Arab-Ajam (non-Arab, Persian) rivalry remains to this day, as do blasphemy laws in the territories where the histories played out. Shi'a fiqh or shari'a evolved mainly in Iran, while Sunni fiqh or shari'a evolved in other parts of the Islamic world according to different schools of thought; both fiqh, whether Shi'a or Sunni, have their own blasphemy laws or versions thereof. To sum up, the political splits and reaches for power of the caliphs following Muhammad spawned the rivalries between the Shi'a and the Sunni, which led to their respective blasphemy laws and the labeling of the other as infidels. These laws grew out of political rivalry and not out of Muhammad's sunna or the Qur'an.

CHAPTER 3

BLASPHEMY LAWS' EVOLUTION

THIS CHAPTER EXPLORES THE CLAIM that the Islamic state has historically used blasphemy laws for political and social control. A brief background of Islamic law after the Prophet's death is given to throw light on how the laws evolved. It is important to understand how the use of blasphemy charges evolved in conjunction with the state's relationship with its subjects and how Islam was used as a binding force to bring people together as well as a force for controlling them. This is consistent with the discussion that *bid'a* (heresy) and *kufr* (blasphemy) are relative terms that have been used interchangeably, mainly for political purposes, in the Islamic state. Drawing from Fatima Mernissi's *The Veil and the Male Elite*, Wael Hallaq's *The Origins and Evolution of Islamic Law*, and Moulavi Cheragh 'Ali's *Proposed Political, Legal, and Social Reforms under Muslim Rule*, it will be possible to see that although Islamic law evolved according to elements of local customs, tribal laws were also integrated into the system.[1] However, interpreting and incorporating local elements into shari'a has been at the whim of the state and whatever has suited it at a particular time.

The shari'a has never been a fixed document. It evolves as jurists and jurisconsults interpret the Qur'an and the sunna (examples from the Prophet's life) in a particular context or situation according to their own judgment, and seeking guidance from the customary laws of the region is not unheard of.[2] The growing needs of the Muslim empire, according to Cheragh 'Ali, led to the formation of several schools of jurisprudence based on the various systems of interpreting the Qur'an and the different methods of testing and accepting the authority of the oral traditions. Thus, facets of Islamic law were sometimes different in Turkey and India, or as currently, differences exist in Islamic law between Egypt and Pakistan such as in matters of divorce. Social and cultural context was always taken into consideration. Both Mernissi and Ayesha Siddiqa assert that codifying the shari'a was initiated under the ʿAbbasids, who had their own agendas, and thus their jurists worked on their shariʿa accordingly.[3] Again, Cheragh ʿAli affirms that, when necessary, every religious, social, and political system was defended to serve the purpose of a caliph, also known as an *amir*, by an appeal to some oral traditions. Muhammad's name was abused to support all manner of lies and absurdities or to satisfy the passion, caprice, or arbitrary will of the despots without consideration of a standard.[4] Later, under the Ottomans the shariʿa was invoked, especially in matters of heresy and blasphemy, when what really was at stake were differences in religious ideology with the Ottoman Sunni state.[5]

Some origins of blasphemy and heresy laws in the Islamic state post-Muhammad seem to be rooted in the fitna (schism) that followed his death, the selection of his successor, and the two fitnas that followed. These schisms divided the community. Each group, whether it was Shiʿa or Sunni, called the other *kafir*, and each group created its own hadith (recording and interpreting the words and deeds of the Prophet) to uphold its claim that it was following the true successor to the Prophet.[6]

PROBLEMS WITH THE HADITH

Many hadith evolved after the death of the Prophet, and Mernissi affirms:

> The winds of discord were blowing strong . . . They [the Muslims] were throwing insults like *kafir* [infidel] and *fasiq* [libertine] at each other . . . The *umma* was now divided into Shiʿites who were pro-ʿAli and the pro-Ummayads . . . the Shiʿites themselves were split into various opposing factions.[7]

People were confused and terrified to see their faith disintegrating, so they sought to fill the vacuum by writing down the Prophet's sayings. In the wake of this effort, self-serving individuals created false hadith and attributed them to the Prophet. It was difficult to collect the true hadith. The main problem was that it was all being collected after the fact, a long time after the Prophet's life.

A secondary problem rested with the reliability of the transmitters. Muhammad ibn Ismail al-Bukhari (810–870), a Sunni Muslim scholar who is generally considered to have collected the authentic sayings of the Prophet and who was born almost 194 years after the Islamic Hijra of the Prophet, did try to evolve some system, but his system also came with its own problems of context. He was relying on how individuals interpreted a particular event and whether or not they were scholars. Hadith, at best, has a historical interest, but the more astute and independent among the Prophet's successors, such as Omar al-Khattab (634–644 as the second pious caliph), used their own judgment in giving legal verdicts rather than depending on hadith attributed to the Prophet. Omar avoided recounting hadith, especially those attributed to the much-quoted hadith transmitter Abu Hurayra.[8] Interestingly, in *A Short History of the Revivalist Movements in India*, Maulana Maududi attributes a number of his claims to Abu Hurayra.[9]

At different times, under the various caliphs, poets and storytellers also played into the hadith traditions. Taha Husayn (1889–1973), who was convicted for apostasy in Egypt, said,

> The storytellers came to recite tales to crowds in provincial mosques. They recounted to them the old stories of the Arabs and non Arabs; they spoke to them of the prophets and used this material to slip in explications of the Koran, the Hadith, and the biography of the Prophet. Military expeditions and conquests were also touched on. These storytellers led the crowds through these subjects, carried along by imagination, knowing nothing of the limits imposed by scientific discipline and the rigor of authentication. The crowds, fascinated by the storytellers, gulped down all the stories they were told. The caliphs and princes quickly realizing the political and religious importance of this new means of communication encouraged and controlled it. They used and exploited it for their own purposes.[10]

Muhammad Abid al-Jabiri gives extensive historical evidence that very early on the rulers realized they could legitimize their authority by associating and justifying acts on the basis of religious citations.[11] According to him, "The famous *'asr al-tadwin*, the era of putting the religious texts into writing, was the beginning of the institutionalizing of censorship." It began in the eighth century CE, in year 134 of the Hijra (AH), when the Muslim bureaucrats began to catalogue the hadith, fiqh, and *tafsir* (explication of the Qur'an) at the "express order of the 'Abbasid state and under its supervision."[12] Modern politicians have continued to wield authority from what they claim is an original Arabic text such as one of the hadith compilations of al-Bukhari or the Qur'an to impress the citizenry. And since most citizens have never bothered to look into the Arabic text, sometimes not even the Qur'an, these politicians have escaped criticism with what they claimed was "authority from the past."[13] Most citizens are afraid to question these pronouncements lest they be branded heretics or commit heresy by questioning an Arabic text.[14] Frankly, many citizens of Islamic states do not have the investigative skills to look into the texts, so the authorities or the agencies have escaped accountability with their claims in the name of Islamic sanctity.

One of the reasons for the increase in fabricated hadith, according to Muhammad Abu Zahra in his chapter titled "The Increase in Lying Concerning the Prophet and the Schisms and Divisions in the Ranks of the *Fuqaha*," is that after the death of the Prophet, the Muslim world was torn by dissent. Beneath the spiritual power evoked by the Prophet were smoldering passions that would lead the *ummah* (Muslim community) to civil wars and produce the schisms that give Islam the sects we know today.[15] Each of the dissenting groups created its own hadith—each with its own justifications and interpretations. How are any of them verifiable, or can one be truer than the other?[16]

GENERAL ZIA-UL-HAQ'S NIZAM-E MUSTAFA

With General Zia-ul-Haq's blasphemy laws deriving legitimacy from the Nizam-e Mustafa (Muhammad's Islam), a rabid fanaticism set in that has made it virtually impossible to have any sane dialogue of tolerance. Pakistani militants derived validation from such fabrications and threatened anyone who challenged the blasphemy laws as challenging Muhammad's Islam; even parliamentary leaders were threatened.

In Pakistan the shari'a discourse started with Zia-ul-Haq. During the so-called Islamization of the laws, he appointed judges to the Shari'at Court who would implement a very limited, orthodox version of the shari'a, a construct foreign to the society at the time. Historically, Pakistan was not a tribal Arab society. Pakistan had a history of centuries of tolerant Muslim rule that generally followed the Hanafi interpretation and was later governed under the British with a set of colonial laws, although Muslim personal law still prevailed in matters of marriage, divorce, and inheritance. The administrative code of British colonial India placed blasphemy under a penal code to prevent conflicts among the numerous religious groups, the Hindus, Sikhs, Muslims, Christians, Parsis, and others. Governing under this model made it possible for each of the different religious sects to govern personal matters according to its own traditions and beliefs.

With Zia-ul-Haq's Islamization policy, blasphemy laws were put under an ostensibly Islamic penal code that resurrected all the schisms of Islam.[17] Matters that had remained buried in the minds of ordinary citizens or handled according to civil jurisdiction within each belief system became a point of contention with the reinterpretation of the laws. Large issues, such as who can be a Muslim and who cannot, the Ahmediyya-Qadiani exclusion being a case in point, rose to the surface. The Ahmediyyas, or Qadianis, until the Khatam-e Nabuvat (finality of prophethood) movement in Z. A. Bhutto's time in the 1970s, had been accepted as part of mainstream Islam, and intermarriage was common with this sect. The Ahmediyya-Qadiani difference with mainstream Islam is in considering Mirza Ghulam Ahmed of Qadian, a religious figure of the mid- to late nineteenth century, as a spiritual force, while mainstream Muslims, especially the orthodox and clerics, believe that revelation was final with Muhammad's ministry. In the 1970s Bhutto succumbed to the pressure of the Jamaat-e Islami and other religious parties through their Khatam-e Nabuvat movement. Consequently, the Ahmediyya-Qadiani were excommunicated from the fold of Islam and were declared non-Muslims.[18] Such exclusion was never an aim of the founding fathers like Jinnah and Iqbal.

As if this were not enough, passport forms and other modes of identification in Pakistan are specifically designed to discriminate against this community. Pakistan's blasphemy laws categorically forbid citizens of this community from claiming themselves as Muslims, as shown in appendix 2. In May 2010 a full-fledged massacre of Ahmediyya-Qadiani was carried out in two of their mosques in Pakistan right under the eyes of the Panjab provincial government in Lahore.[19] This is the same Sharif government under which in 1998 the Islamic parties had become heady, as described in chapter 1. After a backlash, Sharif and his family were granted asylum by the Saudi government in 2000 during General Musharraf's regime. To this Zia-ul-Haq added the deadly Hudood ordinances against women.[20] The penalties under both laws, that is to say, the blasphemy and Hudood laws, are tribal in origin and include arcane punishments such as execution, stoning, lashing, and dismemberment—punishments dating back to the seventh century. A kind and just God would certainly not have wanted such punishments as part of his law, as the Qur'an repeatedly reaffirms kindness and grace. Pakistan's shari'a laws under Zia-ul-Haq were intended to legitimize military rule in Islam's name, silence opposition, and repress freedom of speech. General Zia-ul-Haq became the Amir-ul Momineen (leader of the faithful) to lead the CIA-backed jihad against the Soviets in Afghanistan. And thus Pakistan, which had been a secular state, moved toward a theocracy to fulfill this agenda.

Pakistan's blasphemy laws were, among other things, motivated by the geopolitics of the region.[21] With the fall of the shah of Iran and the takeover by the Shi'a militant orthodoxy under Ayatollah Khomeini and the Soviet incursion into Afghanistan, Pakistan became a frontline state to block the Soviets from accessing the Persian Gulf via Balochistan. The Iranian ayatollahs were not too hostile to the Soviets, and so a diehard Sunni opposition, leaning in favor of Saudi-backed Wahabism, had to be set up through Pakistan. Zia-ul-Haq was suited to lead such a military expedition, as his own upbringing was in the Wahabi clerical tradition.

Zia-ul-Haq thus co-opted Pakistan's Islamic religious parties such as the Jamaat-e Islami and others that had all united under a common banner of the Pakistan National Alliance (PNA) and were connected with Saudi-backed Wahabism. The pact members—Zia-ul-Haq, the Islamic religious parties, Afghan warlords with the local Afghan mujahideen (Islam's soldiers), and Arab-backed entrepreneurs with secret funding from the CIA—armed themselves. They charted what they called an Islamic agenda to bring down the Soviets, defined as the infidel or Islam's enemy in Afghanistan. The Soviets were also projected as threatening Pakistan's borders as well as the Gulf states, a majority of which were Islamic. The communist enemy of the Muslim world, according to this outlook, could only be exterminated through reinforcing rigid Islamic shari'a. But this was an antiquated or skewed shari'a, one that only fulfilled the empire-building dreams of military dictators like Zia-ul-Haq and his cronies, the Islamic religious parties, and others.[22]

Consequently, Pakistani citizens, against their will, were forced to acquiesce to a military dictator who brought laws that were tribal Bedouin practices of Arabia, such as corporal punishments of cutting off body parts, lashing, and stoning, that Zia-ul-Haq justified as part of the shari'a. These practices were not rooted in the secular vision of Pakistan's founder, Muhammad 'Ali Jinnah, and he never spoke of a theocratic Pakistan that the clerics would run. All the militancy in Pakistan and Afghanistan that is perpetrated in Islam's name is justified through Zia-ul-Haq's shari'a, primarily the kufr laws and the Hudood ordinances—blasphemy laws that have no relevance to the Qur'an, the Prophet's *sira* (biographies), or to his sunna. The Prophet only spoke of "nonviolence and equality."[23] The Taliban groups in Swat and Waziristan reinforced these laws. In fact, because of these laws militant groups like the Taliban and their many associates are now taking on the Pakistani state and its writ over its citizens. The 2009 takeover of the military headquarters in Rawalpindi with forty or so high-profile state personnel held as hostages is proof that these radical groups, created by the military state, now believe that the Pakistani state is a sell-out to takfiri (infidel ideologies of the west) and that only they, the Taliban, are capable of delivering the true Islamic state to its citizens. After the recovery of the military headquarters, one of the Taliban leaders issued a statement saying that the takeover was only a small gift to the Pakistani state and its American allies; the

Taliban are capable of taking larger assets. This threat was reinforced in May 2011 when the Taliban seized the Pakistani naval base of Mehran in Karachi to avenge Osama bin Laden's capture from Abbottabad and his consequent killing. Such is the ideology that Zia-ul-Haq's so-called shari'a laws generated. These radical groups are now challenging the Pakistani state and the NATO forces in Afghanistan. Pakistan, if it can survive, will have to renegotiate its priorities: Can it survive as an authoritarian, theocratic, militaristic state? Is such a state politically and economically sustainable?

Insidiously embedded in Pakistan's blasphemy laws are measures that forbid discussion or open debate. This ban on discussion is also tied to the controversy surrounding the Prophet's succession, not simply that the succession was contested but also that it was the exclusive decision of the elite. The election of the first caliph, Abu Bekr, provides an example. The Prophet died on a Monday and his body was left, covered by a cloak, in a corner of his wife 'A'isha's room. Everyone was so busy with the election of the successor that no one thought of washing his body or of the burial. Eventually he was buried, on a Wednesday night.[24]

Only the male elite decided on the successor for the Prophet. They also decided on the qualifications necessary to become a caliph, or amir.[25] The first successor was Abu Bekr; he was an elite Companion of the Prophet and was also his father-in-law. The person who first administered the oath was also an elite tribal leader, another of the Prophet's Companions and, in fact, succeeded Abu Bekr as the next caliph.

Mernissi reports that in Basra in the year 36 of the Hijra, during the first fitna when the ummah did not know which leader to support, 'A'isha bint-e Abu Bekr or 'Ali, common folks did not even know what the quarrel was about. Nor did they know what citizens were to do in the case of an unjust caliph. The people were more concerned about the absence of democracy. Since they had not been involved in the selection of the caliphs, why were they now being involved in the battle? When 'A'isha's supporters were brought to a mosque in Basra to respond to the people's concerns, a young man stood up and asked,

> It is true that you Muhajirun [original migrants from Mecca] were the first to respond to the Prophet's call . . . but everyone had that privilege later and everyone converted to Islam. Then after the death of the Prophet you selected a man from among you without consulting us [common people who were not part of the elite]. After his death you got together and chose another [caliph] still without asking our advice . . . You chose 'Uthman, you swore your allegiance to him, still without consulting us. You became dis-

pleased with his behavior and you decided to declare war without consulting us. You decided still without consulting us, to select 'Ali and swear allegiance to him . . . why have you decided to fight him? . . . Has he done
something reprehensible . . . We must be convinced if we are to take part in
this war . . . Why are you fighting?[26]

Thus, Mernissi confirms that the elite waged the war. The caliphate therefore remained within the male elite, and the tradition continues.

Zia-ul-Haq, by calling himself Amir-ul Momineen in Pakistan, had a similar dream of the caliphate.[27] A prime example of male elite collusion against
citizens is reflected in Zia-ul-Haq's rise to power in Pakistan. He manipulated the shari'a. He declared himself Amir-ul Momineen in collusion with
the mullas, the military, and international agencies for geopolitical gains.
He usurped state authority and enforced Islamic laws created with support
from the judges he appointed to the Shari'at Court. Not only did Zia-ul-
Haq usurp political authority in the name of Nizam-e Mustafa, he also arrested a democratically elected prime minister, Zulfiqar 'Ali Bhutto, and had
him executed after a mock trial.

Pakistan's transformation into a theocracy is embedded in the shari'a
laws that Zia-ul-Haq enforced. The state was not impartial in its leanings.
Rather, it tilted toward one particular segment of the society that upheld his
narrow version of Islam to the exclusion of other Muslim groups and minority groups in the country, such as the Hanafis, <u>Shi</u>'a, Ahmediyya, Christians,
and Hindus. The misogyny of the Hudood ordinances and the pernicious-
ness of the blasphemy laws are reflective of an Islamic state that manipulated
Islamic laws for a political agenda; Pakistan became a theocratic state that
did not have an enlightened vision of twenty-first-century democracy, progress, or the welfare of its citizens at heart.[28] In the succeeding decade, Pakistan openly became a nuclear state, using seemingly Islamic rhetoric against
neighboring India, equally driven by its Hindutva, Hindu nationalistic ideology, when it blasted its first nuclear device at Pokhran.[29] Pakistan blasted
its device at Chagi Hill, Balochistan, in 1998, immediately after the Indian
experiment. However, Pakistan had its nuclear program since 1972, when
Z. A. Bhutto authorized the Pakistan Energy Commission under Munir
Ahmed Khan.

WOMEN AND BLASPHEMY LAWS

Pakistan's blasphemy laws, Section 298-A, forbid any discussion of the
Umm-ul Momineen, the Prophet's wives. This raises serious questions
about the motivation behind imposing silence on events in Islamic history.

The Prophet died in Medina on Monday, June 8, 632. His wife 'A'isha was left a widow at only eighteen years of age. 'A'isha played a major role in the lives of two caliphs: Abu Bekr, her own father, who succeeded the Prophet, and Omar, who was Abu Bekr's successor. She did not, however, support 'Usman, the third caliph, refusing to help him when he was besieged in his own house surrounded by insurgents. It seems clear that she was involved in the politics of her time. In 656, at the age of forty-two, she took to battle at Basra against 'Ali, challenging his legitimacy as the fourth caliph of Islam — another very strong indication of political involvement — calling the population to civil war and sedition against a ruling caliph.[30] She engaged in open warfare against 'Ali, and yet the battle is called the Battle of Camel, after the camel she rode, avoiding all references to her name.[31] What is going on that makes it a crime, punishable under blasphemy laws with imprisonment, to speak about this event? To the male Pakistani elite, were 'A'isha's actions so threatening to an authoritarian system dominated by men — the mullas and the military — that citizens may not speak of this event? As a secular state with a secular constitution, such prohibitions did not need to be built into the country's laws. Matters of history are best left to the history books and do not need to become the business of state politics. Sadly, they did. And the state became a party with one set of beliefs, excluding all others, which it had the power to enforce. In the twenty-first century, a partisan Islamic state is disturbing, and its so-called Islamic laws are simply sinister.

Writers like Muhammad 'Arafa have called 'A'isha's political defiance of the state with 'Ali as the caliph a bid'a (deviation).[32] Muhammad 'Arafa claims that this individual act of 'A'isha was denounced by the greatest of Companions and condemned by the Prophet's other wives and that later she regretted it. Therefore, according to him and others like Said al-Afghani, 'A'isha's actions cannot be held up as positive examples, as they led to the division of the Muslim world into Sunni and Shi'a.[33] Al-Afghani's interpretation of the event is that Allah wanted the ummah to know that women's participation in politics can only lead to dissent.[34] Mernissi questions al-Afghani's sources that led him to proclaim that women be excluded from politics.[35] She further says,

> If the rights of all citizens including women in a Muslim state are a problem for some modern Muslim men it is neither because of the Qur'an nor the Prophet, nor the Islamic tradition, but simply because those rights conflict with the interests of the male elite.[36]

Following the same discussion from Mernissi, under General Zia-ul-Haq's laws, Pakistani citizens may not discuss 'A'isha's role in challenging a caliph or her participation in politics. It is in fact a heresy to speak of either, as demonstrated herein:

Blasphemy Law Section 298-A
Use of derogatory remarks, etc., in respect of holy personages. Whoever by words either spoken or written or by visible representation, or by any imputation, innuendo or insinuation, directly or indirectly defiles a sacred name of any wife (Umm-ul Momineen), or members of the family (Ahle-bait) of the Holy Prophet (PBUH), or any of the righteous caliphs (Khulafa-e Rashideen) or companions (Sahaaba) of the Holy Prophet description for a term which may extend to three years, or with fine, or with both.

By forbidding any discussion of the Umm-ul Momineen, Pakistan's blasphemy laws facilitate excluding women from public and political life. Fearing imprisonment, no woman or anyone else would speak of or reference an Umm-ul Momineen. Furthermore, since the laws are so open to interpretation, violating any one of the sections of Pakistan's blasphemy laws makes a person vulnerable to a death sentence; many a time victims are simply killed in extrajudicial circumstances or by lynch mobs.

The Umm-ul Momineen are highly respected females in the Muslim communities, and one cannot understand why a discussion of them constitutes blasphemy. These were highly intelligent, politically engaged women in the Prophet's council. There is no evidence of women's suppression in the Prophet's life. He loved women, and his wives were outspoken, articulate beings, indeed political: his first wife, Khadija, counseled him throughout the years of his ministry when Muhammad faced the wrath of the Meccan tribes and when he fought battles against them. His wife Hafsah was one of the few persons to have memorized the Qur'an and put it in writing; later, her version of the Qur'an was the basis for a compilation under Caliph 'Usman. His wife Umm-e Salama questioned the Prophet as to why Allah did not send verses about women, and thus several verses in the Qur'an were inspired by her. 'A'isha, the Prophet's youngest wife, besides her political role against 'Ali is considered an authority on Muhammad's hadith.

However, most attorneys in Pakistan are so consumed with protecting plaintiffs from Section 295-C, which carries a death penalty for defiling the sacred name of the Holy Prophet Mohammad, that Section 298-A that I have discussed here regarding the Umm-ul Momineen is overlooked. The issue of blasphemy is indeed overcharged emotionally, especially after Rushdie and the Danish cartoon affair, to the extent that one cannot have a sane debate on issues that have nothing to do with the incidents that happened in Europe. These are two totally different issues: the European blasphemy cases and the situation of Pakistan's blasphemy laws.

Prosecution under blasphemy laws in countries like Pakistan cause human rights violations and call into question whether the state is perpetrating social injustice toward particular segments of the population. Pakistan is a Muslim state with citizens both Muslim and non-Muslim. Attributing its blasphemy laws to the Qur'an is most unfair to the holy text as well as to its transmitter, the Prophet Muhammad. The state is appropriating prophetic authority for political control of its subjects.

The fact that Pakistan's blasphemy laws forbid any discussion of the Prophet's wives is particularly focused on 'A'isha and her active participation in the politics of the time. It is a preventive measure lest Muslim women take her as a role model for political initiatives. Preempted by the restraints on speech in the blasphemy laws, not only are women kept out of politics, but they do not seek public office. This is borne out by the fact that in 1997–1998 during the Nawaz Sharif regime several Muslim women professionals with secular western training and advanced degrees from British and American universities were charged with blasphemy. One woman was the teacher at an English medium school in Islamabad; another was the teacher at a girls' school in Islamabad (described in appendix 5). Two other women were senior professors in English language and literature from British and American universities. Some of these women sought asylum abroad. The women worked in the public sector with education, and they were certainly qualified to seek political office, but they did not. Such instances demonstrate that blasphemy laws, in addition to the Hudood laws that target women, are used to harass females.

Prior to Benazir Bhutto's assassination in 2007, threats from Islamic groups in Pakistan cited the holy text forbidding women from participating in politics. Earlier in Bhutto's career, during one of her tenures in the parliament, a woman named Nisar Apa leveled blasphemy charges against Bhutto. But evidence cannot be found in the Qur'an forbidding women from participating in politics. Furthermore, given that Pakistan is a secular state in the twenty-first century, what purpose would it serve for the government to dabble in theocratic issues that are a matter of history? If Pakistan is to survive it must remain a secular democracy that recognizes pluralism, gender emancipation, rights of minorities, and the mores of social justice. Islam in this setting will be practiced in the private, personal space of the individual and the community and not through a state that uses faith to enforce a political agenda and where the state's vigilantes will impinge on personal beliefs and practices. Islam as a postcolonial rhetoric cannot fill that space.

This was neither Muhammad's vision for his followers nor Jinnah's, who fought for a secular democracy in which all citizens would be free to follow their beliefs although a majority of Pakistan's citizens are Muslim.

Much can be questioned about man-made shari'a laws of the kind that Zia-ul-Haq instituted. While the Meccan verses in the Qur'an deal with the prophetic narratives to include Noah, Abraham, Moses, Jesus, and others that form part of the Abrahamic traditions based on the Old Testament and the New Testament, the Medina verses primarily deal with the issues of day-to-day governance of the Muslim community in Medina after the Prophet migrated there. The Medina verses provide the foundation of Islamic law that the Prophet put into place to govern his fledgling community of followers. In his last sermon he told his followers that he was leaving behind the Qur'an and his own example. He left much to the intelligence and goodwill of his followers that they would progress with the times, that they would keep religion and politics separate, that the political state would evolve to take on the challenges of the time, and that there would be a renaissance in the Muslim world that was seen historically in Baghdad and al-Andalus, or Spain. The theocratic state of Pakistan with contentious "shari'a" laws has only bred violence, with a virtual civil war between the state and segments of its citizenry, with the Taliban and associated militant groups now claiming that they are the custodians of Islamic law. Zia-ul-Haq's shari'a and the weaponry that the state provided to the militant groups to fight the jihad in Afghanistan have bred a monster that is challenging the very state that created it. Nay, the international states that created Frankenstein's monster by arming the militant outfits through the Pakistani military.

The Pakistani state today, with its majority Muslim population, is different from the Prophet's state. This partitioned state has been through many histories and political upheavals including a long period of British colonization in a united India. And although the political state tries to glue the citizenry together through Islam, more goodwill needs to be seen from the state in areas such as economic development, education, and social justice. Most Muslim states, like Pakistan, are postcolonial military dictatorships that propagandize the Islamic rhetoric of the shari'a but fail to deliver the goods to the citizenry even according to the shari'a. The political elites only protect their own fiefdoms; Islam or Islamic law is only for political control of citizens while the elite themselves lead lavish lifestyles far from any version of Islam. Fortunately, detailed images can now be tracked on YouTube, though it becomes too personalized to cite the instances here.[37] It is so simple to trace the hypocrisy of an Islamic discourse compared with the ground realities. The modern Islamic state of Pakistan has not gone beyond that theocratic discourse to deliver on a social welfare program for its citizens: men, women, and children; minorities, laborers, and intellectuals. The Nizam-e Mustafa rhetoric is only to unleash terror on unarmed citizens through Taliban groups, when in reality Muhammad's Islam has all the potential to deliver modern, secular democracy that is compatible with twenty-first-century ideals, Greek Hellenism, secularism, and emancipation that brought about the European Renaissance through the work of Muslim thinkers such as Averroes, Avicenna, and al-Ghazzali. These thinkers established the parameters between faith and reason. Thus, faith is a matter of personal choice and is not the business of the state, and the appropriation of faith in the name of the Nizam-e Mustafa for political gain is a larceny of the faith. Islamic societies are ready for a reformation that is being brought about by liberal thought through secular individuals; despite the terror, scholars and intellectuals are challenging orthodox shari'a interpretations such as Pakistan's blasphemy laws through publications in the western secular academy for global consumption among Muslims and non-Muslims. References are abundantly cited in this manuscript as well as in its bibliography.

EVOLUTION OF ISLAMIC LAW

During his life the Prophet governed according to his own insight and discretion. No doubt, with his extensive travels in the region and his business and commerce negotiations, the Prophet and his followers were conversant with the different laws of the area and used the knowledge these brought to govern the Muslim community of the time. Since Islam evolved in Arabia, which was at the crossroads of the Byzantine and Persian Empires, the laws of both these empires influenced Islamic law and the governance of the Islamic state.[38] In fact, it was during the Prophet's own lifetime that a certain Islamic perception of the law for the community began to emerge.[39] The legal theory and the doctrine of law evolved over the years, and in the centuries that followed these were definitely pluralistic.

The four major schools of Sunni law—Hanafi, Hanbali, Shafi'i, and Maliki—evolved differently in different regions according to their founders: Imam Abu Hanifa (699–767), Imam Ahmed bin Hanbal (780–855), Imam Muhammad bin Idris Shafi'i (767–854), and Imam Malik bin Anas (714–798), respectively. Shi'a law evolved as the Fiqh-e Jafaria mainly after the Battle of Karbala, under Imam Jafar al-Sadiq (702–765).

While Islamic law was struggling to establish itself, Jewish law and the Semitic-Mesopotamian legal traditions were already established.[40] Wael Hallaq challenges Joseph Schacht's claim that the formative period of Islamic law had ended around 860. Schacht (1902–1969) was an Anglo-German professor of Islam at Columbia University in New York. Hallaq argues that Islamic law formed into an identifiable entity by the middle of the tenth century.[41] This may be true of the Arabia, Syria, and Iraq region where Islamic law was evolving in the midst of customary laws that applied to Christians, Jews, Manicheans, and polytheistic faiths. In South Asia the same Islamic law in some areas evolved in different environments where Muslims coexisted with Hindus. Rulers like Akbar (1542–1605) were secular in their administration of the law and removed the *jizya* tax required of non-Muslims, while his great-grandson Aurengzeb reimposed it, contributing to the downfall of the Mughal Empire.

Since Islamic law is tied in with state politics, the law is fuzzy despite the clearly identifiable Sunni schools of fiqh—the Hanafi, Hanbali, Shafi'i, and Maliki. Islamic law has been administered in areas where customs and secular law intertwine, and Islamic law in the hands of intelligent, knowledgeable jurists has the potential to be malleable. Hence, there is no absolute standard for Islamic law: it varies from region to region. For example, divorce laws vary in Muslim countries. In Egypt until 2000, women could not file for divorce, while in Pakistan they could.[42] The Talibanization of Islamic law, especially toward women, is more tribal than Islamic. Broad frameworks of schools are mentioned here that have negotiated with each other where the Qur'an is central, but Qur'anic application of the text and its reading may vary. Canonists may disagree that the Qur'anic text can be interpreted according to context.

At best *qadis* and *proto-qadis* (jurists and protojurists) in the early periods of Islam used independent, discretionary powers, within an Islamic framework, to make their decisions. That framework included their knowledge of the Qur'an and stories about the Prophet's life and his wives as well as his Companions. Furthermore, the qadis were citizens of a polity that was built around the Islamic concepts of justice, tolerance, and the well-being of the community and individual.[43] When decisions were based on other factors, such as imperialism or Islam being the dominant faith, politics played a greater role; examples include decisions to uphold the prestige of a sultan or a caliph, as one sees in the cases of the Christian martyrs in Spain (al-Andalus) and the Neomartyrs in the early Ottoman period. Islam in such instances was used for political purposes, although there was nothing Islamic in the executions of the Cordoba martyrs. This point of view is discussed in chapter 2, on the Prophet's life and quotations from the Holy Qur'an.

Blasphemy or heresy, therefore, according to the position in the Prophet's administrative justice, is not an offense punishable by death. It is certainly not part of the Prophet's Islamic practices and thus not part of his law. There is not a single instance of a blasphemy trial in the Prophet's lifetime, nor is there a reference to execution for blasphemy. This is an innovation of so-called Islamic states like Zia-ul-Haq's, in which blasphemy laws, together with the Hudood laws that reduce a female's testimony to half of a male's, blaspheme the Qur'an. With regard to the Prophet's consorts, the Qur'an says:[44]

> O Consorts of the Prophet
> If any of you were guilty
> Of evident unseemly conduct
> The Punishment would be Doubled to her
> And that is easy for Allah
> But any of you that is
> Devout in the service of
> Allah and His Messenger
> And works righteousness—
> To her shall We grant
> Her reward twice and We
> Have prepared for her
> A generous Sustenance[45]

The verses cited here reference the "doubled" punishment for the Prophet's consorts to emphasize their responsibility, and thus these verses negate Zia-ul-Haq's section of the Hudood laws that reduce a female's testimony to one-half. The verse from the Qur'an also states that for being responsible, the rewards to the Prophet's consorts would be doubled. How, then, is it that a female's testimony is reduced to one-half when according to the position of the present verses the female's testimony ought to be doubled? As such, the blasphemy laws and the Hudood laws are *not* in accordance with the Prophet Muhammad's Islamic vision. Is it because of verses like these that Section 298-A was sneaked into the blasphemy laws lest females start demanding superior treatment by citing the Qur'an in addressing its admonitions or instructions to the Prophet's consorts? Furthermore, when the Prophet chides his consorts to refrain from "unseemly conduct," he is referring to their actions in *all* spheres of life, including the political. This means that females of the Prophet's family could assume political roles as long as their conduct was not unseemly. His wife 'A'isha came into a public sphere against 'Ali ibn Abu Talib. Thus, in the light of such verses, Zia-ul-Haq's laws are the concocted creations of a military dictator whom the

Islamist parties supported in order to seek political control. As such it gave them access to all the country's material and human resources, including its citizenry that included women. Roughly 50 percent of Pakistan's citizens are women, and the Hudood ordinances provide a terrifying but effective way to control them and their resources, such as women's labor and even their sexuality.[46]

HOW LEADERS IN THE ISLAMIC STATE DERIVE THEIR POWER FROM HISTORIC PRECEDENTS

Briefly, the foundations of Islamic law are found in the Qur'an and another document called the Constitution of Medina, a pact that the Prophet reached with the various tribes—polytheists, Christians, Jews, and several Arab clans—on how to coexist in harmony in Medina. The Qur'an as a document was written by various scribes, including the Prophet's wife Hafsah, who was literate; she is also said to have had a written copy of the Qur'an from which Caliph 'Usman reconstructed the Qur'an. Mature Islamic jurists continued to base the shari'a on grounds that since the Prophet had not repealed some customary laws and in fact sanctioned them in his own practice, they were justified.[47]

Likewise, countries like Pakistan that have experienced colonization retain large segments of British colonial law or practices. Some of those old colonial laws have benefited the societies, for example, by granting women an education and allowing them to work in the public sphere. Under colonial law, women had the right to an inheritance, which Islam already granted them, although British colonial law in the military domain enhanced a widow's economic benefits. An interesting example of the mingling of Islamic law with colonial law is that the Pakistani military follows the British inheritance laws: the widow is the major beneficiary of a soldier's pension. This has given autonomy to military widows and has made them economically independent, while in shari'a laws a widow gets only one-eighth, leaving the woman almost totally destitute. Colonial law has thus raised women's economic position as widows. Therefore, in a country like Pakistan with a majority Muslim population, colonial law has intersected with Islamic personal law for women's economic betterment.[48]

With the expansion of the Islamic empire after the Prophet, especially under Omar al-Khattab, when lands were conquered in Egypt, Syria, northern Iraq, and parts of Iran and the Byzantine territory, the mosque in the garrison towns became the center of spiritual and religious practice. The mosque was to become the locus of communal activity. Over the course of time

Qur'anic teachers assisted the military commanders in matters of the law; for example, if the Qur'an suggested lashes for a crime, the same punishment might be applied for drinking. Over time, the punishment for drinking became eighty lashes, and this somehow became a part of the shari'a.[49] Qadis were sent to garrison towns, and slowly they developed a kind of legal administrative system. The qadis used their knowledge of the Qur'an, the sunna, and customary law, together with their own discretionary abilities, to administer justice.[50]

As mentioned, storytelling was part of the hadith tradition. Thus, another early function of the qadis was storytelling. Their appointments included the role of *qussas* (storyteller). The qadis' task was also to enhance the work of the *akhbaris* (poets), who in pre-Islamic days lauded the achievements and glories of leading families and clans. In fact, they took on the role of the poets that was discussed earlier. This happened more so in Iraq than in cities like Medina. Hence, in the early days of Islam, the qadi-storytellers continued to rule communities according to pre-Islamic practices.[51]

By 680, the qadis had started to focus on collecting the prophetic narrative, the hadith, which later became the basis for law and legal theory. Muhammad, the Prophet, derived his authority from the Qur'anic truth, or revealed law. His successors, the caliphs who followed him, derived their authority from being the Companions of the Prophet. Caliphal authority ran parallel to prophetic authority, as the caliphs saw themselves as the defenders of the Qur'anic truth. The caliphs until the middle of the eighth century called themselves God's direct agents who could "implement His statutes, commands and laws."[52] Mulla Omar in Afghanistan and General Zia-ul-Haq saw themselves in similar roles, as upholders of the Qur'anic truth. General Zia-ul-Haq called himself Amir-ul Momineen, and Mulla Omar appeared to his Taliban constituents wearing a cloak that he claimed belonged to the Prophet, although they had no divine right to do so. Simply touting Islamist rhetoric and the force of weaponry gave them such confidence. These individuals wanted a return to the time of the early caliphates of Abu Bekr, Omar, 'Usman, and 'Ali, who were the Prophet's immediate viceregents. It was during the time of these caliphs that some Islamic law evolved.

As the concepts of justice developed, the community and the qadis, under the supervision of the caliphal administration, developed what is known as *'ilm* (knowledge) and *ra'y* (discretionary opinion), which were close to the Prophet's sunna. The people of 'ilm intellectually discussed, arbitrated, and evolved a solution called *ijtihad*, which was based on the Qur'an to offer knowledge, and the sunna and hadith, which allowed for discretionary opinions. A lot of debate was involved in arriving at ijtihad. Another way a community arrived at a consensus was called *ijmʿa*, which involved debate and discussion and reflected the majority opinion.[53]

The qadi remained the central figure in the legal infrastructure, and gradually the system became more complex. Eventually, his office became an established institution that included expert witnesses, scribes, a sheriff, jurisconsults, muftis, and *munadis* (advertisers), whose task it was to announce litigations in public places and seek witnesses to the cases.[54] *Halaqats* (specialized circles of learning) evolved in which religious knowledge was discussed. The caliphs encouraged the growth of halaqats for the evolution of thought that would uphold their own authority as "God's and Muhammad's" deputies on earth.[55] Thus, over time two main schools of Islamic law evolved: the *ahl-e hadith*, the traditionalists who interpreted the law entirely on the Qur'an and the hadith, and the *ahl-e ra'y*, the rationalists who used reasoning and analysis to interpret the Qur'an. Within these two major schools many subdivisions arose. The cities that evolved in the legal enterprises post-Muhammad were Medina, Mecca, Basra, Damascus, Fustat, Yemen, and, marginally, Khurasan. Iran and Iraq emerged as major centers of Shiʿa thought, mainly Qufa.[56]

Therefore, although shariʿa evolved within the frames of the Qur'an and the sunna, hadith, and sira of the Prophet, the jurists administered the law in the name of the ruling dynasties. And while the jurists maintained juristic independence, the community of jurists did serve as the ruler's link to the masses, aiding him in his bid for legitimacy.[57] This ancient role of the jurist was not lost on many of the current leaders in Islamic states. In the cases of blasphemy that are discussed here, the rulers had in place jurists who were willing to interpret religious texts for political purposes. As referenced in the Qur'anic passages cited in chapter 2, *Sura-e Lahab*, the Qur'an leaves the punishment for blasphemy to God: *Haquq-Allah*, rights of God.

Accordingly, punishment or reward can only come from Allah or God. The state cannot take on God's role.[58] Thus the British blasphemy laws that the colonists set in place in India were more humane than Zia-ul-Haq's or those that the Taliban practice in the name of Muhammad's Islam. The latter set of laws gives license for the state and its affiliates to lynch citizens, and such laws violate all mores of social justice and enlightenment. Perpetrators of the Nizam-e Mustafa movement or the Khatam-e Nabuvat (end of prophecy after Muhammad) movement are indeed vigilantes with state support to terrorize the citizenry. The Pakistani state itself now realizes that as a consequence of the challenges posed by militant outfits like the Taliban, this theocratic approach needs to be disbanded if Pakistan is to survive as a political and geographic entity. It may very well be on its way to Balkanization through a takfiri cult in the absence of a tolerant secular democracy. Such laws against its own citizenry are not sustainable for the state's survival.

A TAKFIR CULT

Following the earlier discussion of the shari'a, this section looks specifically at blasphemy called *kufr* (the term refers to one who insults the Prophet). The argument is that it is the kufr or takfiri cult that drives present-day groups like the Taliban and their affiliates, which draw inspiration from Zia-ul-Haq's shari'a and look upon all those who do not subscribe to their militant orthodox version of Islam as kafirs, infidels, including secular Muslims as well as non-Muslims.

A related takfir ideology derived from the root, kufr, started to gain influence in the eighteenth century under Muhammad bin 'Abd al-Wahab (d. 1792). 'Abd al-Wahab set out to reform Islam; he believed it had become impure through interventions such as Sufism, Shi'aism, and rationalism.[59] These he believed were *takfiri*, heretical innovations in Islam. By returning to the pure original text of the Qur'an he believed that Muslims would be better able to cope with the challenges of the modern centuries. Thus, he believed that the Arab version of Islam was the only true faith and all else was takfir.[60]

Muhammad bin 'Abd al-Wahab's takfiri cult of declaring all Muslims not in conformity with his Wahabi Islamic practice as infidels comes from Khawarijism, which originated in the years of the internecine wars that followed the Prophet's death. The Khawarijis were the deserters or rebels who forced Caliph 'Ali ibn Abi Talib to abandon his victory at Siffin against Ma'uviya.[61] Amir 'Ali cites from Abd al-Karim al-Shahristani that the Khawarijis were the men who insisted on the arbitration between Ma'uviya and the caliph, 'Ali.[62] While 'Ali retired to Qufa awaiting the results of the arbitration, 12,000 of these troops revolted against 'Ali and took up arms against him at Nahrwan. The caliph's forces attacked them, and the rebels were defeated in two successive battles. According to Shahristani, some of them escaped to al-Bahrain, where these rebels, "free lances of Islam, spread their noxious doctrines among the wild inhabitants of that tract."[63] Two years later, Khawarijis assassinated 'Ali at a mosque in Qufa. From time to time these rebels resurfaced until leaders such as Abdul Malik drove them to al-Ahsa and al-Bahrain. Under Merwan II, an eighth-century Ommayad caliph, they raised their heads again, this time to be driven into Yemen, Hijaz, and Iraq. They were defeated and forced to retreat to Oman. They spread their ultra-orthodox doctrines among the Berbers of North Africa, and from there they continued to harass the 'Abbasid rulers.[64] Amir 'Ali claims that the Khawarijis are the Calvinists of Islam. He also claims that the K̲h̲awarijis' merciless, fierce doctrines found a voice nine centuries later under Wahabism.[65] Shahristani divides the K̲h̲awarijis into six groups, among which the most important is the Azarika, forerunners of the modern-day Wahabis. According to the Azarika,

> who are the most fanatical, exclusive and narrow . . . every sect besides their own is doomed to perdition, and ought to be forcefully converted or ruthlessly destroyed. No mercy ought to be shown to any infidel or Mushrik (an expansive term, including Moslems, Christians and Jews). To them every sin is of the same degree: murder, fornication, intoxication, smoking, all are damning offences against religion. While the other Muslims, Shi'a as well as Sunni, hold that every child is born into the world in the faith of Islam, and remains so until perverted by education, the Azariki declares that the child of an infidel is an infidel.[66]

After their defeat at the hands of Hajjaj bin Yusuf, the Azarika took refuge in central Arabia. The Wahabis, according to Shahristani, are the direct descendants of the Azarika, as they too brand all other Muslims as nonbelievers and promote their "despoilment and enslavement."[67] It is surprising that as far back as 1922, when Amir 'Ali's *Spirit of Islam* was published, he and Shahristani identified this brand of Sunni Islam to have all the potential for takfir—the capacity to declare all other Islam adherents and non-Muslims heretics—that one now sees embedded at a global level and, more particularly, in the manifestation of Pakistan's blasphemy laws. These laws have the power to condemn some citizens as non-Muslims although they profess to be Muslims and to threaten them with the death penalty should they claim Islam. (In appendix 2, some of sections 298-B and C of Pakistan's blasphemy laws are directed against the Qadianis-Ahmediyyas.) This judgmental attribute derives directly from the Azarika-Wahabi doctrine. For a state like Pakistan to practice this religious fanaticism harks back to the dark ages of the Spanish Inquisition or the terrorism against Catholics under Cromwell.

S̲h̲irk, takfir, mus̲h̲rik, and the whole range of heresy terms are applied to coreligionists in Pakistan today, especially by the upper middle classes that have absorbed the "new" Islam of Muhammad bin 'Abd al-Wahab. These circles are linked to the military establishment, "wannabes," and others, spanned out over the society. It is claimed that "Wahabi" is a term coined by Muhammad bin 'Abd al-Wahab's Ottoman opponents, who suggested that this belief system fell outside mainstream Islam. The implication is that it was based more on a personality cult than on God.[68] The personality was that of 'Abd al-Wahab.

All this is rooted in the politics of the region in the nineteenth and twentieth centuries and most deftly described in Khaled Abou El Fadl's trinity theory of the alliance of the al-Saʿud family, Wahabism, and the British colonizers (1821–1922).[69] While the al-Saʿuds wanted to beat all other contenders in Arabia and enforced their puritanical version of Islam through the Wahabis, the British wanted unchallenged opportunities to explore oil in the region and to weaken the Ottoman Empire and its vast holdings from Turkey to the Iranian border and then deep into Arabia, where the Ottomans held the holy cities of Mecca and Medina. Colonel T. E. Lawrence was also a part of this imperial design. In the 1970s the same enterprise for oil in Central Asia, after the fall of the shah and the rise of a Shiʿa theocracy in Iran, led to the export of Wahabism into Pakistan and Afghanistan.[70]

DeLong-Bas defends ʿAbd al-Wahab, saying that he did not advocate using violence to eliminate shirk, heresy, from among the practicing Muslims but only sought to rid the regions of un-Islamic practices through daʿwa, proselytizing the true Islam.[71] However, the polarization is still reflected in the "us" against "them" discourse. As a consequence, all Muslims who do not subscribe to the Wahabi version of Islam need to be brought into the fold through daʿwa, which literally means "invitation."

Something to this effect was generated during Zia-ul-Haq's period (1979–1989) when at his behest and through a large network of Wahabi groups, both female and male, dars, or proselytizing events, were organized. These took the form of tea parties for women in domestic environments as well as in female educational institutions; for men it was in the mosque sermons as well as through tablighi (proselytes) groups. The groups would go from door to door to reinforce the basic canons of Islam. Participants were indoctrinated into the puritanical Wahabi version of Islam, which strictly forbids any rituals except the five pillars of Islam (profession of faith in God and the Prophet Muhammad, prayer, fasting, charity, and pilgrimage to Mecca). Ritual practices such as commemorating the martyrdom of the Prophet's grandson Hussein in the second fitna of Islam (680) were declared shirk or bidʿa (heresy). In the social sphere a discourse was generated that marked distinctions on sectarian lines: what was shirk and what was not shirk, who was a Sunni and who was not a Sunni, who was a Shiʿa and who was a Qadiani. Such discourse had never been a visible part of social interaction among South Asian Muslim societies that for centuries had lived among non-Muslim communities of Hindus, Sikhs, Christians, and Parsis in a united India. Pluralism was the way of life; faith was the private domain of the citizen. Come Zia-ul-Haq, Wahabi Islam and its template became central to the state.

As a result, Pakistani citizens of all faiths and beliefs are living with blasphemy and Hudood laws—a direct consequence of the influence of the intolerant Wahabism that is spreading throughout the region. The Islamic parties in Pakistan have made it nearly impossible to have any discussion of these laws, as they have threatened the state with takfir (heresy) and have promised violence.[72] Salman Taseer's assassination in 2011 is a case in point. What is even more shocking is that large numbers of attorneys in Pakistan hailed Taseer's assailant as a hero. This is further evident in the daily suicide bombings and the violence of Islamic militants in Pakistan. General Pervez Musharraf's revisions of the Hudood ordinances against women have made only a minimal difference. Extrajudicial killing of Christians continues, and the violations are many. Petty officials and the police insidiously implement their own shariʿa.[73]

ʿAli Eteraz maintains that in 1999, with Musharraf's coup, the country entered a new phase.[74] He claims that in 2002, Musharraf's appointed members to the Council for Islamic Ideology overturned the Hudood ordinances, at least in the area of sex crimes, and in 2005 declared them patently un-Islamic. Eteraz misses the point, however, that the Council for Islamic Ideology is only an advisory body and what it rules does not necessarily change the law. For a full repeal, President Zardari would have to take the law to the Parliament, where the right-wing parties that flaunt the Islamist agenda would veto it. Cosmetic changes like Musharraf's are short-term, ad hoc arrangements that still leave the citizens vulnerable to laws like the blasphemy and Hudood ordinances. Even as this manuscript is written, killings of Christians under blasphemy laws continue—a Christian family cannot keep a Qur'an in the house, as Christians are considered unclean and therefore keeping a Qur'an constitutes blasphemy.

When Benazir Bhutto was prime minister twice, on both these occasions she could have done away with these laws. Even Musharraf, as the martial-law head of state, could have dispensed with them through a martial ordinance, but he buckled under the Islami parties and perhaps his Saudi donors.[75] But the desire to seem "Islamic" has always played into politics, and the laws were not repealed. Attorneys routinely cite the "Objectives Resolution" from the 1973 constitution of Pakistan (inserted into the constitution when Zulfiqar ʿAli Bhutto was the prime minister and Abdul Hafeez Pirzada his law minister):

> Wherein the Muslims shall be enabled to order their lives in the individual and collective spheres in accordance with the teaching and requirements of Islam as set out in the Qur'an and the Sunnah.

This was the beginning of the Islamization process under Zulfiqar ʿAli Bhutto. It may be pointed out that on August 11, 1947, just four decades earlier and just a few days before Pakistan's independence, the founder of the country, Muhammad 'Ali Jinnah, said this in a presidential address to the constituent assembly:

> Dealing with our first function in this Assembly, I cannot make any well-considered pronouncement at this moment, but I shall say a few things as they occur to me. The first and the foremost thing that I would like to emphasize is this: remember that you are now a sovereign legislative body and you have got all the powers. It, therefore, places on you the gravest responsibility as to how you should take your decisions. The first observation that I would like to make is this: You will no doubt agree with me that the first duty of a government is to maintain law and order, so that the life, property and religious beliefs of its subjects are fully protected by the State . . . You are free; you are free to go to your temples, you are free to go to your mosques or to any other place of worship in this State of Pakistan. You may belong to any religion or caste or creed that has nothing to do with the business of the State.[76]

How is it that this secular vision was lost barely four decades after the creation of the country? How did it happen that 3 million to 4 million Qadianis-Ahmediyyas in the country were declared non-Muslims and other minorities like the Christians were threatened and continue to be so? Did Jinnah ever imagine that the very parties that opposed the country's creation as a separate homeland would hijack his dream of a secular Pakistan?

Following the coup that ousted Zulfiqar 'Ali Bhutto, General Zia-ul-Haq took over, and through a presidential ordinance, the Objectives Resolution was modified with the insertion of Article 2–A. Instead of reading "an adequate provision shall be made for the minorities *freely* to profess and practice their religion and develop their culture," the section now reads, "an adequate provision shall be made for the minorities to profess and practice their religion and develop their culture." The Law of Evidence as documented in the Hudood ordinances that reduced the testimony of a female to one-half that of a male was extended to cover minority men and women. One assumes that in the case of minority women it was reduced to one-fourth. The zina clause for women required "evidence of at least four Muslim male witnesses" (appendix 4), and that ruling also was extended to minorities.[77] With one stroke of the pen, the Enforcement of Shari'a Act of 1991 was signed, and all this became law. Why can't the same mechanisms be used to reverse this gross injustice that makes Pakistan a medieval theocracy? This is an unholy military and mulla alliance to keep the citizens terrorized.

'Ali Eteraz observes that while the grounds were being prepared for a pernicious fanaticism in the name of Islam, most western observers missed this radical change because Z. A. Bhutto was a "whiskey-drinking pseudo-socialist from a Westernized family" who was not expected to stand up for Islam.[78] Those who noticed the change ignored it, as Pakistanis were traumatized with the loss of East Pakistan, now Bangladesh. The state had to address other, more pressing issues, such as the return of more than 90,000 Pakistani civilians and military personnel held as prisoners of war in India. Citizens did not have enough distance from the situation to see the creeping changes.

Bhutto proposed the Council for Islamic Ideology, on which eight to twenty religious scholars from different denominations were to represent an Islamic point of view. Eteraz notes that Chapter A of the 1973 constitution, inserted in 1980, gave the government the power to create a federal Shari'at Court, and on that basis, only Muslim judges would interpret the law in light of the Qur'an and the Prophet's sunna.[79] Most of this was implemented under Zia-ul-Haq. But Bhutto's Islamization had sinister elements, as he brought on board 'ulema like Maulana Kausar Niazi, who was also called "Maulana Whiskey," and Maulana Maududi. Bhutto gave this brand of Islam the name "Islamic socialism." Leaders in North Africa like Houari Boumedienne in Algeria followed suit to gain political legitimacy among their people. One has to remember that Islam during the period of colonization in Africa and elsewhere in the Muslim world became a political ideology standing against colonists, especially in Algeria.[80] By Islamizing his political base, Bhutto won the favor of the Gulf monarchies from whom he sought economic assistance.[81] By conceding to the Islamization of Pakistan, Bhutto inserted sections into the constitution that signaled a religious approach, and through cooperating with Jamaat-e Islami's Maulana Maududi, Bhutto opened the door for the Jamaat-e Islami's demand to declare the Ahmediyya community non-Muslim. The foundation for a takfir ideology, the concept of other that is the basis of Pakistan's blasphemy laws, was laid then. Of Bhutto, Eteraz asserts:

> In 1974, he engaged in what became, in the nation-state era, the first collective excommunication in the Muslim world. No postcolonial Muslim state had previously thrown people that self-identified as Muslim officially out of the religion. Contrast this with India, where under a 1971 court case, the Ahmediyya were allowed to refer to themselves as Muslim, even as the vast majority of Muslims were not obligated to acknowledge them as such.[82]

With Z. A. Bhutto's execution and Zia-ul-Haq's military takeover, the latter implemented the Nizam-e Mustafa, and thus Pakistan had a "papal dictator." While Bhutto created the blueprints, Zia-ul-Haq created the Islamic institutions, and the Islami parties heralded him as the savior, Mard-e Mujahid, the man of jihad.[83] Seventeen Islamic scholars were appointed to the Council for Islamic Ideology in 1977. To make sure these men only provided interpretation of Islam consistent with what Zia-ul-Haq approved, he brought in Ma'ruf al-Dawalibi as the chief consultant; this man, a former prime minister in Syria, was Wahabi and had been the president of the World Muslim League as well as an adviser to the Saudi Arabian monarch.[84]

More than ever before, clear-cut language was put into Pakistan's blasphemy laws against the Ahmediyyas, also known as Qadianis (although finer differences do exist between the sects). Under Section 298-C members of this group were prohibited from calling themselves Muslim or their faith Islam. They were forbidden from calling their places of worship mosques, calling the azan (call to prayer), or reciting the Shahada, the Qur'anic proclamation of one's Islamic faith: "There is no God but God and Muhammad is His messenger." In the rabidity that followed the institution of these laws, militants tore down the Shahada from Ahmediyya mosques. No one tried the militants for desecrating the holy text. Nazir Ahmad affirms that this act of the 'ulema was worse than the act of the Meccans when, at the time of the Hudaibiya Treaty in 628, they refused to let "The Messenger of Allah" be written after Muhammad's name.[85]

Connecting Ma'ruf al-Dawalibi's appointment as General Zia-ul-Haq's adviser and the Freedom House report *Saudi Publications on Hate Ideology Fill American Mosques* (2005),[86] it is possible to see parallels between the Pakistani blasphemy laws and the influence of Wahabism in some American mosques. A great deal of the takfir ideology exported to American mosques was based on fatwas issued by 'Abd al-'Aziz Bin 'Abdullah Bin Baz (d. 1999). Bin Baz had been grand mufti under King Fahd in 1993. "His dichotomous mode of thinking, coupled with his persistent demonizing of non-Muslims and tolerant Muslims, runs through almost all the *fatwa* publications exported to American mosques."[87] Some citations that match Pakistan's blasphemy laws against minorities are:

Document No. 2
The one that does not call the Jews and the Christians unbelievers is himself an Unbeliever.[88]

Document No. 52
Whoever believes that churches are houses of God and that God is worshipped therein, or that what Jews and Christians do constitutes the worship of God and or obedience to Him or His Prophet . . . and whoever assists

them to keep their churches open . . . out of a feeling of kinship or out of a sense of obedience—whoever does all these things is an infidel.[89]

These are clear examples of takfir—highlighting division and excommunicating the other. Also built within this very takfir is a section on jihad:

Document No. 2
The effect of this sinful call [interfaith dialogue] is that it erases the difference between Islam and disbelief, between truth and falsehood, good and bad, and it breaks the wall of resentment between Muslims and nonbeliever, so that there is no loyalty and enmity, no more *jihad* and fighting to raise Allah's word on earth.[90]

According to the Freedom House document, tolerant Muslims are also to be condemned as infidels, and under Saudi law they are apostates from Islam who can be condemned to death. In the dualistic worldview of these orthodox believers, only two worlds exist: the Dar-ul Islam, Abode of Peace, and Dar-ul Harb, Abode of War, also known as Dar-ul Kufr, Abode of the Infidel. Pakistan's blasphemy laws seem to be created on the same template as these documents that propagate a takfir cult based on hate as well as division.

However, Cheragh ʿAli maintains that Dar-ul Harb and Dar-ul Kufr distinctions matter only when a dispute exists over property or a crime. For example, if a Muslim has a dispute in Dar-ul Kufr, that person cannot be tried for it in Dar-ul Harb. Cheragh ʿAli also affirms that no such distinctions exist in the Qurʾan.[91] Such is the hate-based ideology not only pumped by Wahabism but also reinforced by other doctrines like that of the Muslim Brotherhood. One of its leaders, Sayyid al-Qutb, takes his declaration of jihad against the state from German Fascist philosopher Carl Schmidt without acknowledging him in his writings.[92] Unfortunately, these are the ideologies that have fed Pakistani and Afghan Islam since the late 1970s, and from these ideologies many of the so-called shariʿa laws have spewed forth.

Many dimensions to this brand of Islam exist, but the discussion in the next chapter will focus mainly on the blasphemy laws, whose net has now widened to *irtidad* (apostasy) and shirk (heresy) for anyone who does not conform to the Wahabi version of Islam.

CHAPTER 4

COLONIAL ORIGINS, AMBIGUITIES, AND EXECUTION OF THE BLASPHEMY LAWS

THIS CHAPTER WILL OFFER FURTHER EXAMPLES that support the claim that blasphemy laws put in place by some Islamic states as part of the shari'a are manipulated for political agendas. As detailed earlier, Pakistan's blasphemy laws under General Zia-ul-Haq emerged as a result of the geopolitics of the region in the 1970s when Pakistan's military led a CIA-backed incursion into Afghanistan to contain the Soviets. Together with the mujahideen, the Afghan warlords, and funding from Saudi Arabia, an Islamic rhetoric was generated to give momentum to the Afghan adventure. Pakistan's extremist religious parties such as the Jamaat-e Islami were on board with General Zia-ul-Haq, and what could legitimize such an undertaking better than the use of so-called shari'a laws derived from medieval tribal Arabia? The medieval laws carried substantive corporal punishments but also served the interests of the ruling male elites, especially the military and the mullas. These laws only served the interests of a segment of the theocratic establishment that Zia-ul-Haq created in which his key supporters were the foreign donors as well as the mullacracy (the clergy).

This chapter also looks at the origins of the blasphemy laws under the British colonists, the template on which Zia-ul-Haq's laws were superimposed. For this discussion data are derived from Siddiqui and Hayat's article "Unholy Laws and Holy Speech" and firsthand observations, such as the charges leveled against Dr. Surriya Shafi and myself.[1]

BLASPHEMY LAWS' PRECEDENTS IN INDIA

Pakistan's blasphemy laws are based on Act 45 of the Indian Penal Code,[2] which the British colonial government put in place in 1860. In Chapter 15 of the code, "Of Offences Relating to Religion," the law commissioners of the British government declared their intent to include the following in the Indian Penal Code:

The principle on which this chapter has been framed is a principle on which it would be desirable that all governments should act but from which the British Government cannot depart without risking the dissolution of society; it is this, that every man should be suffered to profess his own religion and that no man should be suffered to insult the religion of another.[3]

The British colonial administrators created these blasphemy laws to keep peace in a heterogeneous society like India, where the majority were Hindus, with strong numbers of Muslims, Sikhs, Buddhists, Parsis, Christians, and others. The British ensured the "writ of the state" through these laws, which are as follows:

Section 295
Whoever destroys, damages or defiles *any place of worship, or any object held sacred by any class of persons* with the intention of thereby *insulting the religion of any class of persons* or with the knowledge that *any class of persons is likely to consider such destruction, damage or defilement as an insult to their religion*, shall be punished with imprisonment of either description for a term that may extend to two years, or with fine, or with both.[4]

Section 298
Whoever, with the *deliberate intention* [emphasis mine] of *wounding the religious feelings of any person* utters any word or makes any sound in the hearing of that person or makes any gesture in the sight of that person, or places any object in the sight of that person, shall be punished with imprisonment of either description for a term which may extend to one year, or with fine or with both.[5]

In 1927, Section 295 A was added to the Indian Penal Code through the Criminal Law Amendment Act (25 of 1927), which says,[6]

Section 295-A
Whoever, with deliberate and malicious intention of outraging *the religious feelings of any class of His Majesty's subjects* by words either spoken or written,[7] or by visual representations, *insults or attempts to insult the religious beliefs of that class*, shall be punished with imprisonment of either description for a term which may extend to two years, or with fine, or with both.[8]

Through these laws the British superseded some remnants of Muhammadan law that prevailed in India until the British came. It should be pointed out that although Muslims were a religious minority in India, the Muslim rulers who arrived in India with Muhammad bin Qasim's 711–713 invasion of Sind ruled until 1857. They established a system of administration that incorporated Islamic law with the local customs, referred to as "Muhammadan law" by the British colonists. The Muslim rule in India eroded in 1857 with the Indian war of independence and the fall of the last Mughal emperor, Bahadur Shah Zafar. Sovereignty passed to the British, who exiled Bahadur Shah Zafar to Rangoon.

AMBIGUITIES IN PAKISTAN'S BLASPHEMY LAWS

Pakistani jurists maintain that the British created the blasphemy laws through the Indian Penal Code in large part to protect the interests of Muslims, who were a minority in undivided India.[9] However, Zia-ul-Haq's reinterpretation of these laws, originally meant to protect all religions, instead to protect only one orthodox version of Islam also had deliberate ambiguities. In a research project that I conducted in the spring of 2009 for my course Islamic State, Heresy, and Freedom of Speech at SUNY Purchase, I used Siddiqui and Hayat's article together with the text of Pakistan's blasphemy laws to look at the ambiguities in the language. One of the linguistic ambiguities that the students worked on was the use of "etc." (etcetera). "Etcetera" is used at least five times in the text and is poorly contextualized. "Etcetera" in the *American Heritage Dictionary* is defined as "other unspecified things of the same class; and so forth from the Latin, *et cetera*, and the rest." A student of mine wrote of Section 295-C, which makes derogatory remarks against the Prophet punishable by death, "The brevity of the law is daunting. Should a law which may impose death not have incredibly specific instructions for its application? It appears the use of the term, 'etc.' is of what could be interpreted as a violation of the code." Another paper says of "derogatory remarks" that "the question is one of complete subjectivity . . . though the written word is premeditated thought, speaking is much more candid[,] . . . potentially cryptic and sometimes unintentional."

Minority jurists in Pakistan have spoken out on the ambiguity of Pakistan's blasphemy laws. Justice Durab Patel, one of the dissenting jurists on Zulfiqar 'Ali Bhutto's death sentence, has said of Pakistan's blasphemy laws:

> I am not the only person disturbed by the vague and arbitrary definition of blasphemy in Section 295-C. The bill for enacting this section was first passed by the Senate and became law after it has been passed without any change by the National Assembly. But to its credit the Law and Justice

Committee had stated in its minutes that the definition of blasphemy in the section was very vague and that the bill should be sent to the Council for Islamic Ideology for redefining the offence. The committee had also stated that inquiry should be made from other Muslim countries about the penalty of blaspheming the Prophet. Instead of complying with the recommendation of the Law and Justice Committee of the Senate, the government of Mr. Nawaz Sharif rushed the bill through the National Assembly so that it would become law without any delay. As Mr. Nawaz Sharif had a very comfortable majority in parliament, his haste in rushing this bill through the National Assembly reflected his desire to please the handful of members in parliament from the religious parties.[10]

Justice Durab Patel further says,

295-B and 295-C have introduced a new and dangerous principle in our jurisprudence by punishing acts done in the privacy of one's house even though these acts may not violate the rights of other persons. This section will therefore give the police a pretext for searching houses without a search warrant, just as it led to hooligans to break into Dr. Farooq Sajjad's house and kill him.[11]

Siddiqui and Hayat find the ambiguities in the design of Pakistan's blasphemy laws deliberately malicious because the "requirement of intent" is left out. The British Indian Penal Code on which they are based is clear about emphasizing the "intention of the accused." Furthermore, the authors assert that in the Indian Penal Code the proof of intent was a prerequisite of all the sections. For Section 295 the law commissioners were clear that "where there is no intention to wound the religious susceptibilities there will be no offence." Citing Nizami, the authors affirm,

Under this section it must be distinctly proved that there was an intention on the part of the accused to insult the religion of a class of persons. This intention could be ascertained from the nature of the act done. Where there is no intention to wound the religious susceptibilities there will be no offence.[12]

AMBIGUITIES IN THE LAW

THE CASE AGAINST DR. YOUNAS SHAIKH

A case in point is that of Dr. Muhammad Younas Shaikh, who was registered for charges of blasphemy on October 2, 2000, based on an allegation by Maulana Abdul Rauf. In the police report Rauf refers to himself as "Amir Majlis-e Khatam-e Nabuvat" (Leader of the Organization on the Finality of Prophethood). Maulana Rauf submitted with his charges a petition signed by eleven of Dr. Shaikh's students at a private medical college in Islamabad, although only one, Muhammad Asghar 'Ali Khan, a fanatic, was actually present when the so-called crime happened.

The first investigation report (FIR) against Dr. Shaikh claimed that he had insulted the Holy Prophet during a lecture.[13] In response to a student's question regarding Arab practices pre-Islam, Dr. Shaikh said that Muhammad was a non-Muslim until he was forty; that he had not been circumcised until he was forty; that he married for the first time at the age of twenty-five when he was neither a prophet nor a Muslim and therefore his *nikah* (Islamic marriage contract) was not solemnized; that at the age of forty his armpit and pubic hair had not been removed; and that his parents were non-Muslims.

Dr. Shaikh's attorney Abid Hassan Minto, a senior lawyer of the Supreme Court of Pakistan, asserted that this was a true answer.[14] The intent factor was missing in this discourse between Dr. Shaikh and his students. He had not intended to hurt anyone's religious feelings, as this was not a premeditated act. He was only stating facts and clarifying a point of view. However, according to Siddiqui and Hayat, "all these defense arguments were unavailable to the defendant, since Section 295-C makes desecration of the Prophet's name [PBUH] the basis for a blasphemy conviction, regardless of the intention of the accused."[15] Siddiqui and Hayat quote the persecutors' FIR:

First Information Report (FIR): Case of Dr Younus Shaikh
The English translation of FIR registered against Dr. Younus.
Police Station: Margela, Islamabad, October 2, 2000.
Time of reporting: 4-10-2000 5.10 evening
Name/address of Applicant: Maulana Abdul Rauf, Amir Aalami Majlis Tahafaz-e-Khatam-e-Nabowat; 1159/, B Sector G-6/1/3, Islamabad
Crime: 295-C, PPC
SHO: Margela, Islamabad
Sir, I am President of Majlis-e-Tahafiz-e-Khatam-Nabawat, Islamabad. On October 3, 2000, I along with Qari Abdul Waheed Qasmi, Nazim, Majlis Tahafaze Khatam-e-Nabowat, Islamabad and Mufti Khalid Mir were present in our office G-6/1, House No: 1159-B, Street No: 49 that Mohammed Asghar Khan s/o Arbab Khan Afridi of House No: 86/19/B, G-9/2 came there and handed over to me a photo copy of an application bearing signatures of 11 persons. He told me verbally that we all companions were doing course at Capital College G-9, Markaz, Islamabad. On October 2, 2000,

Professor. Dr. Younus Shaikh during a lecture passed some derogatory remarks against Holy Prophet (Peace Be Upon Him) which falls under Section 285-C PPC (Blasphemy Act). Prophet Moahmmed (PBUH) was a non-
Muslim till the age of 40. (2) He had not been incisionsed (khatna) till 40.
(3) Holy Prophet (PBUH) married for fist time at 25. At that time he was
neither a prophet nor a Muslim, therefore his "Nikah" was not solemnized.
(4) At 40 his "Baghal' (armpit) and "zer-naaf" (under-navel) hair were
not removed. (5) His parents were non-Muslims. We cut a very sorry figure, after hearing him and going through this petition. After hearing and
reading application we were extremely sad and we immediately convened
a meeting. During the meeting it was decided that a case against the blasphemer Dr Shaikh Younus should be registered. It is therefore, requested
that a case be instituted against the accused and he may be punished accordingly. 1. Maulana Abdul Rauf, Amir World Majlis Tahafaz-e-Khatam-e-
Nabowat (Signed) 2. Abdul Wahedd Qasmi, Nazim Khateeb Jamia Masjid
Farooq Azam, Islamabad (Signed) 3. Mufti Khalid Mir, Mubaligh Khatim-e-
Nabowat, Islamabad (Signed).[16]

Dr. Muhammad Younas Shaikh was born in Chishtian, Pakistan, in 1952.
He was a medical doctor who had studied in Pakistan as well as in Dub-
lin and London. He had worked in the United Kingdom between 1981 and
1988 and was teaching at a medical college in Islamabad. He was a rights
activist in Pakistan and had started an organization called The Enlightenment, inspired by the ideas of the Renaissance and the European Enlightenment. He was also active in the Pakistan-India Forum for Peace and Democracy. At a meeting of the South Asia Union on October 2, 2000, Shaikh
suggested that in the interest of the people of Kashmir the line of control
between Pakistan and India should become the international border. A Pakistani government official was offended by this suggestion, and on October 3, Dr. Younas Shaikh was suspended from the college without an explanation. Later that evening, an employee of the Pakistan Foreign Office who
was also Dr. Shaikh's student complained to a cleric that Dr. Shaikh had
made blasphemous remarks about the Prophet of Islam. On the evening of
October 4, 2000, Dr. Shaikh was arrested and charged with blasphemy.[17]
    Because blasphemy victims cannot seek bail, they must remain in jail,
as did Dr. Shaikh until 2003, when he was released in utmost secrecy. He
was tried in the Lahore High Court, where Islamists were present and
threatened the attorneys and the jurists. A death sentence was handed to
Dr. Shaikh. The matter was referred back to the lower court, where, due to
the threats that the Islamic militants hurled at the judges and the attorneys,
Dr. Younas Shaikh defended his own case, which was decided in his favor.

Despite the ruling in his favor, for his own safety he sought asylum abroad.[18] Dr. Shaikh called this "Islamic terrorism through the abuse of law and of the state apparatus." These laws certainly are no part of Muhammad's Islam or his shari'a. It is a case of fanaticism at its worst.

SALAMAT MASIH AND ANOTHER VERSUS THE STATE

Another highly publicized case that Siddiqui and Hayat report is that of *Salamat Masih and Another versus the State*. The victim, in this case a thirteen-year-old Christian boy, was framed under Section 295-C, and he was sentenced to death for blasphemy in 1995. The charge against Salamat was that he wrote offensive words on the walls of a mosque. Two others, the co-accused, Rehmat Masih and Manzoor Masih, were also booked. During the trial at a sessions court, militants assassinated Manzoor Masih. Salamat and Rehmat were given the death penalty. The same militants had attacked them as well.

Salamat's and Rehmat's appeal at the Lahore High Court was successful, as the bench reprimanded the sessions court at the lower level for disregard of evidentiary requirements and for basing the case on tenuous grounds. The hearings of this court were held for seven days, while Islamic zealots demonstrated outside the High Court building and the mall road leading to it. The militants threatened Salamat and Rehmat, demanding death for the accused, and they also threatened the defense attorneys and the judges. Asma Jehangir, one of the defense attorneys, argued that the first witness in the case had withdrawn his accusation and did not wish to pursue the case, and thus the FIR stood invalidated. Then she said the evidence of the other two witnesses was contradictory. The timing of when the alleged derogatory remarks were written on the mosque wall and when the matter was reported to the police did not tally. Seven of the eight amicus curiae argued that the prosecution lacked evidence and that these were baseless convictions. The lower court was criticized for delivering a guilty verdict on such inadequate evidence.

> The investigating agency, the Public Prosecutor and the trial court failed to perform their duties in a case based on a serious charge . . . [The] Deputy District Attorney failed to perform his duty, [and] did not confront the prosecution witness with each fact of the FIR, the P.Ws did not state anything regarding any word defiling, the sacred name of the Holy Prophet (pbuh) and despite that the learned trial Court convicted the appellants.[19]

Siddiqui and Hayat state that human rights activists had proposed that before filing an FIR, there ought to be a pretrial investigation of witnesses, as is stipulated in Islamic law, since the law seems to be derived from that source. The claim was based on the Qur'an, that for a *hadd* (serious) crime, the penal code of Islam requires a pretrial credibility verification, and since blasphemy is a hadd crime, it needs to be dealt with according to the Qur'an, where it is called *tazkiat-us-shaoor*.[20]

In this case the High Court pointed to the possibility of personal vendetta. Rehmat Masih claimed that he had collected signatures within the Christian community and had lodged a report against a local teacher who had refused to teach Christian children. The teacher had threatened to teach him a lesson. Rehmat claimed that Manzoor Masih's murder and his own injuries were due to these people. Once Salamat and Rehmat were acquitted, according to Siddiqui and Hayat, Jamaat-e Ahl-e Sunnat, a religious organization, offered a prize of 1 million rupees to anyone for killing the two accused. The Mutahidda 'Ulema Council, another religious organization, offered 300,000 rupees for the same undertaking. Under these circumstances, Salamat and Rehmat could not continue to live in Pakistan. Their families and twenty others had already left their villages in Ratta Dhotran in Gujranwala. In February 1995, Salamat and Rehmat Masih left for Germany, where they were granted asylum.[21]

However, the story did not end there. Militants continued to riot, as they believed that the government, the churches, and the defense attorney had all colluded. A National Solidarity Council was established that brought together twenty-one religious parties. The defense attorney's car and driver were attacked, which called for police protection. Her family was threatened; her sister, Hina Jilani, also a rights lawyer, together with her family were attacked in their house by men who had a sack full of instruments for shooting, strangling, or otherwise slaying them. Police arrived in time to protect the household members, but the chief assailant escaped along with four others who were subsequently arrested.[22]

Justice Arif Iqbal Bhatti, a senior member of the High Court bench that acquitted Salamat and Rehmat Masih, continued to receive death threats. On October 10, 1997, a person pretending to be a client entered Justice Bhatti's chamber where he practiced as an attorney after retiring from the bench, shot him five times in the face and stomach, and walked away quietly. Justice Bhatti expired on the way to the hospital. Justice Bhatti's family claims that his assassination was a result of the verdict he and others gave in the Salamat and Rehmat Masih case, as he had continued to receive threatening and abusive calls from activists of a religious organization.[23] This was all in accordance with a takfir, a blasphemy ideology, that the extremist religious parties advocated.

BISHOP JOSEPH'S SUICIDE

While discussing Pakistan's blasphemy laws one must not forget Bishop Joseph's suicide in Sahiwal.[24] Bishop Joseph shot himself in front of the sessions court in that city on May 6, 1998, when he could not help one of his parishioners, Ayub Masih, in a blasphemy case for which Ayub received a death sentence. Ayub Masih had said that Salman Rushdie was right in whatever he wrote. Bishop Joseph was actually the Catholic priest in Faisalabad and had gone to hear the verdict on Ayub Masih's case that was held in camera, inside the jail, and where no journalist was allowed. Bishop Joseph's suicide and Ayub Masih's alleged insistence on supporting Salman Rushdie appear to be very much in the tradition of the Christian martyrs in Spain and the Neomartyrs under the Ottomans. The Christian community and minorities like the Ahmediyya have brought much attention to these laws at the international level through their websites. Asma Jehangir, who defended the Masihs in 1995, said of Bishop Joseph's funeral service in Khushpur village that he was "a martyr for human rights." The 1997 report of the Human Rights Commission of Pakistan says that blasphemy cases are slammed on members of Pakistan's minority communities to settle land and other disputes.[25]

BLASPHEMY CASE STATISTICS

The statistics from Pakistan shown in tables 4.1–4.5 indicate the extensive application of the blasphemy laws and their abuses. Since minorities such as Christians and Ahmediyyas are the main targets, Siddiqui and Hayat affirm that in 50 percent of the 1980–2007 cases the accused were non-Muslims.

Tables 4.1 and 4.2 indicate the number of cases decided in different jurisdictions beginning in 1960. The British colonists structured Pakistan's judicial system as follows. Cases are first tried on the local, district level in the sessions court. Subject to the outcome, plaintiffs can take their cases to the High Court. Each of the four provinces in the country—Sind, Pakhtunkhwa, Balochistan, and Panjab—has a High Court in its capital, respectively: Karachi, Peshwar, Quetta, and Lahore. Depending on the plaintiff's decision a case may finally end up in the Supreme Court, which is in the capital city of Islamabad. Under British colonial rule each of these courts used Islamic personal law in family matters such as divorce, inheritance, and custody of children. Zia-ul-Haq added an independent judiciary under the Shari'at Court system based totally on shari'a law. However, the jurisdiction of the Supreme Court is final, as it is the apex court.

As shown in tables 4.4 and 4.5, the number of blasphemy cases in Pakistani

Table 4.1. High Court cases in Pakistan 1960–2007, by regional jurisdiction

Lahore	Karachi	Peshawar	Quetta	Shari'at Court*	Total
62	21	6	1	1	91

Source: Adapted from Siddiqui and Hayat
*Azad Jammu and Kashmir, High Court and Shari'at Court

Table 4.2. Apex Court cases in Pakistan 1960–2007, by court jurisdiction

Supreme Court	Federal Shari'at Court	Supreme Court*	Shari'at Court*	Total
10	1	1	1	13

Source: Adapted from Siddiqui and Hayat
*Azad Jammu and Kashmir

Table 4.3. Number of blasphemy cases 1960–2007, by Pakistan Penal Code section

Section	Number of cases
295*	12
295-A	39
295-B	29
295-C	16
295-C and other Chapter 15 provisions	41
296	0
297	5
298*	5
298-A	5
298-B	4
298-C	19
Total	175

Source: Adapted from Siddiqui and Hayat, 324

Table 4.4. Blasphemy cases in Pakistan 1980–2007, by year

Year	Number of cases	Year	Number of cases	Year	Number of cases
1980	1	1990	1	2000	8
1981	0	1991	3	2001	6
1982	0	1992	5	2002	5
1983	0	1993	7	2003	8
1984	0	1994	4	2004	4
1985	0	1995	3	2005	6
1986	0	1996	5	2006	8
1987	3	1997	3	2007	3
1988	5	1998	4		
1989	3	1999	2		

Source: Adapted from Siddiqui and Hayat, 324–325

Table 4.5. Blasphemy cases 1980–2007, by decade

Decade	Number of cases
1980–1989	12
1990–1999	37
2000–2007	48
Total	97

Source: Adapted from Siddiqui and Hayat, 324–325

Table 4.6. Populations of Muslim countries with prominent blasphemy contexts

Country	Population
Indonesia	237,512,352
Pakistan	172,800,048
Bangladesh	153,546,896
Egypt	81,713,520
Afghanistan	32,738,376
Saudi Arabia	27,601,038
Sudan	30,855,000

courts grew fourfold from the 1980s to the 2000s. And although the statistics demonstrate the increasing use of blasphemy laws against citizens, they do not illustrate the many unregistered cases in which blasphemy laws have been used for intimidation against both women and men, especially against government officials, as detailed earlier.

JUSTICE JAVED IQBAL'S INTERVIEW IN *THE NATION*

Dr. Javed Iqbal, a retired judge of the High Court and son of Dr. Muhammad Iqbal, the founding poet of Pakistan, said in a July 1994 report in

LAHORE: PML(N) MPAs Sahibzada Fazal Karim, Mian Saeed Ahmad and Inamullah Khan Niazi shouting at Treasury members for showing reluctance in moving resolution, asking the Federal government to retain death penalty for offence under blasphemy laws (section 295-C)—Dawn photo

4.1. Extremists from Islamic religious parties in Parliament demand the death penalty for blasphemy. *Dawn* photo reprinted in Amritsari, *Blasphemy Law: From Ordinance to Murder.*

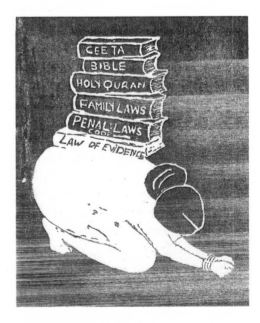

4.2. Shari'a applications under Hudood ordinances against women. Artist unknown. Reproduced in Amritsari, *Blasphemy Law: From Ordinance to Murder.* The publisher Idara-e Amn-O Insaf burned down. Images and materials kindly provided by Shirkat Gah, Karachi.

The Nation newspaper that the religious laws of Islam applied exclusively to Muslims, and non-Muslims are excluded from the hadd, the penal provisions of the blasphemy laws.[26] Justice Javed Iqbal affirmed in the article that although the matter of blasphemy is a sensitive one, he wished citizens to know that in the Mughal Empire and in the pre-Mughal Muslim sultanates when the shariʿa prevailed, the substantive shariʿa laws were divided into three categories: purely religious, criminal, and civil. Officials called *mohtasibs* who had their own separate departments supervised the general rules of morality. Justice Iqbal said the laws that applied to non-Muslims are documented in the *Fatwa-e Alamgiri*.[27] The Sultan's Firmans (also known as the Emperor's Instructions) would be sought when there was no specific law that could be found for non-Muslims, Justice Iqbal affirmed. He further said, "Then such portions of the laws were made applicable to them as were not specifically identified with the tenets of the Islamic faith."[28] The senator and retired justice said that generally the purely religious laws of Islam concerning blasphemy, apostasy, and other such offenses were applied exclusively to Muslims, and non-Muslims were excluded from the provisions of such laws.[29]

In *The Nation*'s report, Dr. Javed Iqbal cited the work of Justice M. B. Ahmad, relying on the Qur'anic verse *Lakum denukum waliya din*;[30] the fatwa said, "They (non-Muslims) could not be persecuted for selling or eating pig or for denying the Prophet Muhammad (PBUH) position as the messenger of God for which the Muslims alone could be punished." Justice Iqbal said the shariʿa law is derived from *usul ul fiqh* and in fact was intended for the believers in faith, and nonbelievers were to be let alone.[31]

For the criminal law of Islam, Justice Iqbal said that it was applied equally to all citizens, Muslims and non-Muslims. For instance, in the case of zina and drunkenness, Muslims were subject to more severe penalties, while non-Muslims were sometimes granted full reprieve by the sultan. Justice Iqbal said the Mughals and pre-Mughals had established a much more tolerant Islamic state than the one that we see today. He affirmed that Quaid-e Azam Muhammad ʿAli Jinnah, the founder of Pakistan, was a liberal attorney and politician who protected the rights of minorities. Justice Iqbal cited his own father as well.

Justice Iqbal said that in his father's book *The Reconstruction of Religious Thought in Islam*, his father, Dr. Muhammad Iqbal, stated that since there is no likelihood of another revelation, Muslims ought to be among the most emancipated people on earth, and Muslims emerging out of the spiritual slavery of dominant colonialism were not in a position to appreciate the basic significance of this idea.[32] Justice Iqbal advocated a spiritual democracy based on his father's philosophy that combined progressive renaissance thought with spiritual Islam. Muhammad Iqbal, his father, was one of the founding thinkers of the Pakistan Movement and was a Sufi philosopher like Rumi. Justice Javed Iqbal stated that it was the responsibility of Pakistani citizens to implement a tolerant Islam based on Quaid-e Azam Jinnah and Muhammad Iqbal's dream, or they will drift in another direction. Javed Iqbal said he considers himself a freethinker who follows the principles of the founding fathers of Pakistan, such as his father and Jinnah.[33]

In direct opposition to the principles of Iqbal and Jinnah stand all the statistics that Siddiqui and Hayat cite on blasphemy cases during Zia-ul-Haq's time and later. They are disturbing, especially as they are used against minorities. Justice Durab Patel said of these instances that unfortunately, the sections that deal with the Ahmadis are dangerous, as police officers in the Panjab were pressured against their consciences to register cases against them. Section 295-B and 295-C violate Article 8 of the constitution and the fundamental rights granted in it. Also, they violate Articles 14, 20, and 25 of the constitution.[34]

All of this reaffirms my conviction that in order to survive, the Pakistani state has to look toward a secular democracy with liberal spiritual goals according to the vision of its founding fathers and not toward a theocratic, intolerant state that uses a skewed version of an Islamic shariʿa to marginalize its own citizens. And certainly blasphemy laws are no part of Muhammad's shariʿa or his Qurʾan. Furthermore, if a woman and her donkey could travel alone from Arabia to Jerusalem in the caliph Omar's time, why is it that in the second millennium some contemporary Islamic states will not permit a woman to drive?[35]

CHAPTER 5

RISKY KNOWLEDGE, PERILOUS TIMES:
HISTORY'S MARTYR MANSUR HALLAJ

A CONFERENCE PAPER THAT I PRESENTED at Duke University's Center for Human Rights in 2004 inspires this chapter. The conference theme was "Beautiful Minds, Risky Times." As such, this chapter addresses the connection of the Pakistani state with its liberal intellectuals and freethinkers.[1] I will frame the discussion here within the context of Hanafi Islam and its institutions of Sufism, Sufi poetry, and Sufi shrines in South Asia, as this is my area of research and one of the major reasons for a blasphemy charge against me from the administration of the Allama Iqbal Open University in the capital of Islamabad in 1998. My PhD in 1992 from the University of Texas at Austin was on the oral traditions of Sufism in both Pakistan and India; furthermore, I was working on a book about the female voice in Sufi ritual in Pakistan and India for the University of Texas Press when the charge of blasphemy was brought against me. Not only was the theme of Sufism a red flag for the clerics-turned-faculty at the Open University, the matter was aggravated by my inclusion of India in the study, as really the Sufi tradition of poetry and music predates the creation of Pakistan when the region was a united India.

Sufism in South Asia evolved in an eclectic environment surrounded by the domains of Hinduism, Buddhism, Christianity, Sikhism, Zoroastrianism (Parsi), and other faith systems, though Islam was central to the discourse. Until the charge was leveled against me and I left for the United States on a sabbatical to complete my book, I was not aware of the traditional hostility between the clerics and the Sufis. A female colleague who herself was a scholar of Sufism brought this to my notice; we met at an ethnomusicology conference at the University of Texas at Austin in 1999. She said, "Well of course the Sufis and mullas have never gotten along. You should have known." I did not indeed know that I was working with risky knowledge in perilous times.[2] Hence, the title for this chapter.

Mansur Hallaj (executed 922) is central to my discourse, as he is a known universalist in Islamic thought who was executed for being a political threat to the "Islamic" state. The state appropriated Muhammad's Islam and the interpretation of his Qur'an, while Hallaj advocated a wider, independent interpretation of Muhammad's life, his times, and the Qur'an. Briefly, this chapter explores the relationships of state, religion, and politics, leading to the subject of divine authority. To build a context, some earlier historical Islamic empires are investigated, along with the Prophet Muhammad's fledgling state of Medina, connecting it to present-day Pakistan.

My position is that some Islamic states manipulated Muhammad's sunna and his Qur'an to establish political and social control. Under the guise of "a divinely interpreted" shari'a that quelled questioning and instilled fear, the political state used kufr, or blasphemy laws, as its instrument of control. The state appropriated the holy text, endowing itself as God's appointed authority or viceregent on earth. Since citizens were subjected to state-ordained laws, some divinely authorized, they were caught in a double bind: questioning the kufr laws was heresy, which was punishable under the laws. Citizens were never permitted to interpret the law because they did not have the ascendancy over the canon, whether intellectual or political, as shall be examined later in the case of Husayn ibn Mansur al-Hallaj (b. 858, d. 922), a teacher of Sufism who was executed for heresy. The interpretation of the canon belonged to the state and its officials, who were also the creators of the canon as God's divine representatives. The present state of Saudi Arabia and its Wahabi canon is an example.

A case study of the historical trial and execution of Mansur Hallaj argues that the 'Abbasid state, in Baghdad, wielding divine authority in Islam's name, persecuted a freethinker who claimed to be spiritual in his practice of Islam but who, at the same time, was also involved in issues of social justice that threatened the 'Abbasid state. Thus, the state was motivated to use its shari'a laws to level charges of blasphemy, heresy, heterodoxy, and apostasy against Hallaj.[3] The state's motives were not religious; in fact, they were decidedly political. The state claimed authority from Islam and its own interpretation of Qur'anic law and the Prophet's sunna. Many times the state's interpretations were derived from the sunna of the Companions, or the Pious Ones, the four caliphs who followed the Prophet—not the Prophet's sunna.[4]

When the state was threatened by the political and philosophical views of individuals like Hallaj, rather than charge these citizens for their political transgressions, the state used divine injunctions that gave it greater authority. First, it is important to clarify some terms.[5]

"Blasphemy" is defamation of one or more gods, profane language, irreverence, impiety, insult to the Prophet, or insult to his Companions.

In Perso-Arabic, *sabb* is a term that is also expressed as *kufr, tauhin,
adam ehtram*, or *sabb-e din*. Also, *sabb* can be extended to *sabb-e rasul* or
sabb-e sahaba.

"Apostasy" is defection or revolt, abandonment, or renunciation of one's
religion.

In Perso-Arabic, it is *riddah* or *shar*, an apostate is also called a *murtad* or *munafiq*, as in the case of Abdullah ibn Ubbay in the Battle of the
Trench (when the Prophet fought against the Quraysh). Thus, the Medinites who betrayed the Prophet were called the *munafiqin*.

"Heresy" is unorthodox religious belief, a belief or idea that is in opposition
to established views. The *Oxford English Dictionary* describes heresy as
"an opinion or doctrine in philosophy, politics, science, art, etc. at variance with those generally accepted as authoritative."

In Perso-Arabic, it is *shirk, mushriq, biddat (bid'a), takfir*, or *ilhad*.

"Heterodoxy" is any opinion or doctrine at variance with an official or orthodox position. It is dissidence, dissident, unorthodoxy.

In Perso-Arabic, it is *murtaqat* or *biddat*.

Each of the terms given here in Perso-Arabic has a distinct meaning: blasphemy (*kufr, tauhin*, or *adam ehtram*), heresy (*shirk*), heterodoxy (*murtaqat* or *biddat*), apostasy (*riddah*), *sabb* (insulting established belief systems), and apostasy (*murtadat*). However, rulers in Muslim states have
applied charges, on the advice of their jurisconsults, to best suit them and
their political agendas at the time. Some additional case studies are discussed in this chapter. And yet, so creative were the states in leveling accusations that no two cases were the same and no two charges were the same.

HALLAJ AS A CASE STUDY

Among Muslims the world over, Husayn ibn Mansur al-Hallaj (858–922) is
the model for *qawwali* and *sufiana-kalam* (Sufi music) singers for his spirituality and true understanding of the faith in its plurality and its universal-
ity. Yet, he is also a controversial figure. A hero among Muslim liberals, he
is also condemned as a heretic among the orthodox mullas and imams. The
fatwas of Ibn Taymiya (Islamic scholar 1263–1328) against Hallaj are well
known.[6]

The two questions put to Ibn Taymiya about Hallaj were:

1) Is this an honest (*siddiq*) or perfidious (*zindiq*) man? Is this a venerable saint (*wali muttaqi*), the possessor of divine grace (*hal rahmani*) or an adept at magic, and

2) Was he executed for *zandaqa* [magic or fire-worship] in accordance with the opinion of the assembly of 'ulama of Islam? Or was he in fact unjustly (executed)?[7]

Answer:

Hallaj was justly condemned. And anyone who is not of this opinion is either hypocritical or ignorant; and whoever approves of him must be killed like him (*wajib-ul qatal*).[8]

After examining Hallaj's life and travels, some of his written discourses, their themes, and his trials and punishments, Ibn Taymiya concluded that he was an unrepentant satanic being.[9]

In the second fatwa, Ibn Taymiya again vehemently dismissed claims from Hallaj's followers sanctifying his practices, his mystical ecstasies, his ideas and utterances. Ibn Taymiya affirms that

for us 'ulama, we have the formula of divine unity (Tawhid) which has been prescribed for us, the way of God that has been laid down for us, and from both we have learned, that "what Hallaj said is only falsehood" (quoting Ibn Dawud, Hallaj's rival) and that those like him deserve death.[10]

In the third fatwa, Ibn Taymiya reinforced the arguments from Hallaj's own Sufi contemporaries who opposed his intense mysticism of union with God that he called *ishq* (divine love) and *Anal Haqq* (I am the divine truth). Ibn Taymiya argued two points:

A. Ecstasy had temporarily cut off Hallaj's reason so he spoke in an amorous delirium, or

B. he was lucid and he revealed the mystery, even that of *Tawhid*, which made his execution necessary.[11]

Ibn Taymiya argued that because of accusation "A" Hallaj could not be pardoned. Furthermore, he was justly condemned for blasphemy against the Qur'an. His execution was justified for his teaching that the hajj could be performed fully outside Mecca (other states at the time had permitted such practices). He was a sorcerer whom the demons served.[12]

Hallaj was a threat to the 'Abbasid state because he traveled widely in the empire disseminating his egalitarian views that showed sympathy with the working classes. This was a vast Sunni empire comprised of citizens from different faiths as well as those who differed from the mainstream Sunni populations, such as the Shi'a and the Isma'ilis (figure 6.1, "Blasphemy Trajectories" chart). The 'Abbasids had to keep scrutiny on their subjects, and thus they had laws in place to deal with kufr and zandaqa that were perhaps a substitute for modern-day sedition laws. The 'Abbasids felt a continuous threat from various segments of their citizenry despite the sophisticated administrative machinery that they had instituted to run their empire. Yet, even with all its safeguards, the 'Abbasid dynasty that persecuted and then executed Hallaj was terminated with Halagu Khan's Mongol invasion of Baghdad in 1258. And with that invasion a great civilization came to an end, together with its "Islamic" laws.

THE CHALLENGE OF INTERPRETING THE QUR'AN

Drawing on the clear and accessible writing of French professor and Islamist Louis Massignon's four volumes on Hallaj and on Herbert Mason's abridged version of Massignon's work, together with Wael Hallaq's *Origins and Evolution of Islamic Law*, I present the argument for understanding a very intricate and challenging judicial matter, especially Ibn Dawud's (the orthodox canonical jurist in Hallaj's case) elaborate arguments that he draws from classical Arabic grammarians, a field that is not necessarily Qur'anic and that the canonists in Islamic *fiqh* (jurisprudence) have appropriated for themselves. The layperson, however, does not have the knowledge of the Arabic grammar, which is the language of the Qur'an. Furthermore, in all likelihood, the average Muslim does not have a grounding in Islamic history, which then leaves the matter of interpreting the holy text open to either charlatans or the state authority. It was this hegemonic appropriation of the holy text that led Hallaj to speak to the laypeople about Qur'anic knowledge in ways they could understand. Naturally, this took away from the state's power that was upheld through appropriation of Qur'anic language and the Prophet's sunna. Hallaj was a threat to state authority and had to be dealt with in the name of Islam: in other words through the shari'a and the manipulation of blasphemy and heresy laws that the state machinery applied to his case.

Hallaj communicated with ordinary people in their own language. Hallaj spoke of divine love, *ishq* and *mahaba*, that could exist between man and the creator. Ibn Dawud gave *ishq* a sexual, sensuous interpretation that was not Hallaj's intent.

Opposing Ibn Dawud in his extensive textual argument derived from hard-core Arabic grammar, Ibn Surayj, another jurist, gave the matter a beautiful defense. He defended Hallaj through his short, concise fatwa that what Hallaj experienced and spoke about was outside the domain of the *word*. In other words, it was a matter of consciousness, of the inner self, a world that dreams are made of and hence inexplicable, yet true. Freud, Jung, and Adler have written extensively on this concept. They wrote about the world of the collective conscious and the collective unconscious, which would now clarify Hallaj's ideas. Hallaj, from such a point of view, was ahead of his time—even as his ideas are today.

The grounds on which Ibn Dawud argued the case was *usul fiqh* (the principles of jurisprudence), while Ibn Surayj argued the case on *ruh*, or the soul. Both points of view are valid in the world of Islam. And both served as the basis of the two fitnas in Islam: one based on the canon in which Muhammad's immediate successors, especially the first three caliphs, upheld the Qur'anic *word*, and the other on the inner, esoteric self of the kind in which the Prophet's *mi'raj*, or nocturnal spiritual journey, was made.[13] The latter point of view was upheld by Muhammad's family that claimed descent through his daughter Fatima and her husband, 'Ali ibn Abi Talib, who believed that only Muhammad's family could interpret the inner, spiritual experience of divine revelation. However, believers of this claim were branded as heretics. In claiming the inner self thus, Hallaj threatened the 'Abbasid state that upheld Sunni Islam and the canonical authority of the Qur'an and the Prophet's sunna, following the first three caliphs, who were Sunnis. Moreover, Hallaj's family members were converts to Islam, and they brought their indigenous, Persianized practices to Islam. That Hallaj had diverse views and so many connections among Muslim and non-Muslim communities all over the empire placed him under the suspicion of the state. The state eventually imprisoned him for being a political threat, but the charges that were brought against him were framed as shari'a laws of kufr.

THE CONSEQUENCES OF HALLAJ'S SENSE OF SOCIAL JUSTICE

Mansur Hallaj, whose full name was Abu al-Mughis Husayn ibn Mansur al-Hallaj, was born to Persian parents in a village of southwestern Iran called Tur. This was an Arabized village, and though he was an Arabic-speaking citizen who also wrote in Arabic, his father was a Zoroastrian convert to Islam; his grandfather Mahamma remained a Zoroastrian. Mansur's father was a wool carder, or *hallaj*. As such, Mansur took the name Hallaj and traveled in the textile centers of Ahwaz and Tustar, settling his family in Wasit, a traditional Sunni town of southern Iraq, in 868.[14] Sahl, a Sunni Qur'anic scholar who was himself trained in Hasan al-Basri's Sufi mystical chain of transmissions (*isnad*), was among Hallaj's earliest mentors.

Hasan al-Basri was born of Persian parents, and although his Persian name was Pirouz, his Arab name was Abul Hasan. The Prophet's wife Umm-e Salama is said to have nursed al-Basri when he came to her as part of the booty in a war between the Arabs and the Persians. She later gifted al-Basri to a young couple, who released him from indenture. Al-Basri's brand of Islamic practice was tempered with Persian mysticism, although he followed austerity and asceticism; his beliefs were a fearless remonstrance of political authority. His philosophy was based on free will called "Qadarism" (capability, man's ability to act) versus predestination.[15] Consequently, Hallaj was intellectually and spiritually groomed in the Perso-Arab school of thought versus a pure Arab tribal brand of thought. He spoke and wrote in Arabic although he lived among the Persianized Arab communities. In his early years Hallaj was associated with Junayd, a Sufi of standing, and it was under Junayd's influence that Hallaj married the daughter of Abu Yaqub Aqta, a secretary of Junayd. This was Hallaj's only marriage, from which he had three sons and a daughter. Much of Hallaj's biography has been built from the narratives of his son Hamd, which are extensively documented in Massignon's study. After Hallaj's execution, the 'Abbasids executed Hamd also for attempting to sustain Hallajism.

Hallaj's marriage into Junayd's network was not favored by his other Sufi mentor, Amr Makki, who opposed this marriage strongly. Sufis too can be competitive. Irrespective, Junayd counseled Hallaj to be patient with the criticism to his marriage. Accordingly, Hallaj went to live with his family in Basra, which was also the home of his in-laws. It was here in Basra that Hallaj's education and development as a Sufi grew. Basra at that time was the literary center of the region with the expansion of Islam into Mesopotamia and Persia. After the Prophet's death it became a significant literary center with the migration of scholars from Medina, which during the Prophet's life was the center of Islamic discourse, law, jurisprudence, and practice. (Medina was the Prophet's adopted city and where he received sanctuary from his opposition, the Quraysh clansmen.) Basra was the center of Qur'anic language in Hallaj's time, and it was here that Hallaj acquired the "imprint upon his language of mystical thought, and from its older Arabic heritage, styles of didactic and lyric poetry; and quickening of his consciousness of social injustice."[16]

The map from Massignon's work (map 5.1) shows why under threat from

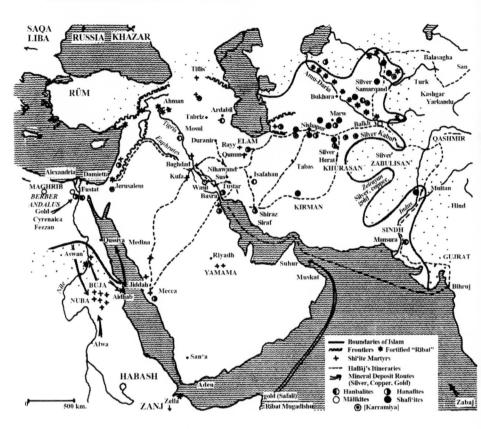

MAP 5.1. Regions in which Hallaj traveled. Adapted by Arlen Nydam from Massignon, *Passion of al-Hallaj*, 1982. © Editions Gallimard, 1975.

the Shi'a kingdoms around the 'Abbasid Empire, the state had to keep a strict eye on a universalist and pluralist like Hallaj; he had to be kept under surveillance, for he had class and faith sympathies with diverse groups. The map is useful not only for understanding how Hallaj and others like him were a political threat to the 'Abbasid state, but it also offers a geographic understanding of the fatwas, the religious decrees, that the Ottoman *seyhul-islams* (jurisconsults) or muftis issued against the Shi'a citizens and kingdoms around Ottoman territories,[17] as will be discussed in detail later.

In a discussion of Hallaj's biography several events stand out. Because he had lived a large part of his life in the textile centers of Ahwaz and Tustar and he was from the artisan class of wool carders himself, he knew the circumstances of the working classes and could be sensitive to class consciousness. He was somehow involved through his in-laws, the Karnaba'i family in Basra, in the revolt of the Zanj, which was a social and economic calamity.[18] Hallaj found himself in the middle of political controversies generated through the diverse ethnic and religious communities in which he circulated. The ʿAbbasids under Caliph Muwaffaq finally put down the Zanj uprising, but Hallaj's alleged sympathies with the revolt would have far-reaching consequences for his trial in later years.

ZANDAQA, THE ACCUSATION OF MAGIC

Hallaj was also allegedly involved with zandaqa, the Manichean heresy. *Zandaqa* is a word of Persian origin. Manicheans were persecuted, even by the ʿAbbasids, for *zandiki* or *zanda* (magic), and generally a *zandiqi* was considered one who practiced magic and was thus heretical.[19] The Sassanids also persecuted the Manicheans, who practiced a mix of Christianity tempered with Zoroastrianism and Buddhism.[20] They seem to have converted to Islam without much conviction and continued to practice their indigenous religions, which made them victims of the zandaqa, or the "Persian heresy."[21]

Generally, during this period *zandaqa* was a term the state used for any form of sedition or political opposition to it, and the officer in charge of such persecution was called the *sahib al-zanadaqi* or ʿarif al-zanadaqi. Individuals who showed irreverence toward the shariʿa or showed libertarian tendencies were also persecuted for zandaqa. Many well-known poets, both *mawali* (non-Arab Muslims) and Arab Muslims, were implicated in zandaqa charges, notably the poets Bashar ibn Burd, Hammad Ajrad, and Ishaq ibn Khalaf, among many others. Poets accused each other of zandaqa, too.[22] To be found guilty of being a *zindiq* (sorcerer) meant punishment by death. One wonders if Pakistan's all-encompassing blasphemy laws instituted by General Zia-ul-Haq were derived from this model of the zandaqa.

Among notable Arab poets against whom the ʿAbbasids used the zandaqa was one Yaqub ibn Fadl, a descendant of ʿAbd al-Mutallib of the Beni Hashem; simply because of being a Hashemite his life was spared, but he languished in jail until he died. Yaqub's daughter was also charged with zandaqa.[23]

Hallaj's first trial was for kufr. He was accused of takfir (heresy) under shariʿa. His invocations, or *shat* proclaiming love for God, made him enemies with Ibn Dawud, a professed Zahirite of the Hanbali school who believed only in the canon and the grammar of the Qurʾan. Hallaj, on the other hand, professed a connection with the inner self of the intuitive world and the soul through which one could connect with the deity and thus achieve divine knowledge. Hallaj's claim of Anal Haqq, "I am the divine truth," emanated from such beliefs. Many, including Ibn Dawud, were offended by such Hallajian claims, as if the mystic was appropriating divine attributes. Ibn Dawud insisted on the pure canon derived from the divine text and its esoteric Arabic grammar. Ibn Dawud found Hallaj's claims of love for the deity absolutely heretical, as he saw love to be something only sexual, something that existed only in the temporal world. Somehow, through his influence in the court and his connections with well-placed officials in the 'Abbasid court, Hallaj was able to escape punishment. His first trial is extremely interesting, however, in the arguments that were used against him by Ibn Dawud and in his defense by Ibn Surayj, a Shafi'ite jurisconsult.

HALLAJ'S TRIALS

As a missionary Hallaj preached widely in the 'Abbasid Empire and also outside it. He traveled into India right up to Gujrat and then north into Afghanistan and Kashmir. He went to Mecca and Medina in the west and moved around in the regions identified in map 5.1. Not only was Hallaj associated with the Zanj revolt, he was also associated with Shi'a as well as orthodox Sunni movements that criticized the 'Abbasid court of Caliph Mu'tatid (895–932).[24] He questioned the tax policies of the state, and he further threatened the authority of the 'Abbasid state by preaching eclectic Islam in public places to the people. In short, the 'Abbasid state found that "Hallaj and his followers were a threat to law and order."[25]

Hallaj was political. He upheld human rights and condemned social injustices. The ordinary people rallied around him as he spoke of matters that affected the grassroots populations. He was one of them. In this he deviated from his Sufi mentors like Junayd who kept an ascetic, apolitical position. Hallaj's critics accused him of being a charlatan who knew how to play with words that got him access to the 'Abbasid court and its top administrators.

Not only did Hallaj dabble in politics, his views on personal intuition (*ilham*) were intensely radical; it was as if he was appropriating spiritual and religious authority, especially with his claim of Anal Haqq. In this shat or locution, Hallaj claimed that it was possible for ordinary human beings to reach the core of their spiritual selves that is the source of divine vision. People from all walks of life rallied around him as they sought his counsel. The poor as well as the rich were attracted to his charisma. He moved in diverse circles of Sufis, Shi'a, Sunnis, Christians, Hindus, Zoroastrians, and Manicheans. Caliph Mu'tatid's mother, Queen Shagab, who was Greek, was Hallaj's devotee and protector. For a long time with her support and with defense from Ibn Surayj, Hallaj escaped punishment.

The charge of *zandaqa* on Hallaj for heresy is not surprising. Although he preached Islam in the areas where the zandaqa was quite strong (among the Turk Uyghur populations, for example), his eclectic interpretation of Islam inspired a threat to the ʿAbbasid court, and as such he was watched wherever he went. Even when he went to India, an envoy of Caliph Muʿtatid was sent to accompany him.[26]

Ibn Dawud, the Zahirite assessor and expert witness of Hallaj who believed in the canon, built the case against Hallaj. Ibn Dawud claimed that the interpretation of the Qurʾan and the Prophet's sunna could only be based on the obvious meaning of the "Arabic lexicon." He based his argument on authoritative examples that he drew from the grammarians of classical Arabic—what Ibn Dawud claimed was the *zahir* (overt meaning) of the words. Ibn Dawud's position also drew from the Hellenistic position of logical syllogisms, an approach through which he and the Zahirites interpreted the holy text. On the other hand, Hallaj claimed through his doctrine that words also have a *batin* (covert meaning). Hallaj, like his Sufi mentors, believed that the Qurʾanic text had hidden meanings, or *isharat*. Hallaj thus claimed that God could also be approached on a human, intuitive level in the manner that God revealed himself to the Prophet. Hallaj followed his Sufi school of Basra that believed in asceticism and prayer and that God loves the soul.[27]

This was the classic argument between the Zahirites and the Sufis. The Sufis, like the metaphysical poets, have given an esoteric meaning to the relationship between God and man, basing it on the Prophet's *miʿraj*, nocturnal journey, in which the divine veil is lifted through *kashf*, enlightenment, where a human's soul becomes one with the divine. For a Zahirite like Ibn Dawud, however, such a claim constituted blasphemy and heresy. Hallaj thus was considered a blasphemer claiming divine authority. Hallaj attempted to explain in human terms, for example, Moses's experience at Mount Sinai. His Anal Haqq meant that through prayer and asceticism human beings could connect with the *ruh* (soul). Hallaj's Sufi mentors had warned him not to preach such experiences in public or to the "uninitiated" audiences without the requisite training and initiation into the spiritual discipline. Hallaj's trials for kufr and later for zandaqa are evidence of the wisdom of this advice.

IBN SURAYJ'S DEFENSE

In Massignon's four-volume work and Mason's abridged work of Massignon, I found Ibn Surayj's arguments in defense of Hallaj most convincing, in fact competitive with the concept of giving the accused the benefit of the doubt. Thus, Ibn Surayj eventually gives a "suspensive" fatwa, or legal opinion, that he calls *tawaquff*: that he is not qualified to pronounce on such matters and that the qadi is also not competent to apply through analogical reasoning any legal sanctions. Quite simply, Ibn Surayj's fatwa "suspends" any legal opinion against Hallaj. According to an interpretation by Ibn Surayj,

> This falls within the category of *sarira*, of the inward consciousness of every person, which will be revealed only on Judgment Day (*yawma tubla'l sara'ir*, Qur'an 86:9), for it is the secret of love (*liawa'l-nufusi sariratun la tu'lamu*) unknowable by science; hidden even from angels, of the khulla of the abdal.[28]

A contemporary, S̲h̲afi'ite Abu 'Amr A-b-Nasr Khaffaf (d. 911), gave a similar suspensive fatwa. Ibn Surayj's response to Ibn Dawud's charge was, "This is a man (*rajul*) [Hallaj], whose inspiration I cannot grasp. So, I shall not attempt a doctrinal evaluation on it."[29]

According to Ibn Surayj, despite his own short fatwa, he considered Hallaj a sincere believer who was not an imposter or a heretic. Ibn Surayj's fatwa established the independence of mysticism in Islam versus canonical courts; in the face of mystic states of consciousness, the jurisconsult suspends his judgment.[30] In contemporary times, this is something Pakistani attorneys plead in Section 295-C of Pakistan's blasphemy laws when their plaintiffs' situations are absolutely hopeless.[31]

According to Massignon, S̲h̲afi'ites like Ibn Surayj believed in metaphysical stages of *ahwal, wajd, ilham* (instantaneous ecstasy), sincerity (*sidq*), and private inspiration that is "not prophetic."[32] Another term is *wahy*, intuition. All these are terms in the metaphysical realm in which Hallaj indulged. Some of Ibn Surayj's discourses on Hallaj have been preserved in Ghazzali's *Sirr al-'alamayn* (39), where he says,

> What should I say about a man who in jurisprudence knows more than I do and who in mysticism speaks a language I do not understand.[33]

In the *Akhbar al Hallaj*, no. 72, Ibn Surayj is reported to have said,

> As for me, I attest that he is a *hafiz* (one who knows the Qur'an by heart), that he is trained in jurisprudence and learned in hadith, traditions and customs, that he fasts continually, prays all night, preaches good morals, weeps out of contrition; it is not because I do not understand the language he uses that I can condemn him as a kafir.[34]

In the same collection of *Akhbar al Hallaj*, no. 71, Ibn Surayj was asked by an anti-Hallajian Sufi, "What do you say regarding the fatwa of those who demand his execution?" He replied, "They must have forgotten the words of God: Would you kill a man because he says, 'my master is God?'" (Qur'an 40:28).

Thus, says Massignon, Ibn Surayj's fatwa removed for good the takfir procedure from trials that involved mystics. The charges against Hallaj then had to be "politicized" for him to be retried under zandaqa and not kufr. However, as will be discussed later, this was not the case in the Ottoman fatwas in which Sufi *raqs* (dances) and *sama* (musical concerts) are punishable as "deviant behavior."

Ibn Dawud reported Hallaj to Caliph Mu'tatid, whose targets were the illiterate preachers (*qussas*) who spoke in the marketplaces. Hallaj's sermons, although reckless, were based on argumentation. He spoke to the people directly in language they could understand, as some Sufis have always done in contradistinction to the canonists. He spoke to the people directly about God without going through the official channels. He was well informed on all the schools of Islamic thought, the Mu'tazilites, Imamites, Sunnis, and others. He was politically and socially dangerous to the state, as he knew too much of the complexities of the holy text. He could not be allowed to have influence over the Arab audiences of Karkh and Bab Basra in Baghdad, where Hallaj gave public speeches to his diverse audiences. He could not be allowed to give spiritual leadership and reasons for hope to an entire population that was made up of nomads driven by famine and ex-Bedouins from Yamama and Ahsa retreating from Basra and Qufa under pressure from the Qarmathian social revolution.[35]

Hallaj's first trial was from 910 to 913, and the second one was in 921–922. By the time of Hallaj's second trial, Ibn Surayj, who was sympathetic toward him, had died, and others willing to please the 'Abbasid caliphate now took over the judicial matter. At the end of the second trial, Hallaj was crucified like Jesus; he was executed, and his body was burned together with a major collection of his works. Massignon resurrected Hallaj's discourses centuries later from different sources in Iraq and elsewhere; this included Hallaj's *Akhbar* discourses.

HALLAJ AND ALTERNATIVE POLITICAL AUTHORITY

Hallaj therefore became a model for Sufi poets who brought Qur'anic knowledge to the people in an idiom they could understand, thus making the Sufis competitors in Qur'anic interpretations with the state.[36]

The conflict between Hallaj and Ibn Dawud was not simply about determining a matter of heresy; it was also a conflict over who has the right to claim spiritual and religious authority. That fight continues to pose problems even today between the Sufis (spiritualists) and the canonists or grammarians like Ibn Dawud. The matter is one of followers or spiritual constituency whether Sufis win the field against the canonists. I say it is Sufi or liberal Islam that has won the hearts and minds of Muslim populations for centuries.[37] For example, the Sufi poetry of Pakistan and India that is sung in the oral traditions among the people glorifies the Prophet's mi'raj, the metaphor of the veil or cloud that is lifted and man becomes one with the deity. Sindhi Sufi poetry romanticizes the bridegroom Prophet as he meets the deity.[38] Gender identification disappears in such poetry.

Panjabi Sufi poetry works with something similar, in which kashf is achieved; the veil is lifted and the boundaries of reason are dismantled in a relationship between the human and the deity. In such poetry the devotee supplicates the deity as a lover; all is embedded in an erotic metaphor. This for Ibn Dawud was plain and simple kufr, blasphemy, in the charge that he brought against Hallaj, and it continues to be a point of conflict in contemporary Pakistan and elsewhere in the Muslim world where Sufi shrines are attacked. The Sufi shrine of Data Ganj Bakhsh al-Hujweiri was bombed in 2010; likewise Sufi shrines have lately been attacked in Iraq. Sufi masters thus have cautioned against impetuous speech and have counseled careful language, isharat. Until recently, Sufis have not permitted the uninitiated into their assemblies.[39]

HALLAJISM AND SUFI POETRY

Sufi practitioners like Maulana Jalaluddin Rumi in Turkey and Sufi poets like Shah Abdul Latif in Sind and Bulle Shah in the Panjab created poetry in indigenous languages, such as Persian, Sindhi, and Panjabi that glorified Hallaj, who went to the gallows questioning the fixed text or rigid interpretation of the holy text that the state had appropriated for political control. Sufi disciples of Hallaj have sung about him so his message would reach the people that all about the Qur'an, Islam, and the Prophet's life is not embedded in the classical Arabic text but is also in the lived experience, the context of a social life and a spiritual morality that the Prophet transmitted. Hallaj and his followers affirmed that such experience can be transmitted in any language and in any culture by those who have committed themselves to the divine path—which may not necessarily be in the orthodoxy that the state or its officials uphold.[40]

I bring my own knowledge and training as a sociolinguist in the oral Islamic traditions to the subject so that the information is disseminated within the framework of the oral traditions: Hallaj spoke to his audiences through speech; Hallaj spoke in public places that made his speeches threatening to the authority of the 'Abbasid state. Here, Hallaj's public discourses and his poetry are looked at through the paradigm of speech communication, and his example is used for contemporary times when Muslims are working toward enlightened communities that can take on the challenges of the second millennium.[41]

The audiences for this book are Muslims who, like myself, are trying to find a voice in turbulent times, my peers in the academy, which includes other Muslims with whom I am in continuous dialogue about what constitutes Islam and about who has the authority to interpret Islam. Is it the orthodox state with its agendas or the citizens in the second millennium? Is it the FM-radio mullas of Swat who took over the province in 2009 or the citizens who for centuries have practiced an enlightened version of Islam that persisted and grew around Buddhism?[42] It can be seen in the stupendous Buddhist civilization of the Swat Valley, which until recently was well preserved, and of Taxila, which absorbed the cultural and artistic dimensions of Alexander's invasion as he came through the northern passes of the Hindu Kush that now constitutes Pakistan.

I have lived in these regions and I grew up in these regions, and thus I bring my own experiences of an enlightened Islam to this monograph as I question the "new shar'iat" and the "new Islam" that Zia-ul-Haq bestowed on Pakistan's citizens against their will.

Many times it was a military state or a monarchical oligarchy that had its own economic and global agenda for enforcing the "Islam" whose victim was a Hallaj. Citizens in such situations are hardly the state's concern; if anything, they are the ones who receive the fallout of reckless state policies such as the Swati citizens did in the civil war between the Taliban and the Pakistani military in 2009. In this recent conflict 1.5 million civilians—children, women, the old, and men—have become displaced to live in refugee camps in the country like the Afghan refugees. The same pattern is repeated in the Waziristan offensive now. And this is done all in Islam's name, as one sees in Hallaj's trial.

This book is being written for students like mine, past and future, so that blasphemy in the modern state that claims to uphold "Islam" can be understood as well as challenged. This is a term that has been used freely like the 'Abbasid zandaqa against anyone who was outside the domain of *sarkari*, official state Islam. This work is furthermore being written for my own understanding of a state, starting with General Zia-ul-Haq and his so-called shari'a laws that turned the world upside down for Pakistani citizens. The blasphemy laws have now become an ideology of the state-supported Taliban and the al-Qaeda groups as they terrorize citizens locally and globally, Muslims included. It is not rare to see graffiti written on the walls in public markets in Pakistan threatening citizens for not subscribing to the militants' version of Islam: in 2008, I read slogans in Urdu on walls in Saddar bazaar in Rawalpindi and even on the boundary walls of the prestigious army race course in the cantonment—something to the effect of "Jo nahin hain talib *khatam-e nabuvat*, vo nahin hai yar-e Muhammad, hai vo g̲h̲adar-e Muhammad (One who does not seek the end of prophecy is not a friend of Muhammad, is a traitor to Muhammad). Similar slogans are splashed in major markets such as Aabpara in Islamabad.

What greater example does one need to demonstrate the abuse that Pakistan's blasphemy laws generate? Aren't the laws full of language that incites one set of citizens against another? And one set of Muslims against another? One cannot drive past a street or a market without feeling fear and with one's freedom of speech gagged. The lynch mobs of the state-backed Islamic parties make their presence known through graffiti like the above and the additional antagonistic loudspeaker sermons from the major Wahabi-funded mosques, especially during the Friday prayers.[43]

HALLAJ AND FREE WILL

Hallaj as a state adversary was a mystic who is most sung about, directly and through isharat, allusion in the Sufi poetry of Pakistan and India. Allama Muhammad Iqbal (1877–1938), the national poet and ideological founder of Pakistan, repeatedly referred to this audacious mystic who was executed in the most inhuman cruelty of the 'Abbasid state. The state held Hallaj's crucifixion up as an example so that no mystic or Sufi would ever use Hallaj's discourse or philosophy in the future. Interestingly, Allama Muhammad Iqbal received a fatwa from the mullas for writing "Shikwa," a poem in which the poet complains to God about the downfall of the Muslims following the disintegration of the Ottoman Empire and its caliphate starting with World War I. Iqbal was, as a result of his western education and commitment to Sufism, an adherent of free will; he questioned Muslims on their state of despair due to their lack of enterprise and apathy to rid themselves of their orthodox mold. Because of the mullas' fatwa on him, Iqbal wrote "Jawab-e Shikwa" (Response to the Complaint) in order to placate this community of clerics.[44]

Sources report that before Hallaj was crucified, his body was dismem-

bered part by part—a foot at a time, a hand at a time—before the crucifixion was carried out. His dismemberment continued for more than a day
in public view. This is a practice that Saudi Arabia continues to this day and
that Zia-ul-Haq tried to follow but into which the medical profession refused to be co-opted. Dismemberments and executions were done publicly
in Saudi Arabia as the public square in Riyadh was prepared for such events
on Friday. I was in Saudi Arabia in the 1970s when such events were reported.[45] (A poster of similar tortures in the Zia-ul-Haq period is presented
in figures 1.12–1.16.) Present-day Taliban and al-Qaeda groups have followed
similar practices, seeking their inspiration from Wahabi Islam and General Zia-ul-Haq's Islam, which has now appropriated global Islam through
armed groups. General Pervez Musharraf in his memoir, *In the Line of Fire*,
confirms that a similar process was followed to execute Daniel Pearl, the
Wall Street Journal reporter, when al-Qaeda operatives picked him up outside his hotel in Karachi post-9/11. Hence, the ideas and concepts discussed
in this chapter are derived from sources like the 'Abbasids in Baghdad. Pakistan's blasphemy laws follow such templates and models derived from contemporary Saudi Arabia.

MISINTERPRETATIONS OF THE QUR'AN

Massignon reports that in the case of a zindiq (freethinker) like Hallaj and
others, the following Qur'anic text from the Sura al-Ma'idah was applied for
punishment.[46] For the discussion here the text is derived from 'Abdullah Yusuf 'Ali's translation:[47]

> *The punishment of those*
> *Who wage war against Allah*
> *And His Messenger, and strive*
> *With might and main*
> *For mischief through the land*
> *Is: execution or crucifixion*
> *Or cutting off of hands*
> *And feet from opposite sides,*
> *Or exile from the land*[48]

'Abdullah Yusuf 'Ali in his footnote to the translation says these laws
were applied for sedition against the state as well as for treason against Allah. These, he wrote, were features of the criminal law at the time, derived—among other aspects of "Islamic" law—from pagan sources, as is

pointed out below. It seems that General Zia-ul-Haq was advised to resurrect these hadd, or corporal punishments, completely out of context with present times in his so-called shariʿat laws. The general's legacy continues to this day among the Taliban and al-Qaeda networks, as was seen in the brutal slaughterhouses these groups established in Swat in 2008–2009 to punish officials of Pakistan's security forces. Ironically, the very state that created these groups and gave them the militant ideology through its shariʿa became their victim: the state created its own monster that it continues to battle. This very act of having created a monstrous shariʿa threatens the theocracy that Zia-ul-Haq established through his support from the CIA and others who took part in the Afghanistan adventure.

Another instance that Massignon notes in relation to the accusations against Hallaj is the punishment the pharaoh prescribed for his magicians as cited in the Qur'an. However, in this instance the Qur'an is only narrating the story of the pharaoh who spoke to his magicians after Moses converted them. It is not a Qur'anic injunction. Many narratives from the Old Testament are cited in the Qur'an that are only historical incidents but not necessarily advocated as punishments, and this is one among many:

> *Be sure I will cut off*
> *Your hands and feet*
> *On opposite sides, and I*
> *Will have you crucified*
> *On trunks of palm trees*[49]

And yet another section that Massignon cites from the Qur'an is,

> *Said (Pharaoh): "Believe ye*
> *In Him before I give you permission*
> *. . .*
> *"Be sure I will cut off*
> *Your hands and your feet on*
> *Opposite sides*
> *And I*
> *Will cause you all*
> *To die on the cross!"*[50]

These last two suras are interesting and at the same time challenging. How is it that an "Islamic state" like Pakistan under Zia-ul-Haq accepted pharaonic laws like the ones mentioned in these two suras? The pharaoh was a pagan. Does this mean a pagan law governs Pakistan? Really, what the Qur'an is talking about in these last two suras is the pharaoh's stories of punishing his people for believing in Moses, an Abrahamic prophet of the Qur'an. The punishments for execution in Pakistan's blasphemy laws are derived from a pagan source, a pharaoh. This is why understanding the social context is so critical when interpreting the Qur'an. A Qur'anic narrative referring to Moses and the pharaoh is not necessarily a punishment to which the Qur'an subscribes. Can we thus say that Pakistan's blasphemy laws are botched, mala fide, and of pagan origin?

Two of the most significant suras many Muslims read daily from the Qur'an stand out for *zindiqi* (sorcerers and magicians). One is Sura al-Falaq:

Say: I seek refuge in the Lord of the dawn, that is, "In the Lord who brings out the light of the dawn from the darkness of night." From the evil of everything that He has created, and from the evil of darkness of night when it overspreads, for the reason that crimes and wickedness are mostly committed at night and the harmful animals that come out at night, and from the evil of the "blowers" (magicians, men and women) into knots, and from the evil of the envious when he envies, that is when he tries to do some harm out of jealousy.[51]

The other is Sura Anas:

Say: I seek refuge in the Lord of Mankind, the King of mankind, the real God of mankind from the evil of the whisperer, who returns over and over again, that is, when he does not succeed in deluding a person by whispering the evil once he withdraws, and then returns to whisper again and this he goes on doing over and over again who whispers (evil) into the hearts of men, whether he be from among the jinn or mankind. That is, "Whether this whisperer be from among mankind or from the jinn (satans), I seek refuge from the evil of both."[52]

Within a social context theory (that speech and language are generated in a specific social environment), the two previous suras are part of the Qur'an for the faithful to recite as a *zikr*, an incantation, a prayer for strength, a reminder in times of doubt. In the framework of the social context theory, the Qur'an was revealed to the Prophet based on a particular situation, as different parts of the Qur'an speak to different situations. These two suras were revealed in the early period of the Prophet's career, when soothsayers and magicians were rampant in Arabian society and challenged his message of Islam. Thus, it is binding for the jurisconsults to look into the Qur'anic texts and apply them for justice.[53]

The Qur'an is a fixed text that is open to interpretation. Its discourse is an emerging, evolving discourse, which is a position that ijtihad (independent reasoning) assumes. This is a nonfundamentalist position, one that Ustad Mahmoud Mohammad Taha adopted in the 1970s under Jaafar Nimeiri's regime, a military dictatorship like General Zia-ul-Haq's. Ustad Mahmoud Mohammad Taha was dubbed an apostate, tried, and eventually executed. The judges gave a decision after the execution that it was uncalled-for, as Ustad Taha "repented" before he was executed. The semantics of the judges' decree was still couched in fear, though this spiritualist and intellectual lost his life; Ustad Mahmoud Taha's interpretation threatened the state and its version of Islam. Ustad Taha's family insisted on this decree to save his image from infamy. Consequently, in Zia-ul-Haq's Islam, too, *ijtihad* has become a prohibitive term; it has been replaced with the more conservative *ijm'a* (the collective opinion of state-appointed jurists of the Wahabi school).[54]

BLASPHEMY, THE PAKISTANI STATE, AND HALLAJISM

It is important to place the blasphemy theme within a historical perspective to see how this area of Islamic law has evolved. To do that effectively requires looking at cases from other societies, such as the Ottomans in Turkey and, as has been done, the 'Abbasids in Iraq. But Pakistan and Afghanistan are still central to the discourse.

The blasphemy, apostasy, and heresy virus currently is worldwide and needs to be treated through disseminating information in the language of everyday use. Citizens cannot leave the interpretation of Islam to the state or its cronies because their interpretations and subsequent laws violate the ideals of freedom of speech and freedom of belief advocated by Muhammad. Their skewed vision of Islam is affecting the lives of millions of Muslims and non-Muslims the world over in total violation of human rights. The blasphemy ideologies backed with violence are coming from state laws instituted in the name of shari'a when really there is no shari'at about these laws, as has been argued in the previous chapters. If truant states cannot be forced to uphold human rights, at least advocates who strive to put the record straight through looking at arguments from the Islamic point of view can shame them.

Islam, which means "submission," is for everyone who seeks it and is not the *ijaradari*, possession, of only the obscurantists, state mullas, or the state itself. And that is why the case studies pertaining to the 'Abbasids and the Ottomans are necessary. It is a way to uphold the argument that despite their complexities and their cultural and scientific achievements, the 'Abbasids and the Ottomans together with modernist states like Pakistan have manipulated Islamic shari'a for political agendas. Islamic shari'a is rich, sophisticated, and nuanced, having grown over fourteen centuries in different cultural and anthropological contexts with the Qur'an as the basis, a Qur'an whose language is mystical, rich, and textured and a Qur'an that speaks to situations according to the context but that is a text that has been grossly misrepresented and grossly misinterpreted.

The influence of Hallaj extended to the area that is now Pakistan. Sufi poets absorbed Hallaj's influence and used it to protest social and economic injustice. Two Sufi poets who will be discussed are Shah Abdul Latif (1689–1752) and Bulle Shah (1680–1758). Both poets' compositions absorb the Hallajian paradigm of divine love tempered with a defiance of political authority: this poetry was a protest against injustice and social and economic oppression. The favorite themes of this poetry are the state and its collusion with the clergy. Therefore, among the clergy and orthodox state institutions such as the ahl-e hadith, Sufi poetry constitutes heresy (bid'a) and blasphemy (kufr). However, Shah Abdul Latif escaped persecution because first, he was a roving minstrel, an identity that many outriders acquired to protect themselves from the establishment, and second, he embedded his coding in myth and metaphor. This is not to say he did not hold the Qur'an and the Prophet in the highest esteem. Much like Hallaj, Shah Abdul Latif was a roving preacher, poet, and spiritual mentor available to his constituents in the language of everyday speech.

Bulle Shah (from a region that at the time was India), on the other hand, was impetuous like Hallaj and a political *baghi*, a rebel, in his interpretation of the faith as it took on caste and gender demarcations.[55] Bulle Shah is a controversial figure whom the establishment considered dangerous for the language he used against the religious and political authorities of his time—to the extent that even his mentor, Shah Inayat, banished him. As a result, he went and lived among dancing girls for several years. He eventually returned and danced before his mentor to win him back.[56] He knew his mentor liked dance; he came back dressed like a dancing girl, veiled in a *ghunghat*. The Sufi poets in this region took on the veil as an image to represent the mi'raj, in which removing the veil leads to enlightenment, kashf, the Prophet's meeting with the deity. They called it *ishq-e haqiqi*, divine love, as opposed to *ishq-e majazi*, earthly love.[57] The divine expression is of lover and beloved, the lover being the woman and the beloved a male. To frame the love between man and the deity in human terms is considered extremely blasphemous in the orthodox canon.[58] For saying the same, Hallaj was executed.

And yet, the rulers of the time in India, the Muslims who ruled from 711 to 1857, did not interfere in the indigenous practices. In fact, Rizvi reports in his study of Sufism in India that Hindu musicians who had converted to Islam continued to integrate the myths of Radha and Krishna into qawwali poetry to chant about divine love in the Sufi assemblies.[59] Many among the Muslim aristocracy and royalty were participants of these assemblies, and this poetry was for their consumption as well. It was in the state's interest to promote religious integration, and therefore such poetry was not branded heretical. Besides, the Muslim aristocracy that ruled India and promoted Islam in this region was generally Central Asian: Mongols, Iranians, and Turks whose Islamic vision was vastly different from that of the Arabs. This aristocracy brought the diverse heritage of their own indigenous cultures to Islam in India in contrast to the more homogeneous tribal Arabian Islam.

In conclusion, one may say that South Asian Islam is distinctly different from Arab Islam, and thus the present trend that Zia-ul-Haq initiated to return this Islam to a more pristine Arab base through his "Islamic" laws has only bred militancy and division within civil society, now leading to a failure in governance of the Pakistani state.

CHAPTER 6

BLASPHEMY CULTURES AND ISLAMIC EMPIRES

THE PRESENT CHAPTER NEEDS to be understood according to the "Blasphemy Trajectories" chart in figure 6.1. The chart has three vertical sections. On the left side in the chart is "Western Arab/Turkish Islam," which was largely Sunni with populations of Shiʻa Islam that had Shiʻa sympathies. The center section, "Arab Islam," is about the dynasties that succeeded Muhammad in the Arab regions. In the "Arab Islam" section, the two significant dynasties are the Ommayads and the ʻAbbasids, in whose empires formidable blasphemy discourse evolved. On the right side of the chart is "Eastern Persian Islam," which is about the geographical regions that had Shiʻa sympathies.

This chart was created to understand how a blasphemy culture evolved in the Islamic states in which the shariʻa was engineered to uphold the empires that followed the Prophet Muhammad and appropriated the Prophet's divine authority to legitimize themselves. My argument is that the blasphemy laws the empires devised are neither Qurʼanic nor based on Muhammad's practices, as discussed in chapter 2. The chart makes clear the ethnic structures of the states that evolved after Muhammad; these states had their own political agendas, in which Islam was used to uphold their authority. Blasphemy laws were central to state control. In the case of the ʻAbbasids and even of the Ommayads in al-Andalus (Spain),[1] the rulers were a Muslim minority who ruled over large populations of Christians, Jews, and other faiths, as mapped out in the chart, especially in the "Eastern Persian Islam" section.

When citizens have differed with Islamic states on politics, civil rights, and social issues, the states have resorted to using blasphemy or zandaqa laws against them. This is discussed in detail in chapter 5 on Hallaj's trial under the ʻAbbasids in Iraq. Hallaj was executed in 922.

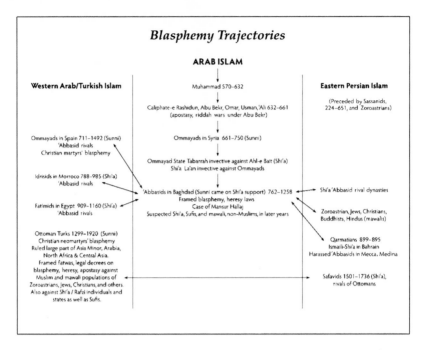

Blasphemy Trajectories

ARAB ISLAM

Western Arab/Turkish Islam	Muhammad 570–632	Eastern Persian Islam
	Caliphate-e Rashidun, Abu Bekr, Omar, Usman, 'Ali 632–661 (apostasy, riddah wars under Abu Bekr)	(Preceded by Sassanids, 224–651, and Zoroastrians)
Ommayads in Spain 711–1492 (Sunni) 'Abbasid rivals Christian martyrs' blasphemy	Ommayads in Syria 661–750 (Sunni)	
Idrisids in Morroco 788–985 (Shi'a) 'Abbasid rivals	Ommayad State Tabarrah invective against Ahl-e Bait (Shi'a) Shi'a La'an invective against Ommayads	
Fatimids in Egypt 909–1160 (Shi'a) 'Abbasid rivals	'Abbasids in Baghdad (Sunni came on Shi'a support) 762–1258 Framed blasphemy, heresy laws Case of Mansur Hallaj Suspected Shi'a, Sufis, and mawali, non-Muslims, in later years	Shi'a 'Abbasid rival dynasties / Zoroastrian, Jews, Christians, Buddhists, Hindus (mawalis)
Ottoman Turks 1299–1920 (Sunni) Christian neomartyrs' blasphemy Ruled large part of Asia Minor, Arabia, North Africa & Central Asia. Framed fatwas, legal decrees on blasphemy, heresy, apostasy against Muslim and mawali populations of Zoroastrians, Jews, Christians, and others. Also against Shi'a / Rafzi individuals and states as well as Sufis.		Qarmatians 899–895 Ismaili-Shi'a in Bahrain Harassed 'Abbasids in Mecca, Medina / Safavids 1501–1736 (Shi'a), rivals of Ottomans

6.1. Shemeem Abbas, 2009. Inspired by descriptions in Rizvi, *Religious and Intellectual History*, 1975.

HOW THE BLASPHEMY LAWS SPREAD

The blasphemy laws mushroomed among various Muslim empires, starting from the caliph Abu Bekr (632–634), who fought the riddah wars against the tribes that rebelled against Islam in the years that followed the Prophet Muhammad's death. These Arab tribes claimed that their pact was with Muhammad to follow Islam, and now that he was gone they were no longer bound by the terms of that treaty. Once these tribes extricated themselves from their obligation to the Islamic state, they started to attack other Muslim tribes. This was viewed politically as sedition against the Islamic state. Therefore, the caliph Abu Bekr branded it as riddah (apostasy) and put down the rebellion. And perhaps it was then that Muslims began to assert that Muhammad was the last and greatest of prophets.[2] As such, apostasy was built into the shari'a. It is misused today in countries like Afghanistan where individuals who change faith, say, from Islam to Christianity are tried and threatened with execution. Contrary to this, the Qur'an does not restrict the choice of one's faith. Moulavi Cheragh 'Ali cites Sura-e Kafirun 109, a chapter on the infidels, from the Qu'ran:[3]

Say: O Ye Unbelievers!
I worship not what ye worship,
And ye are not worshippers of what I worship;
And I am not a worshipper of what ye have worshipped,
And ye are not worshippers of what I worship,
To you your religion; and to me my religion

Furthermore, Cheragh ʿAli cites *Tanvir-ul Abshar*:[4] "No fetva or legal opinion could be given for a Moslem's apostasy, when his words might be construed into a good meaning, or when there be a difference of opinion even by the least authentic of traditions."

Not only did the riddah wars create instability for the Islamic state, the Shiʿa-Sunni rift further aggravated it. Maʿuviya, the son of Abu Sufyan and an opponent of Caliph ʿAli in the Battle of Siffin, allegedly initiated the practice of *tabarrah* (invective) against the Ahl-e Bait (Shiʿa). The Shiʿa were called *rafzi*, nonbelievers. The Shiʿa in return initiated the *laʾan* practice that returned the insult to the Ommayads and their supporters, including the first three Pious Caliphs. This was all based on the politics of Muhammad's succession.

In the center of the chart (figure 6.1) can be seen the successors of the Ommayads. These were the ʿAbbasids who came with Shiʿa support promising to avenge the Karbala martyrs.[5] The ʿAbbasids claimed descent through the Prophet's uncle ʿAbbas and hence furthered their entitlement to Muhammad's succession. Eventually, the ʿAbbasids parted ways with the Shiʿa, and in fact, as the chart shows, the Shiʿa Persian dynasties to the east were looked upon as rival dynasties by the ʿAbbasids. To the west, the Fatimid and Idrisid dynasties, both with Shiʿa connections, competed with the ʿAbbasids. In the east also were smaller Shiʿa kingdoms of Persia, among them the Qarmathians in eastern Bahrain, an Ismaʿili Shiʿa dynasty tracing its roots from Imam Jafar al-Sadiq.[6] The Qarmathians challenged ʿAbbasid authority in Mecca and Medina by massacring 20,000 pilgrims returning from the hajj. They ransacked both the holy cities, blocked the Zam Zam Spring, and took away the Black Stone of Kaʿaba. They extracted a large sum from the ʿAbbasids to return the Black Stone to the city, thus humiliating the dynasty. The ʿAbbasids therefore on both the east and the west were threatened by Shiʿa kingdoms. As a result, the ʿAbbasids put blasphemy laws in place and maintained surveillance to prevent sedition within the kingdom from citizens whom the state suspected.

It may also be pointed out that when the ʿAbbasids carried out the revolution of 749–750 and overthrew the Ommayads, they massacred the entire line; the ruling Ommaya caliph of the time, Merwan II, was killed as he sought refuge in Egypt. Only one member survived the massacre, and that was Abdur Rehman Ommaya. He fled to Spain and, through his mother's Berber North African tribal connections, established the Muslim empire in Spain known as al-Andalus and Muslims as Moors. As he was of Arab descent from the Ommayads, the empire he established was the Ommayad empire of al-Andalus, the Arabic name for Spain. "Moors" is really a generic name for the Ommayads and other, smaller Muslim kingdoms in al-Andalus. Prior to Abdur Rehman Ommaya's arrival, this empire in Spain became a rival of the Arabian 'Abbasid empire, as can be seen from the dates in the chart in figure 6.1 and the arrows that connect them.

The 'Abbasids in Iraq and the Ommayads in Spain, as well as the Ommayads in Syria, shared the same practices of the blasphemy laws, as the shari'a was common to all of them, going back to the customary practices that evolved among the Arab tribes. Both the 'Abbasids and the Ommayads in Spain were Arabs. The severity of the blasphemy laws emanates from the common Near East practices dating back to the Jews and later taken up by the Christians. Nothing much changed in the customary practices in the centuries that followed the Prophet Muhammad.[7] The Ommayads in al-Andalus followed the same shari'a practices that the 'Abbasids followed in Arab lands, except that in Spain, the Maliki school of fiqh (jurisprudence) was predominant. The Maliki school "adopted a rigorist interpretation of the Koran and the law, hostile to innovation and rationalist interpretation."[8]

In addition to the Shi'a states that surrounded the 'Abbasids' lands, the citizens living in the largely Sunni 'Abbasid empire were also Christians, Jews, Zoroastrians, Hindus, Buddhists, Manicheans, and Sufis. Such a diverse population and such a large empire required surveillance. Consequently, the 'Abbasids had in place a legal system with jurists and jurisconsults that gave a strict interpretation of Islamic law, as can be seen in the trial for blasphemy of Mansur Hallaj. I will develop this idea of "strict interpretation" further in the present chapter.

My position is that blasphemy and its related offenses such as heresy, heterodoxy, and apostasy are justifications, under an Islamic cover, for the state to repress independent thinking—disagreement, dissenting political opinion, or *ijtihad-e ra'y*. The state establishes authority through faith, as did states like England through the divine right of kings until the Reformation changed the politics of faith.

The Cordoba Christian martyrs movement (850–859) was part of this resistance against the Muslim empire; the martyrs used blasphemy as a tool against the Islamic empire by inviting their own martyrdom, which in turn roused others to oppose Islamic rule. This was the Christian martyrs' mode of resistance. Later occupants of the Byzantine Empire, the Ottoman Sunni state in Turkey (1299–1922), followed the models of the Muslim Ommayad rulers of Spain, the Arab Ommayads, and the 'Abbasids.[9] The Ottomans dealt severely with the Christian Neomartyrs (1437–1860) when the latter used blasphemy against the Prophet Muhammad as a political tool to solicit their own martyrdom. The Ottomans used the same types of blasphemy laws their Islamic forerunners did to deal with political dissent in which faith played a large part. Thus, the blasphemy laws using religion, *sabb-e din* (insult to religion), *sabb-e rasul* (insult to the Prophet), and *sabb-e sahaba* (insult to the Companions) as a tool in the Islamic empires emanated from administrative contingency. These laws were devised by the state, but they are not Qur'anic. I use examples from al-Andalus and the Ottoman Empire to validate my assertion.

What is interesting about the Christian monks who were the martyrs of Cordoba in al-Andalus is that they resurrected the martyrdom tradition of Saint Stephen in the first century.[10] The Christian monks in Cordoba as well as the Neomartyrs under the Ottomans continued the tradition, in which the Christians not only sought execution but were also punished with torture. Extensive details of the martyrdom in Cordoba are available.[11] In both contexts, in Cordoba and in Turkey under the Ottomans, the monks and ordinary citizens sought martyrdom through blaspheming Islam, its Prophet, and its institutions. They thus invoked punishments under Islamic blasphemy laws.

OMMAYADS IN SPAIN

Based on a discussion of some cases of the Christian martyrs of Cordoba, the argument here is that blasphemy and heresy laws were a creation of the Islamic state to establish its writ over citizens. The shari'a was twisted to support the rulers. Whether the Cordoba martyrs were also tortured, what the mode of trial was, and who approved their executions are the limits of this discussion. My discussion is based on the stories of the martyrs, which are paraphrased here from Wheatcroft's study.[12]

The early Muslim rulers in Spain and the Ottomans conquered Christian lands (also populated by Jews, Manicheans, and people of other faiths) and imposed their Islamic ideology. In Muslim Spain, blasphemy laws had nothing to do with the Qur'an or with the Prophet Muhammad's traditions. Through surveillance of its citizens and public executions for blasphemy, the state in al-Andalus ensured civic compliance and acceptance of the divine right of the caliph to be the ruler; through the divinity of his shari'a, implemented by the qadi, citizens were expected to conform to the law. Although such laws were given the divine aura of the shari'a, these were really the creation of the state, which projected itself as a caliphate of the Prophet Muhammad.[13] Any utterance or discourse against Islam was considered an insult to its creator, the Prophet Muhammad, and categorized as sabb-e din, sabb-e rasul, or sabb-e sahaba.

The Muslim minority rulers in Spain established authority through what they proclaimed was divine law, though there was nothing divine about it. In fact, it was contrary to the Qur'an, as non-Muslim citizens do not fall under the purview of Islamic shari'a, which is meant only for Muslims. (This is an age-old issue. In Pakistani courts today these same issues come up in cases against the Christian or Ahmediyya communities.) The status of non-Muslims was that of *zimmis* (protected citizens) who, upon paying the jizya (poll tax), were supposedly free to practice their religions and maintain their lifestyles and their places of worship.

In Muslim Spain, Christian monks in the mid-ninth century resorted to a novel mode of protest in which they were acculturated historically since the first century. That was to seek martyrdom. How did they do it? They blasphemed against the Prophet Muhammad and insulted Islam. This was a sure way to get executed and draw attention.[14] The first Christian martyr was Saint Stephen, whose example the Spanish Christian martyrs followed.[15]

Thus, when the Christian monks resorted to this mode of political protest to challenge the Muslim state, there was no option but to prevent further blaspheming of Islam and its Prophet. It was a question of the writ of the state. Violators had to be executed through the imposition of divine law that really was the customary common law of the Near East.[16]

The case of the martyrs of Cordoba is interesting: the martyrs were punished for insulting the Prophet and Islam. Since the martyrs challenged the political ideology of the state that derived validation from the Prophet and authority from Islam, they had to be tried for blasphemy and consequently executed.[17] Again, this was customary rather than the law of the Qur'an.

The martyrs movement occurred between 850 and 859, when close to fifty members of the Christian community were executed. These martyrdoms in which the Christians were executed for blaspheming the Prophet Muhammad and Islam have been condemned both in Muslim and western Christian scholarship. With regard to enforcing the writ of the state, the divinity of the caliph and his shari'a had the aura of extraction from the law of the Qur'an, with twisted words and situations out of context: the qadi in Muslim Spain was an instrument of implementation. The qadi was an in-

strument of the caliphal authority. There is no mention of outstanding muftis (jurisconsults) in Spain who dealt with these cases, although at the time,
Maliki laws prevailed in the region. Later Ibn Rushd and Ibn al-Arabi influenced intellectual and spiritual thought in Spain, but in the period in question, during the martyrs movement, their speech was treated as outright
blasphemy under shari'a law. It is likely that what applied in Baghdad under the 'Abbasids applied in Spain also, as the Ommayads in Spain and the
'Abbasids in Baghdad were competing empires (figure 6.1).[18] The martyrs
movement in Cordoba therefore continued to undermine Ommayad caliphal authority and the shari'a in al-Andalus. The caliphate in Cordoba did
not encourage a liberal interpretation of the shari'a and used it to uphold its
own agenda.

The Muslim state's objective was not only to enforce compliance but
also to ensure, through public executions, that sedition of the kind that
the Christian martyrs movement sought to instigate was quelled in time.
More than a religious motive, it was a political act. A Christian ideology
could not be permitted to challenge the Islamic state, and since the martyrs blasphemed against Islam's Prophet and his ideology, a set of laws thus
had to be put in place for governance in a country where the native populations were largely converts from Christianity to Islam. Blasphemy laws in
this case were more in line with punishment for treason or sedition, as really,
the Christian movement's intent was a manifesto of defiance. Reclaiming
the bodies of the martyrs and burying them with other "saints" perpetuated
a political defiance against the Muslim presence. Like all political resistance,
this too was a movement to oust the invader.

Western scholarship on the subject of the Cordoba martyrs is controversial:

> Much of the contemporary literature dealing with these martyrdoms is apol-
> ogetic—that is, trying to present the martyrdoms as the result of genu-
> ine religious persecution . . . Many of Eulogius's Christian contemporaries
> who probably found Muslim rule less unbearable—were not at all enthusi-
> astic about the martyrdom movement and were not ready to accept the exe-
> cuted Christians as martyrs. Their objections . . . refer to the incompatibility
> of these martyrdoms with the traditional Christian ones: The persecution,
> it was claimed, was not real because Christians were allowed by Muslims to
> practice their religion. Therefore, the Muslims could not be represented as
> similar to the pagan persecutors of old. Moreover, the Cordoban martyr-
> doms were unlike the early pre-Constantinian martyrdoms for two reasons:
> The Muslims were not pagans, and the Cordoban martyrs were summar-

ily executed without suffering the variety of torments inflicted on the early martyrs.[19]

However, the shrines of the martyrs and their relics furthered the growth of an oral culture that eulogized the martyrs through storytelling and poetry. Basically, the idea was to demonstrate the ugliness of the Muslim conquest and to create an ever-present realization of this archenemy. The Muslim presence was created into something of a "mythopoeia." Consequently, "the Muslim conquest and the martyrdoms are added like a new meat to a stockpot."[20] The Christians theorized the movement as enriching and "invigorating the life of the community with the blood of the martyrs."[21] They kept the ideology "simmering." The martyrs' blood and the tales of their martyrdom were preserved long after the martyrs were gone, and these tales enriched the "spiritual armory" of the true Christians.[22] These martyrdoms seem very much in line with the suicide bombers of today who believe that their martyrdom serves a cause against the "anti-Islamic" forces of the state and society, except that today's suicide bombers take many innocents with them.

However, the Christian martyrs of Muslim Spain, according to Wheatcroft, left behind legends that created their own "irreducible and *generative* multiplicity," a term and concept that he draws from Derrida. The manner in which the martyrs' tales were narrated was a "dissemination" mechanism in speech communication theory.[23] The tales were interpreted and reinterpreted as an ongoing, emerging dialogue that generated more martyrs, and thus the movement continued in its own time and then in the collective memory of communities that told and heard the narratives. Each community interpreted the tale in its own way.[24]

The way it works in speech communication theory is that political protest is built into the existing legends of the land that establishes the communication between speakers and hearers. Within the myth as sung or narrated by the speaker, the hearers in the speech communities establish the communication with the speaker as well as with each other through shared language, icons, symbols, and speech.

Formidable Christian communities in al-Andalus overtly and covertly resisted the Muslim occupation. These were the majority populations of Spain; by 1200, among the estimated 7 million inhabitants, 5.6 million were Muslims, many of them Christians having converted to Islam. The Muslim empire could retain its control only through religious law that was the making of the state and not Qur'anic law. The state, however, made it look like Qur'anic law and thus sacrosanct. As a consequence, the state matched the

Christian insult or resistance with blasphemy laws that were a potent tool for governance over a large population of Muslims, Christians, Jews, and a complex mix of the three faiths through conversions and intermarriage.[25]

Historically, the movement of the martyrs of Cordoba created a "generative multiplicity." One martyrdom inspired another martyrdom, the tales generated the martyrdoms, and the martyrdoms generated the tales. It was all interrelated. A complete mythology was built around it: the tales led to the destruction of Visigothic Christian Spain and then the reemergence of Christian Spain known as the Reconquista.[26] After 770 years, in 1492 the Muslim kingdom of Granada was defeated and overthrown. Investigating the protest texts of the tales that were perpetuated is research that could be undertaken on its own for linguistic anthropology, comparative literature, or comparative religion.

Christian guilt for being lax in preventing the rapid growth of an Islamic civilization in al-Andalus, the development of an Arab literary culture, and the ease with which Christians converted to Islam could only be redeemed with blood and sacrifice in the eyes of zealous Christians. Only self-sacrifice could atone for the Christian vice of compromise. Also, the history of the fall of Visigothic Spain had to be resurrected, and although the Muslim rulers of al-Andalus were just to their Christian and Jewish minorities in accordance with the Qur'an (that they pay the jizya, or the tax, and be free to practice their faiths), the Christian martyrs movement of Cordoba of the mid-ninth century strongly resisted the *convivencia* (assimilation) with the Muslims. The martyrs rejected the gradual decay of their culture and their faith. Arabic had replaced Latin as the elitist language, and a mixture of Arabic, Romance dialects, and Berber had become the street language. Alvarus spoke thus for the Cordoba martyrs:

> My fellow Christians delight in the poems and romances of the Arabs; they study the works of Muhammadan theologians and philosophers not in order to refute them, but to acquire correct and elegant Arabic style. Where today can a layman be found who reads the Latin Commentaries on Holy Scriptures? Who is there that studies the Gospels, the prophets, the Apostles? Alas, the young Christians who are most conspicuous for their talents have no knowledge of any literature or language save the Arabic . . . Christians have forgotten their own tongue, and scarce one in a thousand can be found to be able to compose in fair Latin to a friend.[27]

Thus, al-Andalus demonstrates another context of the evolution of blasphemy laws that the state claimed from the Qur'an, or prophetic authority, but that were really a creation of the caliphal representatives such as the qadi to uphold the empire.

THE NEOMARTYRS IN OTTOMAN LANDS

A similar occurrence that matches the Spanish Christian martyrs movement is that of the Neomartyrs in Ottoman Turkey. In the case of the Neomartyrs, Vaporis documents instances when Christians also deliberately sought torture.[28] The Cordoba martyrs of Spain lived in the ninth century, while the Neomartyrs under the Ottomans lived from 1437 to 1860.

The similarity between Muslim Spain and Ottoman Turkey despite the distance of almost six centuries is that both empires had to contend with majority Christian populations that the Muslims had subjugated. These populations had lived under Christian sovereignty: the Spanish under the Visigoths and the Christian Turks under the Eastern Roman Church. In the Muslim triad that took over lands were the 'Abbasids, the Ommayads of Spain, and the Ottomans in Turkey. The Arabian 'Abbasids (762–1258) and the Spanish Ommayads (711–1492) in historic time were connected. The bonds were strengthened with the Arab interconnectedness of shared shari'a laws. The 'Abbasids had a more developed system of fiqh that dealt with the complex dynamics of applying it to different ethnic groups; the Ommayads in Spain and the Ottomans in Turkey were only beginners in the business of empire building and novices in dealing with large Christian populations. They were building Islamic empires on the foundations of Christianity under the guise of a shari'a they claimed was from the Qur'an. Ironically, these Islamic empires were applying the same set of customary laws that earlier Near Eastern empires had applied. The punishment for blasphemy in these empires was torture and execution. The law for blasphemy was common, customary law that had nothing to do with the Qur'an except in the context of an insult to the Prophet Muhammad (sabb-e rasul).

According to the accounts of the Orthodox Church, many Balkan Christians in the Ottoman Empire solicited martyrdom through execution, and many were successful. They refused to give up their Christian faith to accept Islam. To distinguish them from the early martyrs of Christianity and the martyrs of Spain they were called Neomartyrs. Vaporis documents 166 with detailed narratives, although the sources are anonymous.[29] Some may be legendary, grown in the oral speech communities of the Christians. Although the Ottoman fatwas do not specifically mention this movement, enough references do exist with regard to punishments for blasphemy committed by non-Muslim subjects in the various fatwas of the Ottoman seyhu-lislams (jurisconsults) that applied to the vast lands of the Ottomans.[30]

The Ottoman Empire was a Sunni Muslim state that manipulated the tra-ditional shari'a, or customary laws, borrowed from earlier Muslim states. In response, the Orthodox Christian Church took up the martyrdom move-ment that was started in Spain and had been in practice since the early cen-turies of Christianity when Christians opposed the Roman Empire. In line with the Spanish martyrs, the Turkish Neomartyrs solicited martyrdom through execution, torture, and imprisonment.

Neomartyrdom was one of the few weapons the Orthodox Church had to fight the spread of Islam among its followers. Neomartyrs provided the church with the much-needed moral examples to strengthen Christianity. Over the years, the church needed the martyrs to defy Islam, and the pri-mary tool was blasphemy against the Prophet Muhammad.[31] In the fifteenth century one Neomartyr is reported; fifteen are reported in the sixteenth century, thirty-one in the seventeenth century, thirty-nine in the eighteenth century, and seven in the nineteenth century. The church prepared the mar-tyrs as "kamikazes" against Islam. Very much like the modern-day Taliban, the church prepared young men to die for the faith. These were men who were fully prepared to blaspheme against the Prophet Muhammad in the qadi's presence. Sometimes to defy the Ottoman authorities, a Christian would convert to Islam and then renege on the conversion publicly; some-times it was the church's pressure on some genuine apostates from Christi-anity to achieve martyrdom, and since apostates from Christianity could not be taken back into the monastery, they could achieve salvation only through martyrdom.[32]

The way the Ottoman authorities were baited was that the apostate from Christianity to Islam, after much prayer and fasting, would go before the qadi, throw off his turban, and declare his return to Christianity. The qadi would persuade the apostate to reconsider his decision over some days, and when this did not happen the apostate was executed publicly. Minkov men-tions three anonymous Greeks who posed as tax collectors wearing Muslim clothes and using Muslim salutations. Taking the public display of Muslim symbols as an indication of the actual conversion to Islam, these three were tried as apostates.[33]

Some literature on "coercive conversion" represents Neomartyrdom as a response to Muslim fanaticism and the drive for mass Islamization where those who did not convert to Islam were killed. This does not seem to be supported with evidence. The Neomartyrs knew well that apostasy and blasphemy would be punished under Islamic shari'a, and they deliberately defied the law to become martyrs, as they knew Muslims would be punished for committing such violations. However, in Islamic shari'a such a punishment is only for Muslims, and Christians, being zimmis, did not fall under the shari'a per se.[34]

A further explanation for the growth of Neomartyrs in the eighteenth century may be that there was an increasing number of Christian converts to Islam who upon conversion were not satisfied with their new faith. A number of the fatwa collections of the period document the religious offenses of the new Muslims.[35] Reneging on conversion to Islam was looked upon as an apostasy punishable under blasphemy laws.

Although most of the fatwas of seyhulislams dealt with new Muslims' apostasies, some fatwas also indicate problems with the new Muslims drinking wine or continuing to respect Christian symbols or follow Christian customs. That these fatwas reflect real-life situations, not hypothetical cases imagined by Muslim jurists, cannot be disputed.[36] It is further claimed that the fatwa was often filed in court as a means of assisting deliberation. Thereafter, as recent work has shown, fatwas were not simply discarded or buried in archives; they were collected and systematically incorporated into the larger doctrinal works, or *furu* (Islamic jurisprudence).[37] Furthermore, the shari'a verdicts of the Ottoman seyhulislams embedded in their fatwas should not be treated as a pool of merely noncoercive and nonauthoritative legal opinions, especially in an era when shari'a knowledge was "essential cultural capital" steering the relationships of power and domination.[38]

The fatwas indicate that the new Muslims might have come to the realization that their new faith of Islam did not match their expectations and that they felt nostalgia for what they had left behind. Additionally, the lifestyles of Muslims and Christians had a syncretism that disappeared within the conservatism of Muslim society in the early eighteenth century.[39] Sometimes the conversion isolated the converts from their original communities, and they yearned for that language and culture. The state retained apostasy rights to enforce the converts' assimilation into the new faith communities as well as its growth of a Muslim population. The neo-Muslims in such instances had to contend with unfamiliar situations imposed through the fatwas:

> Zeyd wears a hat for tomfoolery, perhaps as part of an infidel ritual. What is the punishment for him per the shari'a the question is asked: Renovation of faith and marriage.[40]

More details of the Ottoman fatwas will follow. However, with regard to the penalties for apostasies or blasphemies, the fatwas affirm that the punishments were lighter for children, women, and converts whose conversion was carried out while the candidate was deceived or intoxicated. Appeals were made or cases were contested, and the qadi pronounced the punishments accordingly.[41]

However, a distinction exists between unhappy converts and the Neomartyrs. Nomikos Vaporis has found that the martyrs did not correctly understand Islam, and neither did their biographers, who themselves had a skewed perception of it. The Neomartyrs questioned the authenticity of the Prophet Muhammad's ministry while asserting that Jesus Christ had completed the divine revelation and that it was final.[42] They further affirmed that John the Baptist was the last prophet.[43] Most contentious of all for the Ottoman qadis was the Orthodox Church's insistence on the Trinity and that Mary was the mother of God.

Muslim sacred law, the shari'a, was abused during this period. The qadi courts substituted blasphemy for unrelated offenses, such as defiance toward state officials or members of the Ottoman administration. For example, Anastasios fought two soldiers of the Ottoman military who had tried to rape his sister. Anastasios was imprisoned for this, and according to Vaporis, he was invited to convert to Islam. The qadi alleged that he had accepted Islam, but Anastasios denied the qadi's claim. Despite many temptations, he refused the conversion, and on the qadi's orders, "Anastasios was beaten and thrown into jail where his feet were placed in the infamous leg stocks (*podokake*), which caused indescribable pain."[44] Vaporis reports detailed cases of martyrs from the fifteenth to the nineteenth centuries, and although the shari'a permitted a death penalty for treason, most cases were framed under blasphemy. He gives the example of four brothers who were crypto-Christians (outwardly Muslims but in fact Christian in faith); they supported the Greek war of independence in 1821 against the Ottoman Empire but were tried under apostasy and blasphemy laws.[45] The author contends that the Ottoman qadis overextended the death punishment when they treated defiance toward corrupt state officials or converting from Islam to another faith, as in the case of Anastasios, as apostasy or even blasphemy.[46]

Vaporis's study is based on anonymous accounts from the Ottoman qadi courts that meted out punishments on blasphemy and heresy charges, as collected in a manuscript called *Lives*.[47] In his work on the Neomartyrs, Vaporis gives narratives of the different people who sought martyrdom. These were mainly people, both men and women, from the working classes who had no or little formal education, such as tailors, artists, bakers' assistants, barbers, bartenders, and shoemakers, as well as fourteen monks.

The Neomartyrs movement started in places that were formerly Christian lands. Most of the martyrs were punished in Constantinople, now Istanbul. Vaporis cites fifty-four martyrs in this city. Others were in cities that are now in Greece, Crete, Asia Minor, Syria, and Egypt. The Neomartyrs movement during the Ottoman rule was also initiated to prevent apostasy to Islam of Orthodox Christians. The Ottomans' public executions of the martyrs, according to Vaporis, only created more martyrs; the martyrs' relics were precious keepsakes that the church leaders wished to preserve but that the Ottoman administrators prevented them from acquiring. The Orthodox Church kept the movement alive because with the Neomartyrs cult and its sanctification, many were willing to sacrifice themselves as Jesus Christ's witnesses.[48]

The salient point of this discussion is to demonstrate that with a vast empire like the Ottomans', the state invoked a template of the shari'a through blasphemy laws that made it convenient to govern. And although the state was challenged by a tricky Christian Church that used its parishioners to convert to Islam and then renege on the conversion so the resistance movement could be kept alive, the state's safest bet was its reliance on the shari'a-invoked blasphemy laws. Thus, my thesis is validated that blasphemy laws, whether they are of the Pakistani state or any other Islamic state, are for upholding the political identity of that state. The examples cited from the Neomartyrs' cases reinforce this position in the case of the Ottoman Empire.

OTTOMAN FATWAS

In this section I will refer to the Ottoman fatwas based on the "Blasphemy Trajectories" chart (figure 6.1) to show how the Ottoman Empire fits into the matrix of other empires such as those of the 'Abbasids and of the Ommayads in al-Andalus. Beyond the Christians and non-Sunnis, including Shi'a individuals, the Ottoman state also clearly targeted other states for blasphemy or heresy. Such states were referred to as *rafzi*, nonbeliever states, and among them were the Persian Safavids, a rival empire the Ottomans had conquered. During the seventeenth and eighteenth centuries the terms "blasphemy," "heresy," and "apostasy" were used interchangeably as substitutes for "treason" or "sedition." In this section, the different headings under which the Ottoman seyhulislams categorized areas of blasphemy or heresy or apostasy will be demonstrated. Based on the massive, organized bureaucracy of the Ottomans, these matrixes were clearly demarcated, and as has been mentioned earlier, the fatwas were not purely for archival purposes. These were connected with real-life situations and were "often filed in court as a means of assisting deliberation."[49] The major fatwa collections documented here are derived from Tusalp's study and are summarized in table 6.1, which is taken from her chart listing categories of deviant acts and criminal offenses.[50]

Tusalp puts the blasphemy and heresy theme within the Ottoman bureaucracy. This further supports the facts of the revisionist Islamic movements in India in the seventeenth and eighteenth centuries that used Islam as an anticolonial force against the British and foreign intervention. These were resurrected under the Wahabi rubric in the 1970s with international support that put Pakistan's General Zia-ul-Haq in the vanguard to lead an expedition, sponsored by the CIA and Saudi Arabia, into Afghanistan to bring down the Soviet occupation of that country. In the baggage of that expedition came lethal blasphemy laws and Hudood laws against "woman." The laws in the garb of shari'a are still in place and continue to be used by the state apparatus for silencing public opinion and freedom of speech.

The Ottoman fatwas given here are the legal opinions of renowned seyhulislams. They shed light on the workings of the Ottoman bureaucracy and the empire's administrative dealings with its citizens as well as its international outlook toward other states, some of which it branded as rafzi. The Ottoman Empire looked upon blasphemy as "deviant behavior." But the definition of "deviance" allowed for a lot of latitude. My argument is that this was a "frame" that not only the Ottomans used but that also is being used by the present so-called Islamic states like Pakistan, Bangladesh, Afghanistan, and Saudi Arabia to enforce compliance. Any freethinking, independent judgment or ijtihad then becomes deviant and is punishable by death. (Death for deviant behavior or thought, justified by an invocation of blasphemy, happens in the twenty-first century in the states mentioned here.) Unfortunately, this ideology has become so ingrained and indoctrinated that it has become the manifesto of militant groups like the Taliban. To *not* be deemed "deviant," citizens are forced to conform to a fascist-like ideology under the garb of divine law, of shari'a. Consequently, branding freethinking citizens as "deviants" reinforces state and civil militancy that violates citizens' rights and is a threat to international security. Ottoman Turkey, despite its pluralism in some areas, was also autocratic in its fatwas on blasphemy, apostasy, and heresy, as will be seen here. The formalizing of the shari'a into a "fixed" Islamic code, as was done in the fatwas, gave an

Table 6.1. Categories of deviant acts and criminal offenses

			Scholars' sources of interpretations		
Category	Feyziyye	'Ali	'Abdurrahim	'Abdullah	Neticetü'l-Fetava
Theft	Book of theft (Kitab al sariqa)	Book of hadd crimes (Kitab al hudud: bab al sariqa)	Book of hadd crimes	Book of hadd crimes (Kitab al hudud: bab al sariqa)	Book of theft
Intoxication (Drinking of wine)	Book of hadd crimes (Kitab al hudud: bab-i hadd al shurb)	On the hadd crime of wine drinking (fi hadd al shurb)	Book of hadd crimes (Kitab al hudud: bab al shurb)	Book of hadd crimes (Kitab al hudud: bab al shurb)	Book of piety (Kitab al iman)
Crimes of sex (sodomy, bestiality, necrophilia, rape and murder, homosexual intercourse, anal sex, etc.)	Section on discretionary punishment (bab al ta'zir)	Book of hadd crimes (Kitab al hudud: bab al zina)	Book of hadd crimes (Kitab al hudud: fi al livata; fi zina al dhimmi ve'l livata)	Book of hadd crimes (Kitab al hudud: fi hadd al zina); Section on discretionary punishment	Book of piety
Fornication	Book of hadd crimes	Book of hadd crimes (Kitab al hudud: fi hudud al zina)	Book of hadd crimes (Kitab al hudud: fi hadd-i zina)	Book of hadd crimes; Section on discretionary punishment	Book of hadd crimes
Collective crimes (usurpation, plunder, kidnapping, etc.)	Book of hadd crimes (Kitab al hudud: bab-i qat al tarik)	Book of hadd crimes (Kitab al hudud: bab-i qat al tarik; fasl fi al sa'at ve'l zulmet)	Section on discretionary punishment	Book of hadd crimes (Kitab al hudud: bab-i qat al tarik); Section on discretionary punishment	Book of hadd crimes (Kitab al hudud: bab-i qat al tarik)

Crimes of economy (forgery, tax evasion, etc.)	Section on discretionary punishment	Not specified	Not specified	Section on discretionary punishment	Section on discretionary punishment (Fasl fi y al taʿzir)
Defamation	Section on discretionary punishment	Section on discretionary punishment	Section on discretionary punishment	Section on discretionary punishment	Section on discretionary punishment
Acts of disbelief and religious misconduct	Book of piety	Book of piety (Kitab al iman: nev-i ahir fi el sebb)	Section concerning the renovation of faith and marriage ("Bab ma yata" laqu tecdid al iman veʾl nikah)	Book of piety; section on discretionary punishment (Bab al taʿzir: nev ahir fi taʿzir biʾl-katl)	Book of piety
Acts of heresy	Book of the conduct between states (Kitab-i siyar: bab al murtadd)	Book of the conduct between states (Kitab-i siyar: bab al murtadd)	Book of the conduct between states (Kitab-i siyar: bab al murtadd); section on discretionary punishment (bab al taʿzir: fi el raks veʾl sema)	Book of the conduct between states (Kitab-i siyar: nev fi ahkam al murteddin veʾl zanadeqat; fasl fi ahkam al rafidi al acem ve hukm-i diyarhum ve fi nev ahir); section on discretionary punishment	Book of the conduct between states (Kitab-i siyar: fasl fi sair-i ahval-i ehl-i dhimmet veʾl murtaddin)
Other	Section on discretionary punishment	Section on discretionary punishment	Section on discretionary punishment	Section on discretionary punishment	Section on discretionary punishment

Source: Tusalp, adapted and used here with permission

inordinate level of power to the state to be inflexible, labeling a citizen "deviant" should she or he assert any freedom of thought or speech. The long, lethal arm of the state watched for violations while seeking total compliance.

The Ottoman seyhulislam fatwas, adapted here from the Tusalp study, need to be read carefully and in detail. These records show that by this time in the seventeenth and eighteenth centuries, Islamic states like that of the Ottomans were able to identify the populations, and in the case of blasphemy or disbelief, the state had a legal grammar and construct for dealing with the situation. Hadd crimes mentioned here are those that are a part of the shari'a penal code (appendix 2).

For example, in the fatwas called *Fetva-yi Feyziyye: me'an-nukul* (compiled in 1703) by Seyyid Feyzullah Efendi, among the hadd crimes are acts of personal disbelief and religious misconduct. Fatwas about states are listed in the *Book of Conduct between States* in the chapter on apostasy (*Kitab al-Siyar: Bab al murtadd*). Listed in these fatwas are "acts of heresy among states." These are fatwas that deal with the Ottomans and other states, such as the Shi'a states cited in figure 6.1, for example, the Safavids of Iran. In addition are acts of personal disbelief. Other fatwas by known jurisconsults such as the *Fetva-ye 'Ali Efendi* by Catalcali 'Ali Efendi (compiled in 1692) deal with the same categories of hadd crimes, among which are "acts of personal disbelief" and "acts of heresy among states." These fatwas include Sufi dance and music as subject to punishments for disbelief. The legal grammar for nonbelief in the Ottoman state were terms like *kufr* (blasphemy), *zandaqa* (heresy), *ilhad*, *irtidad* (apostasy), *nifak* (dissent), *dallalet* (pimping), *dehri* (atheism), *revafiz* (Shi'a belief), *sahirlik* (magic), *murdar* (unclean), and *zimmi* (non-Muslims). Many other terms are used in context in the hundreds of fatwas of the period.[51]

The Ottomans registered heresy or blasphemy under different categories of hadd crimes or crimes against religion, and the punishments for these were discretionary depending on the qadi at that time in a particular community. With so many categories and terms in place, the state's officials could easily find a heading to register a case against a citizen. The boundaries of blasphemy, heresy, apostasy, and heterodoxy were fuzzy, leaving the state many options.

The current Pakistani situation by comparison to the Ottomans' is much more haphazard, disorganized, and militant, largely also using extrajudicial killings of alleged blasphemers. Among the Ottomans, the state at least had trained, qualified seyhulislams to address the matters of belief and nonbelief. In current Pakistan, layers of power exist to deal with deviance, from the sessions judge to the almost illiterate policeman who wields authority to the rag-tag mosque mulla who can call upon the mob to lynch a "suspect."[52]

Some instances are cited, in order of severity, from the fatwas reported in Tusalp's study of the Ottoman seyhulislams. The examples show how the shari'a was skewed. Ottoman seyhulislams were themselves 'ulema (religious scholars), and thus they colluded with the state to persecute free thought and freedom of speech. Their fatwas prescribed the death sentence for speaking against the 'ulema. An example given here is evidence that the 'ulema placed themselves on par with the Prophet Muhammad, for speaking against either the 'ulema or the Prophet carried a death sentence. This is contrary to Islam, as the faith does not acknowledge a clergy. Anyone in pre-Ottoman times could call the azan from the mosque minaret, and the community bathed its dead, a role the clergy took upon themselves over the course of time. Gradually, the clergy 'ulema became the lawmakers, and now in Pakistan, Bangladesh, Afghanistan, Egypt, and Iran and a large part of the Muslim world they are also the politicians and the fatwa givers. The case of the Islamabad Red Mosque rebellion in 2007 of the clerics against General Musharraf's regime in Pakistan is an example. Maulana Abdul Rashid gave a fatwa that secular democracy was against the shari'a as he set out to establish his own Islamic courts with a gang of stick-wielding male and female vigilantes in black *burqas*.[53]

Here are some citations from Ottoman fatwas for blasphemy against the Prophet Muhammad:

> If it is legally established that Zeyd the *zimmi* has blatantly insulted the Prophet (PBUH) with dissolute and salacious expressions, what is due from him? *Answer:* In fact the Hanafi imams confined him to discretion and long term imprisonment but some subsequent [imams] issued fatwas for his execution but apart from [these] the Shafi and Maliki imams generally stood for his execution and [the now deceased] Ebu el Suud issued fatwas for his execution and it is among the issues that Sultan Suleyman Han has asked about, still the sultan should be resorted and then he should be executed.[54]

Consulting the sultan before implementing execution for kufr, zandaqa, or ilhad seems part of the fatwa manuals of the Ottomans. Pakistan's blasphemy laws in Section 295-C carry the same death penalty for slandering the Prophet, which is not condoned in the Qur'an. This shari'a is the invention of the states that developed after the Prophet Muhammad's death.

Utterances against 'Ulema & Blasphemy
When Zeyd exclaimed that, "If I become the vizier, I swear that I will execute all the 'ulema, beginning from the mufti to the scholar," Amr warns him not to incriminate the 'ulema, and tells him to recant, yet Zeyd refuses

to recant, what happens to Zeyd? *Answer:* If he defames religion [Islam], he is an infidel. If he does not recant and repent, he is to be executed.[55]

Here the 'ulema are upholders of Islam, and among the Ottomans an insult to the upholder is an insult to Islam punishable by death.

———

My own argument, based on research in the oral Sufi traditions of South Asia,[56] matches Tusalp's finding that the 'ulema were frequently ridiculed in Ottoman Turkey, especially among the Bekhtashi Sufis. And indeed, the 'ulema devised to have Dara Shikoh (1615–1659), the Mughal prince, and his Jewish mentor Sarmad executed, although it had more to do with the imperial ambitions of the prince's brother Aurengzeb (1618–1707) to have Dara Shikoh executed with collusion from the 'ulema. After this, Aurengzeb became the emperor, and that led to the demise of the Mughal Empire.[57]

Presently, Saudi Arabia follows the same pattern, in which the 'ulema share authority with the monarchy. The Sufi poetry that Nusrat Fateh 'Ali Khan and Abida Parvin sang was continuously directed against the *'alim-fazils*, the 'ulema. It is an established tradition in the Sufi poetry sung in Pakistan and India in the indigenous languages to ridicule the so-called guardians of religion. Ottoman Turkey most likely set the traditions for Pakistan and Indian Sufi singers. All this raises the question "Who owns Islam?" Behavior that was branded "deviant" in the Ottoman fatwas established state conformity to and control over free speech. The Ottomans forbade speaking against the Prophet or Islam, but the prohibition also extended to the controllers of faith, that is, the state and the 'ulema. Tusalp's study does bring this out clearly through citations from the fatwas.

THE STATUS OF NON-MUSLIMS IN OTTOMAN LANDS

The Ottomans had classes of citizens whom they watched carefully, especially the indigenous non-Muslim populations. A heretic was a kafir, heresy was kufr, and a non-Muslim was a zimmi (a citizen for whom the state was responsible). Not only was speech monitored, but individual action was also gauged within that framework of the grammar. Relations with non-Muslims formed part of the fatwa manuals. The status of subjugation (*istila*) or the zimmi (non-Muslim) status, *nakzu'l-ahd* (annulment of zimmi status by one of the parties) was adequately documented.[58]

Muslim identity was important for the Ottomans. People who crossed boundaries—for example, dressing up in fanciful clothes during the infidels' festivals, talking to infidels in their own language although they knew the Turkish language well, greeting the infidel in the infidel's way, or going to the infidel's house—were suspect in the legal realm.[59] One does not know if that was true in the social world. However, the state had ways to excommunicate such individuals in the shari'a, as we have seen among the converted Muslims who continued to interact with their original faith communities.

The Ottomans did maintain imperial control over their subjects through monitoring and establishing boundaries on acceptable levels of interaction between native Muslim communities and non-Muslim subjects. Tusalp calls this the "imperial framework." Language was indeed important in this control, whether it was the language of ordinary, day-to-day communication or the language of ritual.

Thus, the Ottoman state had fatwas in place that served a sociocultural function, but they were in line with the shari'a, which helped the state to maintain the boundaries between the communities—much like a colonial enterprise to divide and rule communities on the basis of faith. These boundaries restrained the relationships between the communities before the "deregulation market of religious belief" took over.[60] In other words, such restraint occurred before democratic, secular values took over and pluralism, liberty, equality, and fraternity became the norm. However, it is interesting to note that this separation of communities is what the present Islamic state of Pakistan has followed on the encouragement of its Wahabi benefactors: that it divide the Muslim communities further, excommunicating some and "regulating the market of religious belief." Within Islam now, directly influenced by Wahabism, a class structure has taken over, of the Arab versus the non-Arab. I speak here from personal experience after my 2009 sabbatical in Austin, Texas. Among the five mosques in the city, the premier mosque is the one that belongs to the Gulf Arabs, who during the holy month of Ramadan bring some renowned "knowledgeable" Arab imam to lead the *tarawiah* prayers after the breaking of the fast. Non-Arab Muslims throng to listen to the original Arabic-speaking imam, though these non-Arabs say that they are not welcome in the Arab mosque.[61]

Connecting with the above discussion and the blasphemy chart (figure 6.1), the communities that were openly declared heretical in the Ottoman Empire were the syncretic mystical groups like the Hurufis, Sufi groups with their *tariqas* (lineages) and traditions, and the Bayrami Melamis, the Kalendaris, the Halvetis, and the Qizilbashes; also declared heretical were the Shi'a proselytizing movements of the sixteenth century. Soothsayers and astrologers were suspect. All these heretical movements were given the names *zandaqa*, *rafzi*, and *bid'a*—falling in line with the lexicon identified in discussion of Hallaj and Hallajism. Other terms that were used in the fatwas were *kafir* (infidel), *kufr* (heresy), *mulhid* (nonbeliever), and *ehl-e fesad* (people of dissent), especially for the S̲h̲i'a. *Zindiq* was a term used occasionally for a heretic, although the more popular term for regulations against the apostates was *ahkam al-murtadin* in Turkish in the Ottoman fatwas. Sometimes the S̲h̲i'a Qizilbashes were also referred to as *baghi* (rebels), and regulations against apostates most likely were applied to them.[62]

OTTOMANS AND THE S̲H̲I'A

The Ottomans' fear of the S̲h̲i'a, whom they called *rafizis*, together with their fear of the Sufi, emanates from the threat of the Safavids in Iran, originally a Sufi order that had roots in Turkish Azerbaijan in the fourteenth century. Also known as the Qizilbashes, the Safavids were identified by their red turbans. The Safavids had a large following throughout Iran as well as in the surrounding regions of Syria, eastern Anatolia, the Caucasus, and beyond. As their influence grew, so did their ideology, and in the fifteenth century they became a threat to their Sunni neighbors (figure 6.1). The Safavids established themselves as a significant S̲h̲i'a dynasty that traced links from Muhammad and the Ahl-e Bait, the Prophet's descendants through Fatima and his son-in-law 'Ali ibn Abi Talib. At one time, they evicted the Mongols from northern India and themselves became sovereigns. As Safavid influence spread northwestward into eastern Anatolia, the Ottomans decided to stop them. The Ottomans considered the Safavid S̲h̲i'a Sufis heretics, and serious clashes resulted between the parties in the early sixteenth century. When the Ottoman Sultan Bayezid (1482–1511) showed attraction for Sufism, he was deposed.[63] In 1555 Suleiman signed a treaty with the Safavids in which he agreed to leave Azerbaijan and Caucasia; he permitted Persian pilgrims to perform the hajj and visit the holy cities of Mecca and Medina as well as the S̲h̲i'a pilgrim sites in Iraq.[64]

Still, among the heresies and communities that were to be watched were the S̲h̲i'a states. Among the Ottomans, not only were individuals listed for heretical, deviant behavior, there were proper *kanunnamas* (injunctions) about heretical states such as Persia and communities of non-Muslims, categorized as zimmis.

The Ottomans, on one level, redefined the Islamic shari'a's concept of heresy through their relationships with the bordering Safavid S̲h̲i'a kingdom as well as the smaller communities and principalities of S̲h̲i'as and Sufis that threatened the empire. It was the combination of the state and the clergy working in concert that developed the blasphemy and heresy laws that would control dissenting factions within the state; the laws helped prevent alliances between dissenting factions with outside influences. In the absence of sedition laws, religious law and its inquisitional potential were used to establish authority.[65] Sufi protest and interpretation of the law on the hidden meanings of Qur'anic texts are at the other end of the spectrum. The connections between the empire and the religious elite as the shari'a evolved (especially related to blasphemy, heresy, and apostasy) are complex.

FATWAS AGAINST SUFIS

The period of the seventeenth century between 1630 and 1680 was strong in "inquisitional activism," with the orthodox Kadizadeli preachers like Kadizade Mehmed Efendi of Balikesir (d. 1635), Ustuvani Mehmed Efendi of Damascus (d. 1661), and Vani Mehmed Efendi (d. 1685), who viewed Sufis with suspicion.[66]

Sufis and Sufism were alternative authorities on the shari'a, the interpretation of the Qur'anic text, and the Prophet Muhammad's sunna (precedent).[67] The Sufis have taken a humane approach based on love and compassion. Briefly, the Sufi emphasis on the overt and covert meanings of the Qur'anic text, the incantation practices, and the acceptance of the suprasensory world has brought heresy accusations against this community, as is evident in the Ottoman fatwas and rigid sanctions against Sufism. As alternative authorities, the Sufis undermined the hold of the Ottomans. Like the Mongols in India, the Ottomans thus established an empire based on an Islamic ideology that was politicized to legitimize domination.

Sufi groups like the Bekhstasis had *tekkes* (lodges) in Anatolia, and these seminaries were places for Islamic learning in which freethinking was key. Important to this Sufi tradition was also Jalaluddin Rumi (1207–1273), originally an Afghan, who had to leave his land because of the Mongols and through Persia came to Turkey. Many other "nomads" like Rumi received sanctuary in the Sufi tekkes.[68] Rumi and his mentor, Shems-e Tabrizi, belonged to centuries-old mystical traditions that evolved through the interactions of Judaism, Hinduism, Zoroastrianism, Buddhism, and Christianity. These traditions merged within Islam as Sufism. Because of its eclectic nature, orthodox clerics and obscurantists have viewed Sufism with suspicion.

While Sufism advocates freethinking as well as independent reasoning, or ijtihad, followers of orthodox Islam insist on a rigid, inflexible following of only the Qur'anic text and their own creation of a sunna and hadith of the

Prophet that is open to question, as state functionaries in collusion with the clergy have manipulated the sunna and the hadith to fulfill their own political agendas. The Qur'anic text has been quoted out of context, as has the Prophet's hadith. Thus, we find a tension between Sufism and orthodox *mollazade* Islam. These conflicts between Sufism and orthodox Islam are reflected in the judicial system of Islam as well as in the manner in which the Qur'an, the Prophet's life, and his sunna and hadith were interpreted.

In summary, I have investigated the Ommayads in Spain and the Ottomans in Turkey to demonstrate these empires' application of blasphemy laws for administrative control in which the shari'a was used. Many times this shari'a was a concoction of the state and its functionaries. The caliph gave himself divine authority using Islam for validation in an empire that was composed of a large population of non-Muslims; among these non-Muslims, large numbers converted to Islam but continued to practice a syncretic version of Islam. Perhaps this is also the reason for a revisionist Saudi Arabian–backed movement in South Asia and elsewhere in the Muslim world to bring citizens into the fold of codified, canon-based Islam of tribal Arabia, reinvented by Muhammad ibn 'Abd al-Wahab (1703–1792). It would consolidate the Wahabi empire and its ideology.

THE AFFILIATES: WHERE TO?

PAKISTAN'S BLASPHEMY LAWS are the outcome of three empires: the Islamic empires that followed after the death of the Prophet Muhammad, the British Empire in India (1857–1947), and the CIA-led empire in Afghanistan (1978–1989). These laws have nothing to do with the Prophet Muhammad or the Qur'an or the Prophet's sunna. These laws are a kufr, a blasphemy, in the name of Islam.

The writing of this book has been my own emotional, spiritual, and intellectual journey in which I have explored the Prophet Muhammad's Islam, his times, and his community of followers whom he governed in Medina. I have investigated the evolution of blasphemy laws that are being used in a country like Pakistan within that time frame. I have not found a single bit of evidence in the Qur'an about blasphemy except the issue with the Trinity, or in the Constitution of Medina (622) that the Prophet drew up as a treaty with the Jewish, Christian, and polytheist tribes of his time. Neither have I found any evidence of blasphemy in the Treaty of Hudaibiya that the Prophet made with the Quraysh (628), although in that year, when the treaty was made, he and his followers were not permitted to perform the hajj, as the Qurayaish did not permit that, and the Prophet and his followers returned to Medina peacefully.

However, as stated above, what I have discovered in my research is that Pakistan's blasphemy laws are the direct outcome of the Islamic empires, the British Empire in India, and the CIA-led incursion into Afghanistan spearheaded through General Zia-ul-Haq's dictatorship. Zia-ul-Haq's laws violate human rights, deny social justice, and now threaten the international security of non-Muslims and Muslims since they have become a militant ideology for violence, fanaticism, and intolerance. They reflect the absence of governance in a state that claims to represent an Islamic system based on

Muhammad's Nizam-e Mustafa. Midwifed by authoritarian regimes, these laws together with the Hudood ordinances against women reflect poorly on postcolonial states that sought independence as Islamic entities that were never conceived as theocratic polities. With close to 3 million Hindus, 3 million Christians, and a large population of Qadianis in the country, in addition to several denominations of Muslim sects that include 20 percent Shi'a and the rest largely Hanafi Muslims, the citizens cannot be made hostages to a Salafi/Wahabi shari'a simply because the oil-rich Saudi kingdom has its own imperial agenda to export this version of orthodox Islam as the only Islam. The Pakistani state and especially its religious parties have politicized the issue for their own agendas, including regimes like those of General Musharraf and Nawaz Sharif. These laws ought to be a non-issue, especially for a state that needs to address matters of economic development, literacy, health care, housing, flood control, water and sanitation, and security together with a host of other problems of governance.

In the Islamic empires, blasphemy laws evolved over time, such as during the caliphate of the Rashidun when Abu Bekr, the first caliph, fought the riddah wars, also known as the Apostasy Wars (632–633), with some of the Arab tribes that declared autonomy and reneged on their oath to the Prophet Muhammad to follow Islam. Their argument was that their treaty was only with the Prophet Muhammad, and now that he was gone, there was no need for them to follow Islam. Many self-proclaimed prophets emerged on the scene. It was then that Caliph Abu Bekr put apostasy regulations into Islamic law, although this was in oral form, as the writing and codification of Islamic law started only under the ʿAbbasids (758–1258). Also, the Khatam-e Nabuvat, the end of prophethood, is a product of the same time under Abu Bekr, who told the tribes that there would be no prophet after Muhammad.

Then, during the Ommayad rule of Maʿuviya in Damascus, the laʿan practices of the Shi'a evolved as a reaction to the declaration of successors to Muhammad's Islam. Blasphemy and heresy did become issues at the time, even under the Rashidun and later under the Damascus Ommayads, as the Shi'a believe that in the compilation of the Qur'an, certain verses were eliminated.[1] Later, blasphemy and heresy became an issue in the caliphate of the ʿAbbasids in Iraq when large populations of Manicheans, Armenians, Kurds, Persians, Turks, Arab polytheists, and Christians of various ethnicities converted to Islam from sheer expediency for the benefits that could be derived from the conversions. These populations, however, continued to practice their old rituals, and it was then that the ʿAbbasids had the zandaqa (heresy for practicing magic) put in place as part of Islamic law or shari'a.[2] The execution of Mansur al-Hallaj, a Sufi mystic, and his trial by the 'Abbasids is a case in point. It is the beginning of the rift between Sufis and the state.[3]

Since the Ommayads, or the Moors, in al-Andalus were a contemporary competing Islamic empire with the 'Abbasids in Iraq, they created their own blasphemy shari'a in which the caliph's qadi sentenced the Cordoba martyrs to death for seeking martyrdom; Christian monks would come into the city cursing the Prophet Muhammad. These monks would be tried in qadi courts and asked to renege on the cursing; they would refuse to do so and would be executed, thus fulfilling their desire to become martyrs of Christ. Similar practices were put into place in Ottoman Turkey when the Neomartyrs from the Orthodox Christian Church blasphemed against the Prophet Muhammad. They would be tried in qadi courts, and on refusing to renege on the cursing, they would be executed. They too became martyrs of Christ. However, no evidence is found in the Prophet Muhammad's practices to uphold such executions.

Blasphemy laws have a special history in India, part of which is now Pakistan. The history goes back to the execution of Crown Prince Dara Shikoh (1615–1659), a Sufi mystic and intellectual who translated the Sanskrit Upanishads into Persian and believed in an interfaith dialogue with the Hindus and other faiths in India. His translation was called *Sirr-e Akbar*. His grandfather Akbar had also initiated an interfaith dialogue with the Hindus. Dara Shikoh was the eldest son of Shahjehan, the fifth Mughal emperor, who built the Taj Mahal; he was a disciple of Hazrat Mian Mir, a Qadiriyya Sufi whose shrine exists today in Lahore. Dara Shikoh and his sister Jahan Ara were also disciples of Mulla Shah Badakhshi of Kashmir, another Qadiriyya Sufi. Since the Mughals did not have a law of succession, Aurengzeb, a younger brother of Dara Shikoh, imprisoned their father, Shahjehan, in the Agra fort while he was still the emperor, eliminated his brothers, including Dara Shikoh, and became emperor of India. In eliminating his eldest brother, whom his father desired to be the next emperor, Aurengzeb had the support of the clerics around him: a heresy charge was brought against Dara, and he was executed in the most ignominious manner. His face was blackened, and he was paraded around Delhi city on an unwashed, dirty elephant for all to see. Citizens wept as they saw the humiliation of this graceful prince. Dara's head was presented to Shahjehan in the Agra fort.

Thus, the antagonism between the mullas and the Sufis in this region has a history. For General Zia-ul-Haq, Aurengzeb was the model ruler, who reimposed the jizya, the zimmi tax on the non-Muslim population, which Akbar had removed. As such, on motivation from western powers and the funds that he received through the CIA, Zia-ul-Haq brought to the books the most horrendous, brutal, so-called Islamic shariʿa, in which he had the support of Islami parties like the Jamaat-e Islami so that the war against the infidel communist Soviet forces in Afghanistan could be won. Only the combined forces of a militant Islamic jihad could make such an adventure possible. And who was best suited to advise on such a template of militant Islamic jihad but the British? They had seen themselves ousted from India not only by the forces of Gandhi, the Indian congress, and the Muslim League but also by groups like Deobandi Muslim clerics in India. Militant jihad in India against colonial forces was fought for a long time, and thus this model was replicated through General Zia-ul-Haq, this time to oust the Soviets from the region.[4]

As a part of the jihadi ideology, a militaristic jihad was set up with the Afghani mujahideen, made to become the proxies of the Pakistani military, while the forces of the Islami parties in the country were additionally bolstered, as they became advisers to the state. The Islami parties legitimized Zia-ul-Haq's dictatorship and propped him up as the Amir-ul Momineen, leader of the faithful, in the manner of a caliph. Generous funds poured in through the CIA as well as the Gulf monarchies, particularly Saudi Arabia. Saudi Prince Turki al-Faisal, who was head of the kingdom's foreign intelligence services, worked closely with the CIA and Pakistan's Inter-Services Intelligence to ensure the success of the jihad against the Soviets in Afghanistan.

It was also then that Osama bin Laden, a trained civil engineer, was brought in to build the tunnels in Afghanistan.[5] Bin Laden brought his own equipment and funds to participate in the jihad against the Soviets, and it was here that he assumed mythical heroism as a mujahid, a freedom fighter. He was allegedly an ally of the CIA. In return for Saudi patronage, General Zia-ul-Haq enforced a Wahabi-dictated shariʿa on the Pakistani citizens; this meant the imposition of the lethal blasphemy laws as well as the notorious Hudood ordinances against women. Maʿruf al-Dawalibi, the Saudi adviser on Zia-ul-Haq's shariʿa project, personally supervised the insertion of shariʿa laws while at the same time ensuring that shariʿat courts were set up on parallel lines with the civil courts and the higher appellate courts in the country, such as the Supreme Court.

Additionally, Zia-ul-Haq was ordered to give the country an "Islamic" curriculum, which meant glorification of militaristic jihad. In order to promote an Islamic jihadi ideology, Zia-ul-Haq had to produce the ʿulema to validate the Islamization process in the educational domain of the schools, colleges, and universities. Consequently, the ʿulema were brought in from the madrassa seminaries, and a quick fix was arranged: seminary diplomas were given equivalence through the rubber-stamp notifications of the University Grants Commission in Islamabad.

I researched the websites of the various madrassas and religious seminaries to write this conclusion and made interesting discoveries. On the website of the Jamia Ashrafia in Lahore, from which the dean of my faculty at the time of the blasphemy charge against me had received his diploma, I found the equivalence clause mentioned thus:

> Pakistan University Grants Commission has declared the final degree of Jamia Ashrafia Lahore equivalent to Masters in MA Arabic/Islamic Studies: UGC Notification No. 8418/ACAD/84/VOL. VII/227/240 dated Feb 3, 1985.[6]

Thus the diploma for the ʿalimiyya, to be an ʿ*alim* or ʿulema (scholar), was declared equivalent to a master's in Arabic Islamic studies.

During my research, also of interest was the statement that the Dar-ul-ʿuloom Deoband in India had "introduced a two-year full time Diploma in English language and literature for students wishing to pursue higher education in universities."[7] The Dar-ul-ʿuloom Deoband is the model for madrassas throughout the world, including the ones in Pakistan. Was I correct, then, in protesting in 1998 that my department's courses were being plagiarized and hijacked for the Dars-e Nizami, seminary courses? That perhaps also explains why after two meetings I was dropped from the special-interest meetings of the Dars-e Nizami in 1998 while I was chair of the Department of English Language and Applied Linguistics at the Allama Iqbal Open University. Another colleague, who is now dean of the faculty of humanities at the Open University, I am sure delivered the goods, as I was eventually harassed to leave the institution, and the latter replaced me with collusion from the faculty of clerics in my university.

In hindsight as I now look at the situation and the writing comes full circle, it was not just me as the female with an American PhD and the chair of a department who was the target; it was a battle for the heart and soul of the university, and the Department of English Language and Applied Linguistics was the centerpiece. It had been built over three decades by teams of secular Pakistani academics as well as British consultants with input from the British Open University in Milton Keynes. The clerics knew the prestige of the English department, as it was their trophy along with the rest of the open learning system of the Allama Iqbal University that they hijacked for the Dars-e Nizami, the seminary system.[8] Zulfiqar ʿAli Bhutto's People's Open University transitioned into the Allama Iqbal Open University during

Zia-ul-Haq's regime and then perhaps the Dar-ul-ʿuloom Deoband Islami-yya in Nawaz Sharif's regime when he was prime minister.[9]

The quick-fix rubber-stamping of seminary diplomas from the madrassas to create a core of Islamic scholars, ʿulema, during Zia-ul-Haq's Afghanistan adventure is based on British educational policies in India through the various accommodations the colonial administrators made with the madrassas. Foremost was Warren Hastings, the first British governor-general of India (1773–1785). In accordance with the Oriental School of Education Policy, the British patronized madrassa education; this was a political decision of Warren Hastings that he considered necessary for peaceful governance. Other British accommodations in madrassa education were made through the New-Scheme System for Madrassahs in 1915 under the Earl Committee. Archdale Earle was the director of mass education in India then, and as an outcome of studies conducted by him and another study done under the Nathan Committee it was decided that Persian would be discarded from the madrassa curriculum and instead English would be made compulsory together with a local language such as Bangla, mathematics, geography, history, drawing, handicrafts, and drills.[10]

Therefore, the British colonists did make accommodations with the madrassas despite Thomas Macaulay's Minute on Indian Education that he delivered in 1835 in which he said it was the purpose of British imperial rule to produce citizens who were Indians in blood and color but English in taste, opinions, morals, and intellect. Macaulay (1800–1859), who had served on the Supreme Council of India from 1834 to 1838 during Queen Victoria's reign, added significantly to British imperial policy in India: the education policy in India that inducted bilingual education in the system also introduced elitist English schools for boys and girls. Macaulay proposed the following after the Indian Mutiny of 1857 (called the Indian War of Independence in indigenous contexts) that were later enacted: the Indian Penal Code (1860), Criminal Procedure Code (1872), and Civil Procedure Code (1909), all of which are in place in the Pakistani legal system to date. These laws are also applied in Singapore, Bangladesh, Sri Lanka, India, Nigeria, and Zimbabwe. The notorious blasphemy laws are a part of Macaulay's Indian Penal Code, and it was on this template that General Zia-ul-Haq superimposed his own so-called shariʿa-based blasphemy laws. Reducing a female's testimony to one-half of a male's is reworked into the British law of evidence, giving it the color of the shariʿa. Zia-ul-Haq and his advisers built ambivalence and nebulousness into these laws, making them lethal in the hands of a truant state and its administrative machinery, especially its police and now its Islamic vigilante groups like the Taliban. I have cited personal experiences with the Law of Evidence in earlier chapters.

Thus, it was the model of the jihad that the Deobandi madrassas and their affiliates resurrected against the British in India that made it possible for a jihad ideology to be put in place for the Afghan-Pakhtun mujahideen to fight the Soviets. The manuals using visual images of tanks and Kalashnikovs for jihad were printed at the University of Nebraska from 1984 to 1994 through CIA funds for $51 million. The Taliban, who are the former mujahideen, fondly called "the Muj" by Charlie Wilson, use those manuals to this day to fight the West, which they call kafirs, infidels. Thus did we find a proliferation of madrassas in the region beginning in 1978 and continuing to this date. And it was the British accommodation of madrassa education as colonists that was the model that produced the countless "'ulema" to validate the Islamization process in Pakistan and Afghanistan during 1978–1988. That was the "mullaization" period of the Pakistani academy as well as the pattern of governance in the country. Now that Islamization has totally gotten out of hand, it is currently Talibanization funded from the Gulf petrodollars. We have no civil society in either Afghanistan or Pakistan, and this is one of the most dangerous regions of the world, where citizens have no security of life.

The Pakistani military state's relationship with its offspring and its proxies, the Taliban, is questionable. It is a duplicitous relationship that is simple shadow boxing: one time lovers and one time not lovers. The Pakistani military cannot claim to fight the Taliban in Waziristan and then also claim they are a valuable asset; there are no good Taliban and bad Taliban. This liaison of the male, military, and mullas is dangerous; it has spelled disaster for democratic institutions, and the affiliates will have to part ways. The recent discovery of Osama bin Laden having lived for several years in a compound right next to the Kakul military training academy raises searching questions about these liaisons. These illegitimate offspring, the Taliban, born of a military liaison, have been used as a proxy for the Pakistani military in Afghanistan; these offspring need to be provided with means for educating themselves and their communities to change course, which seems to be the path of the Obama administration.

Fortunately, the judiciary and the lawyers in Musharraf's regime of 2007 stood up to authoritarianism. Again, the military regime used the Red Mosque clerics to create a civil war right in the heart of Islamabad to divert attention away from the confrontation with the judiciary and to frighten the western allies that without Musharraf, the region would be overrun by religious extremists like the Red Mosque clerics. The clerics, on their end, heady with state support, now wanted their own shari'a for the entire country without popular vote through the ballot.[11] The military and mulla affiliates quarreled, and since then the citizens have only experienced violence in their cities.[12] Suicide bombings have overtaken the country, for the militants now challenge the state. The Marriot Hotel in Islamabad was bombed during the holy month of Ramadan (September 2008) as citizens broke their fasts during *iftar*. Close to 600 people were killed, and these were mostly workers and staff. Daily bombings are routine in city centers where citizens shop. Girls' schools in northern Pakistan are attacked, and their education is threatened. With support from unknown sources, the militants use violence against anything that is modern, branding secularism as *la din*, meaning without faith. This is a dangerous discourse that right-wing religious organizations have generated. Islam is not exclusive of secularism, as I have always maintained. The ʿAbbasids, the Ommayads in Spain, and the Ottomans in Turkey, despite their reliance on religious law, were secular—especially in promoting the arts and the sciences that ushered in the European Renaissance.[13] The "la din" discourse is indeed dangerous, as it creates polarization in the civic body, like most of Zia-ul-Haq's so-called shariʿa laws.

Religion is a citizen's private domain, and the state cannot pry into individual belief as, sadly, the tendency became with the Zia-ul-Haq–generated shariʿa. During the Red Mosque takeover in Islamabad in July 2007, stick-wielding mullas and *mullanis* (female clerics) were prying into citizens' backyards to see if shariʿa was being followed, who was coming, who was going, and what was being cooked in households. I was threatened by mullas while driving a car in Rawalpindi Cantonment. The mullas had issued threats in Rawalpindi and Islamabad to women that they would be attacked if seen driving cars.

The Prophet Muhammad's was a pluralistic state, as can be read in the Constitution of Medina; some empires that are discussed in this book were also pluralistic, though for political purposes these states appropriated prophetic authority and used blasphemy laws.

If Pakistan is to survive, it has to build its civic institutions through democratic consensus and most of all through educating its citizens. So-called shariʿa laws such as the Hudood ordinances and blasphemy laws need to be totally repealed. It is not a question of amendment. Why should a democratic state have threats dangling over citizens' heads and leave them at the mercy of state minions like an illiterate policeman who is entitled to register an FIR against a citizen, as was done in the case of Dr. Younas Shaikh? Musharraf had promised to repeal the laws, but later, under pressure from the Islamic parties, he reneged. Or perhaps he was pressured by his Gulf paymasters to back off.

A Pakistani state under pressure from the military continuing on this path can only expect its Balkanization, as theocratic states such as Pakistan with no roadmaps for development, education, gender equity, or social justice cannot remain on the world's map for long. Neither can the Gulf monarchies be on the world maps for long with the youth in the Arab Spring taking over. Besides, monarchy as a political institution is not compatible with Islam; it is a bid'a, a heresy. If we are to follow the Prophet Muhammad's sunna, his example, we would recognize that he was never a monarch, nor did he advocate a monarchy. Neither does the Qur'an uphold monarchy as a political institution. None of the four caliphs who followed the Prophet Muhammad were monarchs.

We lost half the country in East Pakistan through military arrogance and that of its politicians like Zulfiqar 'Ali Bhutto. We will lose what now remains if the military and mulla lovers do not part ways and civilian institutions are not allowed to develop. The Taliban ought to be lured into education and social and economic development. The Pakistani military state ought to get out of its mindset of fighting a Hindu India and stop building its stockpile of weapons. We need dialogue with India so the citizens of both countries can live in peace and the resources spent on weaponry and arms instead can be spent on economic and social development.

Unfortunately, because of these so-called shari'a laws, the Pakistani state has failed its citizens. The language of Pakistan's blasphemy laws is shameful in that they are documents of hate speech that discriminate against citizens and incite more hatred. The same applies to the Hudood ordinances. How can a state in today's environment reduce the status of its female population to one-half? Are we living in an age of slavery in which half the citizens have half the rights of the other half? The political state of Pakistan blatantly claims misogyny according to the Hudood ordinances. And the state will not stand up to safeguard half its citizenry because a group of religious mullas with hardly any education want to put down women for the challenge they pose or because the state empowers these mulla vigilantes through the hate language of its blasphemy laws to kill minorities, intellectuals, children, and women. This is not even sustainable for the state's existence in the twenty-first century.

Many of the militant outfits in Pakistan and Afghanistan are indoctrinated in the linguistic creed of the blasphemy laws, and thus we have executions and dismemberments. The Taliban have used these laws with impunity in Afghanistan and in northern Pakistan, such as in Swat and Waziristan. This violence is exacerbated through the Hudood ordinances; these laws have led to physical violations against women in which they were tortured and executed for alleged zina (fornication). A female musician was shot dead in Swat in 2009, and her body was displayed to make her an example. Militant groups continue to bomb girls' schools in northern Pakistan, threaten women's education, and force females to stay at home.

Such violations of human dignity cannot be upheld in the present millennium with citizens taken back to the jahilliya period of pre-Islamic Arabia. Though these laws profess to wield authority from Muhammad, that legitimacy has been challenged with evidence from the Qur'an and the Prophet's life here in this book.

I grew up in the care of a mother who chanted the Qur'an throughout the year, especially in the holy month of Ramadan. She was a Mufti and claimed her lineage with pride. Factory workers going to their jobs at the Pakistan Ordnance Factories in Wah Cantonment, where my father was posted as a military engineer from 1954 to 1958, would dismount their bicycles to listen to my mother's Qur'anic chants during Ramadan. She was a great advocate for women's emancipation, as she kept my daughter so I could finish my graduate degree in England in 1966–1968. She did not let me come back from England although I wept for my daughter. Her letters to me in England always said that she was taking better care of my daughter than I would have myself and that it was absolutely necessary for my own future and my daughter's that I complete my education in England. My mother would never have put up with the Hudood ordinances. She was all for a western education for women, no *purdah* (veiling), and no shackling of women. She refused to wear a nose ring (*nath*) for her wedding, saying that it was a sign of female enslavement. She taught me to stand up for myself and to always speak the truth, no matter what the price. And hence this book.

Accordingly, it is absolutely essential to address this matter of a skewed shari'a operating in Pakistan that is nothing but terror and naked aggression against citizens. This was never the vision of the founding fathers. Pakistan, if it survives the absence of governance, the violence, and the near–civil war situation in the country, needs to work toward structural reform. Civic institutions ought to be developed. The Taliban challenge the writ of the state from their Waziristan sanctuary and in fact all over the country. They need to be disarmed and educated; they need to be provided other means of livelihood, as weapons are no solution. Perhaps Pakistani women will have to take over the peace process like the Liberian women did; they may have to force the parties to the negotiating table, as there can be no military solution to violence—it only breeds further violence. The Liberian women forced the warring factions of male militias, Christians and Muslims, to the negotiating table. The women used cultural practices to persuade the men to disarm, and one of the threats they used was to disrobe in public.[14] The males negotiated, and today Liberia has a female president, Ellen Johnson Sirleaf, born October 29, 1938.[15] It is a country at peace now.

The first and foremost move ought to be to disband the shari'a laws Zia-ul-Haq created that incite fanaticism, violence, and intolerance. Section 295-C of Pakistan's blasphemy laws will have to be totally repealed. Justice Durab Patel, who in 1994 was the chairman emeritus of the Human Rights Commission of Pakistan, spoke strongly against the blasphemy laws. He affirmed that Section 295-C must go. The law was so "vague," he said, that anything construed by anyone against the Holy Prophet could be interpreted as "blasphemous." Section 295-C was brought into law during Nawaz Sharif's regime in 1992, making death the only penalty for offenses under it. Justice Patel said that Article 295-A was enough to deal with blasphemy cases; 295-A was a part of the British legacy in which "proof of *intent*" was necessary, and if required, the punishment of imprisonment prescribed under Article 298-A could be raised. Osama Siddiqui speaks about intent, or *mens rea*, at great length in his radio interview for the Harvard Law School. Siddiqui also speaks about Zia-ul-Haq's "controversial laws and legal mechanisms that remain highly contentious to date. . . . [E]xamples include the parallel legal apparatus of the Federal Shari'at Court, Shariat Appellete Bench of the Supreme Court, and various laws regulating personal behavior and proscribing citizen choices on the basis of state-dictated notions of morality."[16]

Section 295-C has frequently been used to settle personal vendettas and land disputes. Niamat Ahmer, a schoolteacher, was charged under this section of the blasphemy law and killed because some of his opponents wanted him transferred. Tahir Iqbal was registered under the same article and killed because of a property dispute. Dr. Akhtar Hameed Khan, a notable social worker and pioneer of the Orangi Educational Project in Karachi, was also implicated in a blasphemy accusation by a person who wanted to take over his office.[17] Other cases have been discussed earlier.

The case of Asea Bibi, a Christian woman and mother of five children, being sentenced to death by a district court is outrageous. It was some small argument between women over drawing water from a village well that blew up into such proportions. Governor Salman Taseer and the minorities minister Shahbaz Bhatti were assassinated in 2011 while attempting to repeal the blasphemy laws in order to save Asea Bibi's life. In other instances as well, schoolteachers and academics take on the role of vigilante seminary mullas (appendix 5). The glorification of Salman Taseer's assassin, Mumtaz Qadri, who was Taseer's bodyguard, is indicative of an extreme vigilante culture in Pakistan bordering on virtual insanity. The attorneys in the court where Qadri was pronounced guilty of manslaughter and thus given the death sentence threw rose petals at him.

Who bred such intolerance? The jihad ideology of General Zia-ul-Haq and the mullas propped up by the imperial western powers as well as the Gulf monarchies to bring down the Soviet Union. The proxies in the war were the Afghan mujahideen.

South Asia at the moment is caught in the great oil game of Central Asia. We have many parties and many players, including the West's interests in the region. We also have religious ideologies and nuclear arms; India is no exception, with its Hindutva nationalism, as was seen during the Ayodha riots of 1993. Muslims in India were terrified through the state machinery as the police watched Hindu fundamentalists tear down the Babari Mosque. Members of India's parliament, too, have been hurling blasphemy charges at each other over this incident. Alternative religious interpretations of the scripture have led to blasphemy accusations in the Indian parliament as well.

One expects sanity will prevail in South Asia in the face of theocratic forces that have been unleashed. Both India and Pakistan flaunt their nuclear status, and that enjoined with theocratic discourse does not bode well for the citizenry of either country. In the best interests of the region, all parties in the conflict need to think outside the frame of religious law. The stress needs to be on dialogue, demilitarization, and secular, liberal discourse that seeks economic development. Social justice ought to be the goal and not dreams of empire. These simply cannot be sustained in the twenty-first century.

The west likewise needs to play its role in the drama that it helped create to bring the Cold War to an end, and the best way to do that is to bring all the parties to the table and let there be a peaceful dialogue between Pakistan and India in the better interests of citizens of both countries. The world has not forgotten the Mumbai disaster of 2008.

In the meantime, Pakistan's blasphemy laws ought to be examined by a council of world academic Islamic scholars, male and female, who have a liberal view of the Prophet Muhammad's life, the Qur'an, and his sunna, definitely not the mullas or the canonists. There ought to be a global debate in the academy and in forums that respect freedom of speech. These laws ought to be examined in the light of the Constitution of Medina, as that was the Prophet's charter with the non-Muslim tribes of his time. And until such time, Pakistan's blasphemy laws together with its misogynist Hudood ordinances ought to be suspended. Like the Arab Spring, when the youth called for social justice, young intellectuals and especially musicians ought to sing about the Constitution of Medina and bring the message of that char-

7.1. Allama Iqbal Open University English language workshop, 1998. Author on the left. Male colleague giving a diploma to a female faculty member from Kinnaird College, Lahore. Author was full professor and chair of the Department of English Language and Applied Linguistics. This photo was taken before the blasphemy charge.

ter to the streets. Let the people and citizens be the ones to choose how they wish to be governed. The Constitution of Medina is easily accessible on the Internet for anyone to read.

I do not see any "blasphemy" or even a reference to that term in the charter. Thus, the conclusion is that Pakistan's blasphemy laws are simple kufr in the name of Islam. And this kufr ought to be obliterated.

Let me also make clear that the demand for a suspension of Pakistan's blasphemy laws is in no way connected to the European blasphemies or the incident of the cartoons. These are totally different issues. Pakistan's blasphemy laws are related to an unjust, militaristic state. The jihad is over in Afghanistan now, and peace ought to return to citizens' lives. The so-called shari'a laws need to be put away, and life ought to return to a civil, democratic system in which citizens decide how they will be governed.

Meantime, I do not see myself as a victim, and neither are the other women faculty at the Allama Iqbal Open University who left and made alternative careers. However, the people of Pakistan, the woman on the street, lost as she is, pay for the education of academics like me.

I have published two books in these thirteen years and several articles since I left Pakistan. And although the ride was bumpy, I now have a tenured position at SUNY Purchase, where I teach courses on Islam. I teach about gender and freedom of speech in Islamic societies and citizens living under Islamic laws. My place now is in the American academy, where my students ask searching questions about gender and sexuality in Islamic societies, and I have an engaging, meaningful dialogue with them in an atmosphere of free speech without fear of being persecuted for blasphemy. This is what Islam is all about: discourse and debate, and this is how Islamic law evolved over the years under the 'Abbasids and the succeeding empires of Muslims, including the Mughals in India. Islamic law evolved in eclectic environments beginning with the Prophet Muhammad's community of followers in Medina. The prime example of the Prophet's eclecticism is the Constitution of Medina and his Qur'an, which needs an intelligent, liberal, semantic interpretation based on ijtihad and freedom of exploration. Islam and secularism are not exclusive of each other. This is a period of reformation for Islam, and hopefully more scholarship of this kind will be forthcoming.

APPENDIX I. FIELDWORK

In addition to bringing to this book the experience of a lifetime living under all of Pakistan's military dictators, namely, Field Marshal Ayub Khan, General Yahya Khan, Zia-ul-Haq, General Musharraf, both the Bhuttos, and the Nawaz Sharif regimes and their military and mulla cohorts, I carried out fieldwork in Pakistan during summer 2008 that included visits in Lahore to the shrine of the eleventh-century Sufi scholar Data Ganj Baksh al-Hajweiri and the shrine of women Shi'a scholars, the Bibi Pak Daman. I conducted interviews with religious scholars; shari'a lawyers; and citizens from the Federally Administered Tribal Areas, where shari'a laws, including blasphemy laws, are enforced through Taliban groups. I further interviewed senior officers of the Pakistani army who had served in Saudi Arabia, including one officer who gave his insights on the radicalization of shari'a laws in Pakistan under Saudi Wahabi influence. In 2008 I observed the lawyers' movement against the Pakistani military state that instituted radical shari'a laws including the blasphemy laws, though generally the protest was a demand for independence of the judiciary. I collected archival materials from the Pakistan Book Foundation and specialty bookstores such as the Oxford University Press in Islamabad in 2008.

Earlier, in the summer of 2007, I conducted fieldwork in Pakistan. Most of the data was collected in Islamabad, Rawalpindi, and Karachi. I was in Islamabad during the armed confrontation between Taliban clerics and the Pakistani military at the Red Mosque in June and July. Although risky, I traveled several times in the area to assess the situation. I interviewed citizens from a broad cross-section of the population, such as citizens' groups and lawyers, to evaluate the prevailing situation in the country.

During this period of 2007 I also traveled to Karachi to interview lawyers and activists at the Human Rights Commission in the city. This I thought was a safer place to speak to individuals as well as collect data, away from the scrutiny of state officials and the numberless intelligence agencies in the capital of Islamabad. At the Human Rights Commission in Karachi I further met with minority members of the parliament whose communities are affected by Pakistan's blasphemy laws. To my knowledge, none of them has since suffered the fate of Governor Salman Taseer, who was assassinated in 2011 as he tried to repeal the blasphemy laws over the judicial order of a death sentence against a Christian citizen in a Panjabi village. However, Shahbaz Bhatti, the minority affairs minister, was gunned down two months after Taseer in Islamabad for trying to have the blasphemy laws repealed. I was provided additional data at the commission. Among others I interviewed in Karachi was Ardeshir Cowasjee, a Parsi journalist who writes for the daily newspaper *Dawn*.

In 2007 I also interviewed the managing director of the Pakistan Law House, a specialty bookstore for judicial materials. He provided crucial material on Pakistan's penal code, in which the blasphemy laws are embedded. He enabled the data collection at the Human Rights Commission as well as at Shirkat Gah, a women's NGO founded by Khawar Mumtaz and Farida Shaheed; these are activists in the women's rights movement in Pakistan. They have worked against the Hudood ordinances as well as against the blasphemy laws. In Karachi I interviewed Akmal Wasim, an associate professor of law in the Hamdard University there. Wasim facilitated my Karachi research, including the above interviews and the materials collection, especially the case studies at the Shirkat Gah resource center. Incidentally, the most valuable materials on blasphemy cases are held in this center away from the scrutiny of the regime as well as the militant Islamic groups. These are publications of the Idara-e Amn-O Insaf, whose offices the militant Islamic parties burned down some years ago but whose publications are preserved at the Shirkat Gah. While in Karachi I happened to visit the site where Daniel Pearl, the *Wall Street Journal* reporter, was abducted; in fact, the hotel where I stayed was also where Pearl had stayed at the time of his abduction.

During both field trips to Pakistan I was able to meet with officials of the Pakistani military, including retired generals, major generals, and admirals. These individuals were willing to share inside information, having retired from the services now.

All spelling, language, and syntactical errors have been left in for the reader to see the ambiguity as well as the absurdity of the laws.

OFFENSES RELATING TO RELIGION: PAKISTAN PENAL CODE

SECTION 295-B

Defiling, etc, of copy of Holy Quran. Whoever, willfully defiles, damages or desecrates a copy of the Holy Quran or an extract therefrom or uses it in any derogatory manner of for any unlawful purpose shall be punishable for imprisonment for life.

SECTION 295-C

Use of derogatory remarks, etc; in respect of the Holy Prophet. Whoever by words, either spoken or written or by visible representation, or by any imputation, innuendo, or insinuation, directly or indirectly, defiles the sacred name of the Holy Prophet Muhammad (PBUH) shall be punished with death, or imprisonment for life, and shall also be liable to fine.

SECTION 298-A

Use of derogatory remarks, etc. . . . , in respect of holy personages. Whoever by words, either spoken or written, or by visible representation, or by any imputation, innuendo, or insinuation, directly or indirectly defiles a sacred name of any wife (Ummul Mumineen), or members of the family (Ahle-bait), of the Holy Prophet (PBUH), or any of the righteous caliphs (Khulafa-e Rashideen) or companions (Sahaaba) of the Holy Prophet description for a term which may extend to three years, or with fine, or with both.

SECTION 298-B

Misuse of epithet, descriptions and titles, etc. Reserved for certain holy personages or places.

1. Any person of the Qadiani group or the Lahori group (who call themselves Ahmadis or by any other name) who by words, either spoken or written or by visible representation:

   a. Refers to or addresses, any person, other than a Caliph or companion of the Holy Prophet Mohammad (PBUH), as "Ameerul Momneen", "Khalifat-ul-Momneen", "Khalifat-ul-Muslimeen", "Sahaabi" or "Razi Allah Anho";

   b. Refers to or addresses, any person, other than a wife of the Holy Prophet Mohammed (PBUH), as Ummul-Mumineen;

   c. Refers to or addresses, any person, other than a member of the family, as the Ahl-e Bait; or

   d. refers to, or names, or calls, his place of worship as Masjid shall be punished with imprisonment or cither description for a term which may extend to three years, and shall also be liable to fine.

2. Any person of the Qadiani group or Lahore group, (who call themselves Ahmadis or by any other names), who by words, either spoken or written, or by visible representations, refers to the mode or from of call to prayers followed by his faith as "Azan" or redites Azan as used by the Muslims, shall be punished with imprisonment of either description for a term which may extend to three years and shall also be liable to fine.

SECTION 298-C

Persons of Qadiani group, etc, calling himself a Muslim or preaching or propagating his faith. Any person of the Qadiani group or the Lahori group (who call themselves Ahmadis or any other name), who directly or indirectly, posses himself as a Muslim, or calls, or refers to, his faith as Islam, or preaches or propagates his faith, or invites others to accept his faith, by words, either spoken or written, or by visible representation or in any manner whatsoever outrages the religious feelings of Muslims, shall be punished with imprisonment of either description for a term which may extend to three years and shall also be liable to fine.

Last edited 02/28/2001.

Quoted from *Muhammadanism* at http://www.muhammadanism.org/Government/Government_Pakistan_Blasphemy.htm.

PAKISTAN: Teachers are taking over the responsibilities of the mullahs and turning educational institutions into seminaries.
September 30, 2011

The misuse of blasphemy laws are no longer the prerogative of religious bigots or fundamentalists. It is now being used in every section of society, particularly members of the
teaching staff who are eager to contribute in pushing the country towards a religious intolerant state. Indeed, the enthusiasm of the educational staff in this instance was so high that
they accused a student of a minority community of blasphemy without following the basic
concepts of the ethics of imparting education.

These ethics are being violated when the secrecy of examination papers are dishon-
oured. When an examiner asks a question of a student if he or she is not satisfied with the
student's answer the examiner has the right to fail that student. However, the examiner
does not have the right to disclose the student's answer which is the personal opinion held
by that student. The attitude of the teaching staff now is to gain points from the religious
leaders by pointing out those students who they believe to have made blasphemous comments mistakenly or otherwise.

In a recent case a ten-year-old Christian girl, Ms. Faryal Bhatti, misplaced a full stop
in her Urdu examination paper on September 22, 2011, which has made hers and her
mother's life unbearable. Faryal was a student in Sir Syed Girls High School, Pakistan
Ordinance Factory Colony, Havelian. They have been accused of hatching a conspiracy
against Islam and its Last Prophet (PBUH).

When completing her paper the girl, who has not studied Islam and is therefore unfamiliar with the terminology of the religion, inadvertently placed a dot incorrectly in the
word, Naat, meaning a poem in praise of the Last Prophet which changed it into the word,
Lanaat which means the opposite: a curse.

The teacher, Mrs. Fareeda sternly rebuked Faryal in front of the class and took the matter to the headmaster, even though the child defended herself by saying that it was a mistake. The news of her alleged transgression spread outside the school into the community
and she was labeled a blasphemer. The mosque loud speakers helped to spread the news
and rallies were arranged in protest against the mother and daughter. In response to these
protests the administrators of the Pakistan Ordinance Factory Colony immediately transferred the mother who was serving as a nurse at the colony's hospital. They were asked to
leave the colony immediately. Despite the mother's abject apology and explanation that it
was the simple error of a young girl who was in a hurry to complete the paper because of
the time limit, no understanding was shown by the teaching staff who were more interested in gaining the favour of the uneducated and illiterate mullahs.

This is not the first case of this type. Earlier this year a 17-year-old student, Syed Samiullah, an intermediate student and resident of Mujtaba Colony Malir Halt was charged
with writing derogatory remarks against the Last Prophet (PBUH) in his Urdu, Islamiat
and Physics papers. The incident was reported to the police by the Controller of Examina-

tions of the Intermediate Board of Education, Karachi, who attached copies of Samiullah's answers sheets as evidence of his alleged blasphemy. He was arrested on January 28, 2011.

Syed apologised at every level from the board of education to the police and the magistrate but the educational officers, as in the case of Faryal, wanted to become more mullah-like than the mullahs and filed an FIR against him.

Syed and his family were pressurised by the educational authorities to the point where he had to confess to having committed blasphemy. The situation was exacerbated by the murder of the governor of Punjab province for his stand against the amendments to the blasphemy laws and the glorification of his assassin. No doubt Syed and his family saw a similar fate in store for him.

There are enough people in Pakistan today spreading religious hatred and intolerance and there is no need for the educationalists to swell their ranks. Teachers have the duty to teach and nothing more. While each and every person has the right to his or her own religious beliefs those beliefs should not colour their thinking when practising their professions. Contrary to the religious teachers educationalists are supposed to teach tolerance and enlightenment. The educational system must at all times remain unbiased and free from hatred. However, judging from the number of minority students and teachers themselves who are harassed because of their religious beliefs this is obviously not the case in Pakistan.

The degeneration of the teaching staff has reached the point where they are turning schools and colleges into Islamic madressas (seminaries) which are run by the very antithesis of a teacher, illiterate and uneducated mullahs. While they are receiving all the benefits, salaries and perks as required by the government grading system they are, in fact, doing the work of the mullahs. If this is not stopped now it will be harder for the government ministers and generals to [rein] them in at any time in the future.

The innocent error of a young girl has ruined her life and that of her mother. The government must put a stop to this biased and misguided use of the blasphemy laws. The appeasement policy of the government with regard to religious fundamentalists and their treatment of the minorities, the Ahmadis, Christians, Hindus and others, will only make it more difficult for them to act when it becomes necessary.

Quoted from http://www.humanrights.asia/news/ahrc-news/AHRC-STM-130-2011.

About AHRC: The Asian Human Rights Commission is a regional nongovernmental organization that monitors human rights in Asia, documents violations, and advocates for justice and institutional reform to ensure the protection and promotion of these rights. The Hong Kong–based group was founded in 1984.

APPENDIX 4. THE HUDOOD ORDINANCE;
QANUN-E SHAHADAT OR THE LAW OF EVIDENCE

The discussion here is based on Rashida Patel, *Islamization of Laws in Pakistan?* (Karachi: Faiza, 1986), 44, 78–86.

The Law of Evidence, which is a part of Zia-ul-Haq's Hudood ordinances, was prepared by the Council for Islamic Ideology. Like the blasphemy laws, these sets of laws too were based on an earlier Evidence Act of 1872 that was created under British colonial rule in India. Although the main sections of the 1872 Evidence Act were repeated in these laws, other sections too were added and the new conglomerate was packaged as the Qanun-e Shahadat Order 1984, which replaced the 1872 Evidence Act. The Qanun-e Shahadat (Law of Evidence) was issued as a Martial Law order in order to "revise, amend and consolidate the law of evidence" to conform with Islamic injunctions per the holy Qur'an and the Prophet's *sunna* (example). Sections of the 1872 Evidence Act were rearranged and renumbered. An instance that is quoted is Section 118 of the 1872 Evidence Act read:

> All persons shall be competent to testify unless the court considers that they are prevented from understanding the questions put to them, or from giving rational answers to those questions, by tender years, extreme old age, diseases, whether of body or mind, or any other cause of the same kind.

Under the Qanun-e Shahadat, a redefinition was created on the "competency of a witness," which was to be determined by the court according to the "injunctions of the Holy Qur'an and the *Sunnah* for witness, and where such witness is not forthcoming, the court may take the evidence of the witness, who may be available" (PLD 1985, CS p14; GP October 29, 1984).

The law opened the door for the hundreds of courts in the country and petty government officials to determine a witness's competence according to their whims: what according to them were their injunctions of Islam. The framers of the law created ambiguities that have been exploited by the state's minions. (Accordingly, as a female I have encountered such situations when dealing with male officials in the state bureaucracy my witness was questioned. I have given instances in the book.)

Among the Hudood laws are also sections that apply to *zina* or *zina-bil jabr* (rape), for which defense requires

> at least four Muslim adult male witnesses about whom the Court is satisfied having regard to the requirements of *tazkiyah al shudood* that they are truthful persons and abstain from major sins (*Kabair*) give evidence as eye witnesses of the act of penetration necessary to the offence.

Such sections raise major questions, such as why would *zina-bil jabr* occur if four Muslim adult witnesses were present? Patel, the author of this reference, questions of the witnesses, "Why did they do nothing to stop it? Is that not a major sin in itself?"

It may be pointed out that after many years of activism by women's organizations and human rights groups, General Pervez Musharraf's government issued the Protection of Women (Criminal Laws Amendment) Act, 2006, which suggested some cosmetic changes to the mode of registration of zina (rape) in a competent civil court, which is not a shari'a court. Punishments for zina are specified in the new act, though many sections of the earlier Hudood ordinance remain intact even in the 2006 act.

The Protection of Women (Criminal Laws Amendment), 2006, and an update from December 2010 are posted by pakistani.org at http://www.pakistani.org/pakistan/legislation/2006/wpb.html. The laws also are discussed in Ameena Ulfat and G. M. Chaudhry, *Women and Protection of Women Rights* (Rawalpindi, Pakistan: Federal Law House, 2007).

APPENDIX 5. FATE OF A TEACHER ACCUSED OF BLASPHEMY TO BE DECIDED TODAY

Wasim Abbasi, *The Nation* (Pakistan)

ISLAMABAD—The inquiry committee of ʿulema and teachers will meet today (Tuesday) to decide the fate of an Arabic teacher of the Federal Government College, G-10-4, who had allegedly passed blasphemous remarks against the Holy Prophet (PBUH) during a class lecture, sources told *The Nation* on Monday.

Director General of Federal Directorate of Education (FDE) Brig. (Retd) Maqsood-ul-Hassan had suspended the accused teacher on Monday after an initial inquiry. While another lecturer who had quarreled with the accused teacher for passing blasphemous remarks and sent on forced leave has been asked to resume the duty.

The accused teacher had allegedly passed blasphemous remarks against the Holy Prophet (PBUH) while delivering a lecture in the college a few days back. However, according to sources, she stated before the inquiry committee that the incident was a result of a misunderstanding as she had never been involved in any undesirable activity throughout her 20-year career.

"I cannot even think of such an act," she said and added, "I always performed my duties with honesty and religious tolerance."

The inquiry committee includes Maulana Abdul Aziz, Maulana Zamir Ahmed Sajid, Maulana Muhammad Sharif, Maulana Sajid Naqvi, Principal of Commerce College, Ch. Muneer Ahmed and Principal of Margalla College, Farhat Mujtaba.

After examining the lessons of the Arabic book, the committee would give a final decision on whether or not the accused teacher committed blasphemy.

Following the incident, ʿulema representing Almi Majlis Tahafuz-e Khatam-e Nabuwat (AMTKN) had called for a protest demonstration on Monday. But after negotiations with senior officials of the district administration and FDE they withdrew the call and demanded suspension of the accused teacher, restoration of the teacher who had a quarrel with the accused and no action against the protesting students. The ʿulema had given the deadline of 2 p.m. to the district administration for the acceptance of their demands.

The ʿulema included Maulana Tajuddin Madni, Maulana Abdur Rashid, Qazi Ahsan Ahmed, Mufti Khalid Mir and Mufti Mahmood-ul-Hassan. Meanwhile, the inquiry committee submitted the initial report to the DG Federal Directorate of Education who later suspended the accused teacher. The classes were held according to routine. However, due to a tense situation, a heavy contingent of police was deployed around the college.

Quoted from http://www.nation.com.pk/daily/today/national/isb6.htm. Accessed October 29, 2001.

NOTES

PREFACE

1. At that time I was perhaps one of the very few PhDs from an American university and a likely candidate for the vice chancellorship of my university. The prospect caused fear, openly expressed in my presence by the majority seminary clerical faculty, in other words, the mullas of the university.

2. This madrassa along with several others was granted affiliation with Panjab University during Zia-ul-Haq's regime to validate the seminary diplomas.

3. See Jamal Malik, *The Colonization of Islam: Dissolution of Traditional Institutions in Pakistan* (New Delhi: Manohar, 1996).

4. Among the public in Pakistan it was a common joke that appointments to key positions in the country under the Sharif brothers, Nawaz Sharif (prime minister) and Shahbaz Sharif (chief minister of Panjab Province) were made on the recommendation of Mian Sharif, alias Abbaji (Daddy). Mian Sharif/Abbaji was a small-time owner of a steel factory with strong links with the Tablighi Jamaat, which proselytizes Islam. Later the business developed into the giant Ittefaq group. During General Zia-ul-Haq's regime, Mian Sharif/Abbaji reportedly bought influence with the general that enabled Mian Sharif to put up his sons, Nawaz and Shahbaz, in the political arena of Islamist politics. Now the brothers lead the right-wing Muslim League in the country. President Tarar had strong links to the Tablighi Jamaat and was a close associate of Mian Sharif/Abbaji.

5. For privacy the accuser's name is not used.

6. Furthermore, sensational insider stories about gross sexual, academic, and financial misconduct among the clerical elite at the university were continuously being published in a soap-opera style by the tabloid Urdu press in Islamabad. Foremost were the exploits of the dean of humanities, who was my supervisor. None of the stories was contradicted by either the university or the individuals themselves, nor was any legal action taken against the press that reported the stories. Also, a *dharna*, or sit-in, was organized outside the vice chancellor's office in which faculty members and administrators participated for several days. Daily reports of the dharna were communicated to the president's office, that is, to Mr. Tarar.

7. Hindi Kanhyalal, *Tarikh-e Lahore* (Lahore: Majlis-e Tariqi-e Adab, 1977; originally published 1884).

8. Documented in Shemeem Abbas, *The Female Voice in Sufi Ritual: Devotional Practices of Pakistan and India* (Austin: University of Texas Press, 2002).

9. Until 1973, when Ahmediyyas and Qadianis were declared non-Muslims in Zulfiqar 'Ali Bhutto's regime, intermarriage with that sect was acceptable. Bhutto buckled under the clerics to declare Ahmediyyas and Qadianis non-Muslims, although earlier, despite riots in the 1950s, previous governments including General Ayub Khan's had refused to give in to such pressure from the Jamaat-e Islami, an Islamist political party, to declare the Ahmediyyas non-Muslims.

CHAPTER 1

1. In 1983 Safia Bibi, a thirteen–year-old blind girl, reported after she became pregnant that she was raped by her employer and his son. She was convicted for *zina* (fornication),

and her rapists were acquitted. It was only after intense public protest and international pressure that she was released from prison on "her own bond." As reported in the *Calgary Herald* of October 26, 2011, during General Zia-ul-Haq's regime 15,000 rape victims were in jail "because they could not comply with the Islamic condition requiring them to have numerous male witnesses of their victimization." Another instance is that of Mukhtaran Mai, a woman of Muzzafargarh village in Pakistan; in 2002 she was gang-raped by men of the Mastoi clan for "honor revenge." The case dragged on for nine years in the High Court and the Supreme Court of the country while it also drew international publicity. In April 2011 the Supreme Court used the Hudood laws to give a verdict in favor of the accused, who were released for lack of evidence.

2. Despite some alterations under General Pervez Musharraf, these laws are in place even now. In 2006 General Musharraf reformed the ordinances to the Protection of Women Act with the Criminal Laws Amendment, which was signed into law to allow for cases of zina and rape to be tried only in the civil courts and not in the Islamic shari'a courts. The changes are minimal and cosmetic.

3. Taliban militants killed the dancer and singer Shabana in Mingora and threw her dead body into the Green Square for others to learn a lesson. Kushal Yousafzai, "Pakistan: Music Has Died in the Swat Valley," *Freemuse*, April 23, 2009, at http://www.free muse.org/sw33496.asp. Musicians and entertainers, according to the Taliban, are associated with sexual immorality and must therefore be punished under the Hudood laws.

4. Taseer's adult son was kidnapped after a court pronounced the death sentence upon the assailant, Malik Qadri. Taseer's son is still missing as this book goes to press. Taseer's assailant, Qadri, is a hero to many in the country, notably among right-wing attorneys.

5. Karen Armstrong, *Islam: A Short History* (New York: Modern Library, 2002).

6. Statistics here are derived from Ahmed Rashid, *Descent into Chaos: The U.S. and the Disaster in Pakistan, Afghanistan, and Central Asia* (New York: Penguin Books, 2009).

7. Tariq 'Ali, *The Duel: Pakistan on the Flight Path of American Power* (London: Scribner, 2008), 44.

8. For historical contexts and background read Armstrong's *Islam*.

9. As of this writing, two further opinions by South Asian scholars have been documented regarding British colonial agendas in creating the blasphemy laws in undivided India that were adopted to Chapter 15 of the Pakistan Penal Code under General Zia-ul-Haq. The first is in part 1 of Osama Siddiqui's interview in the *Harvard Law School Human Rights Journal* of November 11, 2011, in which the attorney talks about Jeremy Bentham and John Stuart Mills's utilitarianism that led to experimentation in India. In the nineteenth century British colonial administrators were dissatisfied with the prevalent laws in England and, adopting utilitarianism as a philosophy, were using India as a guinea pig to come up with a new set of laws to be eventually adopted in England. The blasphemy laws were among such experiments. At http://harvardhrj.com/2011/11/osama-siddique-interview -part-i/. The other view is found in Asad 'Ali Ahmed, "Specters of Macaulay: Blasphemy, the Indian Penal Code, and Pakistan's Postcolonial Predicament," in *Censorship in South Asia: Cultural Regulation From Sedition to Seduction*, ed. Raminder Kaur and William Mazzarella (Bloomington: Indiana University Press, 2009), 172–205.

10. See the DVD of writer-director Gillo Pontecorvo's 1967 film *The Battle of Algiers* with actors Brahim Hadjadj, Jean Martin, Yacef Saadi, and Samia Kerbash. Criterion Collection DVD, 2004.

11. Discourse derived from Sayyid al-Qutb's writings emphasizes the divide between the "believers" (Muslims) and the "infidels," or enemies of Islam.

12. Fortunately, in January 2010 the Supreme Court of Bangladesh forbade any political party to use the prefix "Islamic" and restricted campaigning based on religion, in a move toward returning the constitution to its secular origins. Women Living Under Muslim Laws, "Dhaka Court Bans Use of Religion in Politics," reprinted from *Dawn* (by AFP), January 5, 2010, in (Shirkat Gah) *Newsheet* 22, no. 1 (March 2010): 1. http://www.shirkatgah.org/publications/Newsheet-2010-03-05.pdf.

13. See Ahmed Rashid, *Taliban: Militant Islam, Oil, and Fundamentalism in Central Asia* (New Haven, CT: Yale University Press, 2000). See also Fawzia Afzal-Khan, *Lahore with Love: Growing Up with Girlfriends Pakistani-Style* (Syracuse, NY: Syracuse University Press, 2010), an excellent memoir of this activist about her adolescent years in Zia-ul-Haq's Pakistan. With regard to the deepening Islamization of government, Afzal-Khan gives details of both Zia-ul-Haq's and Zulfiqar 'Ali Bhutto's tampering with the constitution of the country that led to the excommunication of the Ahmediyya from the fold of Islam in Pakistan. I include her contemporaries Khawar Mumtaz and Farida Shaheed, the founders of Shirkat Gah, a nonprofit organization for women's rights, in the bibliography as well; Khawar Mumtaz and Farida Shaheed, eds., *Women in Pakistan* (London: Zed, 1987). Many valuable source materials in this book were graciously provided by the Shirkat Gah Resource Center in Karachi. Women activists and scholars have been in the forefront of advocating against Pakistan's blasphemy laws as well as the Hudood ordinances against women.

14. For the same reasons, until I left my position at the Open University in Islamabad in 1999, I was always a trusted academic for the selection board at the International Islamic University in the capital, Islamabad.

15. Ironically, the same poet, Allama Muhammad Iqbal, received a blasphemy fatwa, a religious injunction from the clerics, in the 1930s for his poem "Shikwa" (Complaint). The poem was man's complaint to God for the loss of Muslim prestige, perhaps a reference to the loss of the Ottoman lands. As a reconciliation gesture toward the clerics the poet wrote "Javab-e Shikwa" (God's Response to Man's Complaint). The fatwa at that time did not carry a nonbailable arrest warrant or a death sentence. It only meant social and spiritual isolation; such was the power of the mullas even then.

16. See SherAli Tareen's excellent reference about the satellite networks for the Dars-e Nizami madrassa system not only in Pakistan but also in Bangladesh, the Caribbean, South Africa, Britain, and the United States. SherAli Tareen, "The Deoband Madrassa," in *Oxford Bibliographies* (n.d.). http://www.oxfordbibliographiesonline.com/view/document/obo-9780195390155/obo-9780195390155-0019.xml.

17. As chair of the Department of English Language and Applied Linguistics I attended two special-interest-group meetings of the Dars-e Nizami in my university around 1998. Since the dean of my faculty was a mulla, I was eventually dropped from the group, as the mullas were not comfortable with my secular input or my objections to any appropriation of my department's courses.

18. The Prophet never had a revelation on blasphemy, and neither is there any material as such in the Qur'an.

19. This reason was boasted to the faculty in meetings by the dean of humanities and the dean of education. These deans were overtly members of the Islamic militant parties Sipah-e Sahaba and Jamaat-e Islami, respectively.

20. A woman professor of chemistry at Panjab University in Lahore who is my personal friend spoke frankly about the mulla hegemony at the university that politicians supported, including her own husband, who was then a minister for state in the Nawaz Sharif government. She asserted this in her husband's presence.

21. An inspector of the FIA visited me in my office about this time in 1998, before the blasphemy charge was leveled against me. He wanted to know what I was doing at the Institute of Folk Heritage and socializing with the Korean ambassador and his wife. The FIA followed me, as a female official, to make sure I was not fornicating. In the end, when the agency wallas and their clerical cohorts got exasperated at not being able to frame me under zina or Hudood laws, they had only the blasphemy charge to level against me.

22. This question still remains uncovered. We know the Pakistani agencies, but really it was a covert operation. This is one of the questions in the book. It is not simple and is asked here as an exploration.

23. Mukhtaran Mai, the village woman whose case is described above, was gang-raped during Nawaz Sharif's regime of 1998, and Dr. Shazia Manzur was gang-raped during General Musharraf's regime in 2005. The perpetrators are at large, as the Hudood ordinances give them total protection with the clause requiring four adult Muslim male witnesses. Likewise, Zahra Kazemi, an Iranian-born Canadian journalist, was thrown into jail in Iran in 2003 for taking photos of student protests. According to Shirin Ebadi, Kazemi was gang-raped and killed in jail under suspicious assault circumstances. Shirin Ebadi, *Iran Awakening: A Memoir of Revolution and Hope* (New York: Random House, 2006), 199. The present Iranian ayatollahs also have practices in place whereby virgin female victims condemned to death must be raped, the rapist paying the equivalent of five dollars as the bride price to prevent a virgin from going to paradise. According to Islamic belief, a virgin is promised a place in paradise on death; thus, to prevent this from happening and ensure that the accused go to hell, the ayatollahs created a law that condemned virgins be raped before their executions. "Prison Guards Marry and Rape Virgins before Executions," video uploaded to YouTube April 11, 2010, by MDSTVUSA and text attributed to *Fox News* (July 21, 2009) and *Jerusalem Post*, http://www.youtube.com /watch?v=KQTod8Q_R10. In Pakistan the blasphemy laws and the Hudood Ordinances are a double whammy against women; if the state cannot get women under one set of ordinances, it has the instruments to get them through another, as I experienced.

24. See Aitzaz Ahsan, *The Indus Saga and the Making of Pakistan* (Karachi: Oxford University Press, 1996); and Ayesha Jalal, *Partisans of Allah: Jihad in South Asia*, Cambridge, MA: Harvard University Press, 2008.

25. Jalal, *Partisans of Allah*.

26. The 1972 Hamoodur Rehman Commission Report was a classified document that was declassified in 2000 under General Musharraf. Parts of it that documented some of the military atrocities were leaked to the Indian and Pakistani press in 2000.

27. Personal interview with a Pakistani woman medical doctor in 2009. She is absolutely devoted to these sessions in which Saudi-trained *mu'allimas* like Farhat Hashemi propagate the "correct" Wahabi Islam and the textual Qur'anic interpretation. Defense Housing Societies are elite neighborhoods where officials associated with the defense services in Pakistan own land allotted to them by the state.

28. See Fatima Mernissi, *Dreams of Trespass: Tales of a Harem Girlhood* (New York: Perseus Books, 1995).

29. In summer 2007 I had the opportunity to drop off some female associates at one of these parties that were adequately protected with military security arrangements.

30. The Wahabi influx of Islam in South Asia is also in part a result of the large numbers of Pakistani, Indian, and Afghan expatriates working in the Gulf states such as Saudi Arabia. The trend to export Pakistani labor to the Gulf started during Z. A. Bhutto's re-

gime with the creation of an Overseas Pakistani Foundation that channeled the country's manpower abroad.

31. *Khatam-e Nabuvat* is a slogan of the Islamic parties in Pakistan that means prophecy was finalized with the death of the Prophet Muhammad and there would be no prophet after Muhammad.

32. A farshi salam bow is made with one hand raised to the forehead.

33. For complete contexts see Mumtaz and Shaheed; Women Living Under Muslim Laws, *Fatwas against Women in Bangladesh* (1996), http://www.wluml.org/sites/wluml.org/files/import/english/pubs/pdf/misc/fatwa-bangladesh-eng.pdf; Hina Jilani, "Law as an Instrument of Social Control," in *Locating the Self: Perspectives on Women and Multiple Identities*, ed. Nighat Said Khan, Rubina Saigol, and Afiya Shehrbano Zia (Lahore: ASR, 1994); Joanna Liddle and Rama Joshi, *Daughters of Independence* (London: Zed, 1986); Rashida Patel, *Islamization of Laws in Pakistan* (Karachi: Faiza, 1986); Ahmed Rashid, *Taliban: Islam, Oil, and the New Great Game in Central Asia* (London: Tauris, 2000); Rashid, *Descent into Chaos.*

34. The Islamic Religious Police in Afghanistan who enforce "Islamic" punishments on citizens is a ditto of the *mutuaweens*, religious police who carry sticks in their hands and are visible on the Riyadh streets. I was reprimanded by one as I lifted my veil to see where I was walking. *Hisba*, the implementation of a near-Calvinist Islam for public morality, has been in demand in Pakistan's northwestern frontier, now Pakhtunkhwa (bordering Afghanistan), by the Islami parties. If not through the state legislature, then by weapons, the mullas keep the citizens terrorized. I encountered one such stick-carrying cleric terrifying females in a women's bazaar in the Anarkali neighborhood of Lahore and shouting at them to cover their heads. This was in 1998. I encountered something similar in the same bazaar in 1980, at the peak of Zia-ul-Haq's Islamization.

35. I was personally affected by the Law of Evidence when in 1994 a clerk at the Capital Development Authority in Islamabad insisted that I bring my *mehram*, my male caretaker, to verify the sale deed of an estate that I was registering. I was fifty-one years old then. As recently as 2008, when I was renewing my national identity card called the NICOP, the head of the division at NADRA (the National Database and Registration Authority) that handles these matters insisted that I send a male family member with an identity card or a male colleague to witness the application form at the office in Islamabad. I had to arrange the male witnesses from New York to represent me in Islamabad. The official would not have it any other way. As I attest in this book, the Talibanization of the Pakistani bureaucracy is subtle and pernicious. With such sly application of practices resulting from the Law of Evidence or Qanun-e Shahadat, I fear that the time is not far when Pakistani women will have to show male guardians' approval to leave the country, a practice Saudi Arabia follows.

36. See W. Montgomery Watt, *Muhammad at Medina* (Karachi: Oxford University Press, 2006), 221–249.

CHAPTER 2

1. See also William Shepard, *Introducing Islam* (New York: Routledge, 2009).

2. Barnaby Rogerson, *Prophet Muhammad: A Biography* (London: Abacus, 2003).

3. Syed Abu A'la Maududi, trans., *The Holy Qu'ran*, Arabic and English (Lahore: Islamic Publications, 1981).

4. 'Abdullah Yusuf 'Ali, trans., *The Meaning of the Holy Qur'an*, 9th edition (Beltsville, MD: Amana, 1997).

5. Muslims believe that Abraham and his son Ishmael built the Ka'aba; Ishmael's mother was Hagar. The hajj ritual symbolizes Hagar's search for water as Ishmael cried for water and she ran between Mounts Saffa and Marwah. The Zam Zam Spring sprouted where the infant Ishmael beat his heels from thirst. The sacrificial ram that substituted Ishmael, whom Abraham was directed in a dream to sacrifice, is ritually celebrated by Muslims around the world through sacrificing an animal after hajj. In the centuries following Abraham, the Ka'aba became a rallying place where Arab tribes in the region met to negotiate trade and politics. It also housed male and female deities. The Ka'aba's guardianship was a coveted role that the tribes took in turn through elections. Both the Beni Hashem and the Beni Ommaya competed for Ka'aba's guardianship. Muhammmad's paternal grandfather held the guardianship of the Ka'aba for some time.

6. Rogerson, 21.

7. Ibid., 17, 23, 57, 58, and index listings.

8. 'Abdullah Yusuf 'Ali, 1738 and index listings under "Gardens of Paradise."

9. Rogerson, 72.

10. Syed Amir 'Ali, *The Spirit of Islam: A History of the Evolution and Ideals of Islam, with a Life of the Prophet* (New Delhi: Kitab Bhavan, 2000; originally published 1922), 10.

11. Rogerson, 93.

12. Emphasis mine. I owe the selection to Nazir Ahmad, *Qur'anic and Non-Qur'anic Islam* (Islamabad: Vanguard Books, 1997), 32. It is Sura al-A'raf, 7–158, as translated by 'Abdullah Yusuf 'Ali, 391. In his commentary on the same page 'Abdullah Yusuf 'Ali explains as follows. 1) Muhammad was not literate, "yet he was full of the highest wisdom and knowledge of previous Scriptures." 2) He was not tutored in a "school" of thought. His message was clear, bold, and from a clean slate. 3) The pagan Arabs, pre-Islam, were "unlettered" and so was the Prophet. 'Ali's argument in his commentary is that they were versed in orality, including the Prophet himself.

13. 'Abdullah Yusuf 'Ali comments (389), "In the reflex of the *Tawrah* as now accepted by the Jews, Moses says: 'The Lord thy God will raise unto thee a Prophet from the midst of thee, of thy brethren, like unto me'" (Deuteronomy 18:15). The Jewish people are from Abraham's son Isaac, the Muslims from Abraham's son Ishmael, born of Hagar. "In the reflex of the Gospel as now accepted by the Christians, Christ promised another Comforter (John 14:16)."

14. Muhammad's grandfather, by tribal custom, had several wives. Abu Lahab was a step-uncle.

15. Sura al-Masad (The Plaited Rope); Sura al-Lahab (The Flame) III: 1–5. 'Abdullah Yusuf 'Ali, 1712.

16. "Father of Flames" was Abu Lahab's nickname. He was a sworn enemy of early Islam. "Fire" is also a reference to the hereafter. Abu Lahab died a week after the first battle the Prophet fought for Islam, the Battle of Badr. Many of the Prophet's enemies perished in that battle. Badr was the first battle the Prophet waged against the Quraysh after he left Mecca and migrated to the sanctuary of Medina, where the tribes invited him to come in order to arbitrate their disputes. Map 2.2 shows the battle sites and dates. Sura al-Lahab also refers to Abu Lahab's wife. She would tie bundles of thorns plaited in ropes made from palm leaves and deposit them in the Prophet's path at night. Metaphorically,

she carried a burden of hate around her neck, and "to carry wood as fuel" also means that she carried tales that spread like fire.

17. Mohammad Asrar Madani, *Verdict of Islamic Law on Blasphemy and Apostasy* (Lahore: Idara-e Islamiat, 1994). Madani uses other Qur'anic verses to justify blasphemy laws. The verses cited here are selections influenced by Nazir Ahmad, who is against the blasphemy laws. I have used Madani for specificity.

18. As chief of the Beni Ommaya, Abu Sufyan fought against the Prophet in the Battle of Badr, Battle of Ohud, Battle of the Trench, and finally the assault of Mecca that led to the city's capitulation with Abu Sufyan's and the Meccan tribes' conversion to Islam. Later, his son Ma'uviya fought with the Prophet's son-in-law 'Ali ibn Abi Talib. Ma'uviya's son Yezid dealt a fatal blow to the Prophet's grandson Hussein at Karbala. Another grandson, Hassan, was quietly poisoned, some believe. The conflict between Muhammad's family and the Ommayas was an ongoing conflict resulting in two fitnas, or schisms, in Islam and was the basis of the Sunni-Shi'a rift that continues to this day.

19. In Rogerson, 153.

20. 'Abdullah Yusuf 'Ali, 1751.

21. Maududi, *Holy Qur'an*, 185–247.

22. References to the poets are derived from Madani, who cites various hadith (92). Albeit militant in interpretation, he has an endless list of names of male and female poets (92–149). Syed Amir 'Ali in *The Spirit of Islam* mentions some of the same names. Interestingly, Madani's work is a response to Salman Rushdie's *Satanic Verses*, Madani calls Rushdie's book a fitna and justifies the fatwa of death against Rushdie.

23. Madani, 100.

24. Follow the CD recording by Muhammad Amman, *Arabie Saoudite: La tradition du Hejaz* (OCRA, Radio France, Paris 2001, 7 94881 66032 2). One of the songs on the CD, "Ya ahl al-hawa" (People of Passion), translates thus: "O men of passion, I want to talk to you / Yesterday, this seductress of an unparalleled beauty spent the night with me / she honored my apartments, leaving her perfume everywhere / After knocking at my door, she said: Peace be on you / I said: And on you too, oh essence of sugar! / I said: My passion in declaring itself had dried me out / And: union is a miracle for the afflicted / She said: yes that's true. Then laughed / And got up at break of dawn."

25. I am indebted to Nazir Ahmad for these selections from *Qur'anic and Non-Qur'anic Islam*, 93.

26. Sura al-Qalam, 68–1, 2; Sura al-Mu'minun 23–60. "Nun" is a consonant in the Qur'an.

27. Rogerson, 146.

28. Madani and others. One can find a great deal of hate literature of this kind written in Urdu in bookstores in the inner cities in Pakistan.

29. Syed Amir 'Ali, *Spirit of Islam*, 59.

30. Ibid. Also see Rogerson.

31. In Syed Amir 'Ali, *A Short History of the Saracens: Being a Concise Account of the Rise and Decline of the Saracenic Power* (New Delhi: Kitab Bhavan, 2001; original 1926), 15.

32. My research revealed that after the Battle of Khaybar against the Jewish tribes, the eventual ownership of the Fadak orchard that had belonged to the Jews became Muhammad's share of war booty. It is a major theme in Shi'a protest discourse, as upon Muhammad's demise the orchard did not pass to his daughter Fatima and her husband,

'Ali ibn Abi Talib, as was expected. The caliphs, Muhammad's viceregents known as the Caliphate-e Rashidun (the Pious Ones), argued that since Muhammad was the state, the orchard should devolve back to the state. In later events control of the Fadak orchard was a source of dissent between Muhammad's descendants and the caliphate. The legacy of Fadak played a formidable role in the first fitna and the second fitna in Islam. As such, in Shi'a literature extensive material exists with reference to Fadak that makes for ideological differences between Shi'a and Sunni Islam.

The Fadak theme is kept alive in Shi'a oral rituals during Muharram and in communal settings. No Shi'a child is kept ignorant of the caliphate that followed Muhammad. Fadak's usurpation is a major theme. In fact, the Shi'a claim that Muhammad's daughter Fatima died from a miscarriage when the caliphate's minions forcibly knocked down the entrance door to the house demanding 'Ali's oath of fealty to the caliph. The child who died was named Mohsen, a popular name among the Shi'a.

33. Rogerson, 208–209. Here in the last sermon, Rogerson cites Muhammad as saying, "Oh my people, no prophet or apostle will come after me and no new faith will be born."

34. Armstrong, 26. In support one can say that the Islamic *kalima* or Shahada that every Muslim child is required to recite as her initiation into the faith and is chanted into every infant's ear at the time of her birth besides the *azan* (call to prayer) is "La illa ha il Allah, Muhammad ur Rasul Allah" (There is no God but God and Muhammad is his messenger). The Shahada is only an affirmation of the faith.

35. Denis Spellberg, *Politics, Gender, and the Islamic Past: The Legacy of 'Aisha bint Abi Bakr* (New York: Columbia University Press, 1994).

36. Syed Amir 'Ali reports in *A Short History of the Saracens*, 51–52, that as the battle was being lost, Ma'uviya ordered his troops to raise Qur'ans on their swords in order to seek peace. This was on advice from Amr al-Aas. 'Ali's troops refused to fight, seeing the Qur'ans on swords. Abu Musa represented 'Ali and Amr al-Aas represented Ma'uviya in an arbitration.

37. It was several centuries later that Muhammad bin 'Abd al-Wahab arose from around this same region to give a very basic Calvinist form of Islam that is now Wahabism and that the Taliban and al-Qaeda groups uphold to be the only Islam. All other sects of Islam accordingly are heretical and need to be brought within the fold, and non-Muslims are kafirs, infidels, who must either be brought within the fold or exterminated.

38. Although Abu Sufyan and his wife Hind did convert to Islam, the tribal animosity was never resolved between the Hashemites and Ommayas. Ommaya hegemony passed from Abu Sufyan to Ma'uviya and then to his son Yezid. Ma'uviya established himself as governor of Damascus through the caliph 'Usman.

CHAPTER 3

1. Fatima Mernissi, *The Veil and the Male Elite: A Feminist Interpretation of Women's Rights in Islam* (New York: Perseus Books, 1992); Wael Hallaq, *The Origins and Evolution of Islamic Law* (New York: Cambridge University Press, 2005), 36; Moulavi Cheragh 'Ali, *The Proposed Political, Legal, and Social Reforms under Moslem Rule* (Bombay: Education Society's Press, Byculla, 1883; reproduced in Google Digitized Books Online, 2009). All these are texts that I have used to teach my classes on Islam and have found useful.

2. Hallaq, *Origins and Evolution*, 36; Cheragh 'Ali. Moulavi Cheragh 'Ali (1844–

1895) was a modern reformist Muslim scholar who worked closely with Sir Syed Ahmed Khan; he later moved to Hyderabad Deccan, where he worked in the administration of the Nizam of Hyderabad. Khan recommended him for appointment as translator for the prime minister of Hyderabad state in India. I am using some of the nineteenth-century Muslim scholars to uphold my arguments, as they represent the moderate South Asian Islam that the majority of people follow in the region.

3. Ayesha Siddiqa, "Many Readings of *Shariʿa*," *Dawn*, April 3, 2009.

4. Cheragh ʿAli, xix. Also see the abridged edition of Louis Massignon's study, *Hallaj: Mystic and Martyr*, ed. and trans. Herbert Mason (Princeton, NJ: Princeton University Press, 1982). I cite my own investigation (see chapter 5) of Mansur al-Hallaj's trial under the ʿAbbasids in Baghdad, which strengthens the argument that Muhammad's name was used inappropriately as a justification for a political end.

5. Inferred from Emine Ekin Tusalp's study "Treating Outlaws and Registering Miscreants in Early Ottoman Society: A Study on the Legal Diagnosis of Deviance in Seyhulislam Fatwas" (master's thesis, Sabanci University, Istanbul, 2005); and from Devin J. Stewart, "The Ottoman Execution of Zayn al-Din al-ʿAmili," (Brill) *Die Welt des Islams* 48 (2008): 289–347. Zayn al-Din al-ʿAmili (d. 1558) was a Twelver Shiʿa jurist who was executed by the Ottomans.

6. Mernissi, *Veil*, 36, citing Mohammed Tabari, *Muhammad, Sceau des prophètes*, trans. Herman Zotenberg (Paris: Sinbad, 1980), 352, and Ibn-Hisham, *Al-Sira al nabawiya* (Beirut: Dar Ihyaʾ al-Tharwa al-ʿArabi, n.d.), vol. 4, p. 314.

7. Mernissi, *Veil*, 36–37, citing Muhammad Abu Zahra, *Malik* (Cairo: Dar al-Fikr al-ʿArabi, n.d.), 146.

8. Omar said of Abu Hurayra, "We have many things to say, but we are afraid to say them, and that man here has no restraint." In Mernissi, *Veil*, 79, citing al-Asqalani, *Isaba*, vol. 7, 440.

9. Maududi, *Short History*, 32.

10. In Mernissi, *Veil*, 47, quoting Taha Husayn, *Fi al-adab al-jahili*, 10th edition (Cairo: Dar al Maʾarif, 1969), 149–150. Taha Husayn was a progressive Egyptian intellectual and university professor who in 1926 was convicted of apostasy for his work *Fi al-shiʿr al-jahili*. The work cited here by way of Mernissi, *Fi al-adab al-jahili*, was written to appease the religious establishment (ʿulema), though the progressive, secular message is still couched in the work.

11. Muhammad Abid al-Jabiri (b. 1936) is a Moroccan intellectual, writer, and professor of Arab and Islamic philosophy who has written extensively about the Islamic world's difficulties with navigating tradition and modernity.

12. In Mernissi, *Veil*, 16, citing al-Jabiri, *Taqwin alʿaql*, vol. 1 (1984), 63.

13. Based on Mernissi, *Veil*.

14. Shirin Ebadi in *Iran Awakening* cites examples when the judge repeatedly accused her of being un-Islamic for questioning seventh-century Arab tribal laws (118). Others lost jobs (52).

15. Mernissi, *Veil*, 36, citing Muhammad Abu Zahra, *Malik*, 146.

16. A pertinent example is in the instances that both the Shiʿa and the Sunni cite as indications of the Prophet's nomination of his successor: the Shiʿa cite the hadith "Mun kunto maula fa ʿAli un maula" (Whoever accepts me as a master, ʿAli is his master too) at Qom Ghadir, where the Prophet expressed his desire for the Arab tribes to choose ʿAli as his successor. Qom Ghadir was a spot where the Prophet rested on his way back from

his last *hajj* (pilgrimage). The Sunni, on the other hand, cite the example of the Prophet nominating his father-in-law Abu Bekr (his wife 'A'isha's father) to lead the prayers when he was too ill to do so himself as proof of the Prophet's intention for Abu Bekr to succeed him in the spiritual leadership of his Islamic community (ummah).

17. See appendix 2 for text of Pakistan's main blasphemy laws.

18. Siddiqui and Hayat state that the status of Ahmediyya-Qadiani citizens is that of non-Muslims in Pakistan's constitution. Osama Siddiqui and Zahra Hayat, "Unholy Laws and Holy Speech: Blasphemy Laws in Pakistan—Controversial Origins, Design Defects and Free Speech Implications," *Minnesota Journal of International Law* 17 (Spring 2008): 312.

19. *New York Times*, May 29, 2010.

20. See appendix 4 for highlights of the Hudood laws against women.

21. From my discussions with members of the Institute for International Education in New York in fall 2005.

22. For greater detail read Ahmed Rashid's *Taliban: Militant Islam, Oil, and Fundamentalism in Central Asia.*

23. Mernissi, *Veil*, 10.

24. Mernissi, *Veil*, 37, citing al-Tabari, *Muhammad, Sceau des prophètes*, 352, and Ibn Hisham, *Sira*, vol. 4, p. 314.

25. Mernissi, *Veil*, 39.

26. Mernissi, *Veil*, 56, citing al-Tabari, *Tarikh al-unam wa al-muluk* (Beirut: Dar al-Fikr, 1979), vol. 5, p. 179.

27. Eventually, the caliphate became dynastic and monarchical, as we find now in the Gulf region and earlier with the Ommayas and the 'Abbasids. However, Islam does not permit a *malkiat* (monarchy), going by the Prophet's precedent. Is the monarchy, then, a bid'a, an innovation against Islam, and therefore a heresy? My discussion here is based on Muhammad Khalid Masud, *Iqbal's Reconstruction of Ijtihad* (Lahore: Iqbal Academy, 1995). Militant Islamists worldwide now have a dream of the caliphate that they claim will resurrect the Prophet's Islamic community.

28. See appendix 2 for text of the blasphemy laws and appendix 4 for details of Hudood law Qanun-e Shahadat (Law of Evidence) against women.

29. Iftikhar Malik, *Jihad, Hindutva, and the Taliban: South Asia at the Crossroads* (Karachi: Oxford University Press, 2005).

30. Mernissi, *Veil*, 5.

31. Ibid.

32. Pakistan section mine. Then Mernissi, *Veil*, 4, citing 'Abdallah Ibn Sulayman 'Arafa, *Huquq al-mar'a fi al Islam*, 3rd edition (Al Maktab al-Islami, 1980), 149. Mernissi refers to 'Arafa's work as a "recent book."

33. Shi'a argue that 'Ali ought to have become the first caliph, as he was Muhammad's adopted son as well as his son-in-law, married to his daughter Fatima. Also, he was a Hashemite like the Prophet. The Sunni argue that Abu Bekr ('A'isha's father), who became Muhammad's immediate viceregent, was chosen for his age, being one of the most senior Companions of the Prophet. As noted earlier, the Sunni back this claim by Muhammad's appointment of Abu Bekr to lead the community in prayers when the Prophet himself was gravely ill.

34. Mernissi, *Veil*, 5–6.

35. Ibid., 6.

36. Ibid., ix.

37. Check YouTube postings regarding General Pervez Musharraf's regime.

38. Shepard; Fazlur Rahman, *Islam* (Chicago: University of Chicago Press, 2002).

39. Hallaq, *Origins and Evolution*, 4.

40. Ibid., 18–21.

41. Ibid., 3.

42. Mona Eltahawy, "Egypt's Sexist Divorce Laws Blamed Not on Islam, but on Men," *Guardian*, February 22, 2000. http://www.guardian.co.uk/world/2000/feb/23/4.

43. Hallaq, *Origins and Evolution*, 18–21.

44. ʿAbdullah Yusuf ʿAli, Sura 30-31: 1065–1066.

45. Also see Qur'an, 4:32 and 9:71, cited in Khaled Abou El Fadl, *The Great Theft: Wrestling Islam from the Extremists* (San Francisco: HarperCollins, 2007), 308.

46. During Zia-ul-Haq's regime, the Muslim Family Ordinance that General Ayub Khan had put into place in 1961 abolishing "unmitigated polygamy" was quietly ignored. As a result several senior army officers took on second wives who were younger women. Some of my male associates in Pakistan's military circles took advantage of the laxity in the Ayub Khan ordinance; several of them, especially those in the medical corps, married nurses, perhaps to ensure that these women would take care of them; these officers kept their first wives as well in separate homes.

47. Hallaq, *Origins and Evolution*, 19–25, citing Muhammad Ibn Hazm, *Muʾjam al-Fiqh* (Damascus: Matbaʿat Jamiʿat Dimashq, 1966), vol. 2, pp. 838–839.

48. One of my Pakistani female friends reports that even the families of clerics are happy to marry their daughters to soldiers in the Pakistani military, as they say that in case of an eventuality their daughters will be the sole beneficiaries because of Angrez ka Qa-nun, the English law. Under Sunni Islamic law a widow receives only one-eighth of her husband's inheritance.

49. Hallaq, *Origins and Evolution*, 33. This is perhaps also the beginning of the tak-fir infidel ideology wherein the Shiʿa supporters of ʿAli ibn Abi Talib were branded as heretics.

50. Ibid., 52.

51. Ibid., 40.

52. Ibid., 43.

53. Ibid., 54.

54. Ibid., 57–78.

55. Ibid., 63–64.

56. Ibid., 64.

57. Ibid., 167.

58. Dr. Zainal Azam B. Abd Rahman, senior fellow and director of the Center for Sya-riah, Law, and Political Science, Institul Kafahaman Islam, Malaysia (IKIM), 1992–2009. Web page downloaded July 15, 2009. I only take the definition of "Haquq-Allah" from it. The application is my own per my study of Sura al-Lahab in the Holy Qur'an.

59. El Fadl, *Great Theft*, 45–46.

60. Ibid.

61. Amir ʿAli, *Spirit of Islam*, 291.

62. Ibid., 291–292, citing Shahristani, *Kitab al Milal wa al-Nihal.* Abd al Karim al-Shahristani (1086–1153) was an influential Persian historian of religion and heresiographer.

63. Ibid.

64. Ibid., 293.

65. Ibid.

66. Ibid.

67. Ibid.

68. Natana J. DeLong-Bas, "Wahabism and the Question of Religious Tolerance," in *Religion and Politics in Saudi Arabia: Wahabism and the State*, ed. Mohammad Ayoob and Hasan Kosebalaban (Boulder, CO: Lynne Rienner, 2009), 11–21.

69. El Fadl, *Great Theft*, 62.

70. The consequential "Islamic" laws of politics in the region are further discussed in Ahmed Rashid's *Taliban: Militant Islam, Oil, and Fundamentalism in Central Asia*. Also see Rashid's *Descent into Chaos*.

71. DeLong-Bas, 11–21.

72. BBC Urdu News reported July 26, 2009, that Maulana Sufi Muhammad of the Tehrik-e Nifaz e Shari'a in Swat said both democracy and the legal system in Pakistan are kufr, blasphemy. This was after none of the self-declared Islamic parties in that area won the vote because a majority of Swat citizens voted for the secular Awami National Party in 2008.

73. These three news sources give examples: Pervez Amirali Hoodbhoy, "Towards Theocracy?" (India) *Frontline*, March 14–27, 2009; Akbar S. Ahmed, "Pakistan's Blasphemy Law: Words Fail Me," *Washington Post*, May 19, 2002; and Tariq Rahman, "Pluralism and Intolerance in Pakistani Society: Attitudes of Pakistani Students towards the Religious 'Other,'" 2007, at http://www.tariqrahman.net.

74. 'Ali Eteraz, "Pakistan Is Already an Islamic State," *Dissent*, April 30, 2009.

75. Benazir Bhutto promised both times before she was elected as prime minister that she would do away with the Hudood ordinances against women, but she remained inactive on the issue. At least Musharraf did something about the laws in 2006 so they would be dealt with by civil courts and not shari'a courts.

76. In *Dawn*, Independence Day Supplement, August 14, 1999, transcribed from printed copy by Shehzaad Nakhoda.

77. Naeem Shakir, "Pakistan: The Blasphemy Law in Pakistan and Its Impact," (Asian Human Rights Commission) *Human Rights Solidarity* 9, no. 7 (July 1999).

78. Eteraz, "Pakistan," n.p.

79. Ibid.

80. See Pontecorvo's film *The Battle of Algiers*.

81. Eteraz, "Pakistan."

82. Ibid. Under pressure from the Islamic parties, similar discrimination was initiated against the Ahmediyyas in Indonesia and Malaysia. Hodri Ariev, Ratno Lukito, and C. Holland Taylor, principal authors, *Illusion of an Islamic State: How an Alliance of Moderates Launched a Successful Jihad against Radicalization and Terrorism in the World's Largest Muslim-Majority Country*, ed. Abdurrahman Wahid (Winston-Salem, NC: LibForAll Foundation Press, 2011). The book, first published in Indonesia in 2009, "helped stem the tide of the Muslim Brotherhood's political ambitions in Indonesia," according to a "product description" at Amazon.com.

83. Eteraz, "Pakistan."

84. Ibid. See also Women Living Under Muslim Laws, *Fatwas against Women in Bangladesh* (1996), at http://www.wluml.org/sites/wluml.org/files/import/english/pubs/pdf/misc/fatwa-bangladesh-eng.pdf.

85. Nazir Ahmad, 96.

86. Freedom House, *Saudi Publications on Hate Ideology Fill American Mosques* (Washington, DC: Center for Religious Freedom, 2005). http://www.freedomhouse.org.

87. Ibid., 4.

88. Ibid., 28.

89. Ibid., 21.

90. Ibid., 57.

91. Cheragh 'Ali, 21–24.

92. El Fadl, *Great Theft*, 83.

CHAPTER 4

1. Osama Siddiqui and Zahra Hayat, "Unholy Laws and Holy Speech: Blasphemy Laws in Pakistan—Controversial Origins, Design Defects, and Free Speech Implications," *Minnesota Journal of International Law* 17, no. 2 (Spring 2008): 303–385.

2. Indian Penal Code, Act 45 of 1860 (Krishen Lal and Co., Law Publishers, 1929), cited in Siddiqui and Hayat, 335–385. Regarding Macaulay's penal code in British India see David Gilmour, *The Ruling Caste: Imperial Lives in the Victorian Raj* (New York: Farrar, Straus, Giroux, 2005), 123–134. Macaulay's penal code is the infrastructure for Zia-ul-Haq's "Islamic" blasphemy laws. Zia-ul-Haq tried to resurrect Muhammadan law as it was prior to British law. Also see Asad 'Ali Ahmed, "Specters of Macaulay."

3. Indian Penal Code at 1322, in Siddiqui and Hayat, 327.

4. Indian Penal Code at 1324, in Siddiqui and Hayat, 338. Italics in original except where noted otherwise.

5. Indian Penal Code at 1341–1342, in Siddiqui and Hayat, 338.

6. Indian Penal Code at 1328, in Siddiqui and Hayat, 338.

7. Pakistan's present blasphemy laws have replaced "his Majesty's subjects" with "the citizens of Pakistan" by Adaptation Order 1961, article 2 (with effect from March 23, 1956). Siddiqui and Hayat, 338.

8. Ibid.

9. In a 2002 case, Justice 'Ali Nawaz Chohan affirmed, "Historically speaking these laws were enacted by the British to protect the religious sentiments of the Muslim minorities in the subcontinent before partition against the Hindu majority." In Siddiqui and Hayat, 337.

10. The text of the speech is derived from Durab Patel, "Blasphemy Law and Fundamental Rights II," cited in *The Blasphemy Law: From Ordinance to Murder*, ed. Felix Qasir G.M. Amritsari (Karachi: Idara-e Amn-O Insaf, 1994), 196–198. Sharif also appeared eager to please the Saudis, who later gave him asylum when he was charged in a terrorist court for trying to divert General Musharraf's plane and thus conspiring to kill him.

11. Ibid. Dr. Farooq Sajjad was the son of one of the leaders of the Jamaat-e Islami, a fundamentalist party. Dr. Sajjad had supported a change in Section 295-B and 295-C of the blasphemy laws. In 1994 he was beaten with sticks, and reportedly his body was burned while he was still alive.

12. Siddiqui and Hayat, 340, citing Muhammad Mazhar Hussain Nizami, *The Pakistan Penal Code with Commentary 269* (All Pakistan Legal Decisions, 1974).

13. Ibid., 343, citing the FIR as posted by Rationalist International at http://www.rationalistinternational.net/Shaikh/fir_dr_shaikh.htm.

14. The British colonists structured Pakistan's judicial system as follows. Cases are first

tried on the local, district level in the sessions court. Subject to the outcome, plaintiffs can take their cases to the High Court. Each of the four provinces in the country—Sind, Pakhtun<u>kh</u>wa, Balochistan, and Panjab—has a High Court in its capital, respectively: Karachi, Peshwar, Quetta, and Lahore. Depending on the plaintiff's decision a case may finally end up in the Supreme Court, which is in the capital city of Islamabad. Under British colonial rule each of these courts used Islamic personal law in family matters such as divorce, inheritance, and custody of children. Zia-ul-Haq added an independent judiciary under the Shar'iat Court system based totally on shari'a law. However, the jurisdiction of the Supreme Court is final, as it is the apex court.

15. Siddiqui and Hayat, 343.

16. Ibid., quoting the FIR posted by *Rationalist International.*

17. *Mukto-mona,* "Mukto-mona Special News," January 23, 2004, http://www.mukto-mona.com/news/shaikh_free.htm.

18. Ibid.

19. Siddiqui and Hayat, 332.

20. Here Siddiqui and Hayat cite as their source Dr. Shaikh's attorney Abid Hassan Minto, in a personal interview on August 20, 2007.

21. Siddiqui and Hayat, 334.

22. Ibid.

23. Ibid., 335, citing Sajid Iqbal, "Former LHC Judge Bhatti Gunned Down in Lahore," *Dawn* Wire Service, October 11, 1997.

24. This event seems to have similarities with the Cordoba martyrs in al-Andalus and the Neomartyrs during the Ottoman period, except that the bishop shot himself to achieve martyrdom against a tyrannical Muslim regime in Pakistan in 2008.

25. Felix Qasir G.M. Amritsari, ed., *The Blasphemy Law: From Commitment to Hara-Kiri* (Karachi: Idara-e Amn-O Insaf, 1998), vol. 3, p. 206.

26. In Amritsari, *Blasphemy Law: From Ordinance to Murder,* 129, citing Javed Iqbal in *The Nation,* July 8, 1994, 5. Citations of Justice Javed Iqbal in text are taken from this report, which Amritsari included in his compilation. These are also the arguments that Muslim scholars like Moulavi Cheragh 'Ali make against the Cordoba martyrs in al-Andalus.

27. Ibid. Here Iqbal cites *Fatwa-e Alamgiri* (Calcutta edition), vol. 2, pp. 347–357.

28. Ibid. Iqbal cites *Fatwa-e Alamgiri,* vol. 2, pp. 357, Sharh Waqayah III, chapter on Qaza.

29. Ibid.

30. The line, from Sura-e al-Kafirun, is translated "To you be your way / And to me mine" in 'Abdullah Yusuf 'Ali, 1708.

31. In Amritsari, *Blasphemy Law: From Ordinance to Murder,* 129–130. In *The Nation,* Justice Iqbal cites M. B. Ahmad, *The Administration of Justice in Medieval India* (Aligarh, India: Aligarh University, 1941), 76–77; and Neil B.E. Baillie, *Muhammadan Law* (Lahore: Premier Book House, 1965; originally published 1799–1883), 74.

32. Muhammad Iqbal, *Reconstruction of Religious Thought in Islam* (Lahore: Institute of Islamic Culture, 1986), 147.

33. In Amritsari, *Blasphemy Law: From Ordinance to Murder,* 130.

34. Ibid., 196–198, citing Durab Patel, "Blasphemy Law and Fundamental Rights II."

35. Khaled Mattawa, a known Libyan American poet now teaching at the University of Michigan, Ann Arbor, made this comment during a discussion at Elizabeth Fernea's Memorial Conference, University of Texas at Austin on October 18, 2009.

CHAPTER 5

1. Pakistan's founder, Muhammad ʿAli Jinnah, was one such person. For details of his biography see Stanley Wolpert, *Jinnah of Pakistan* (New Delhi: Oxford University Press, 2005); Ayesha Jalal, *The Sole Spokesman: Jinnah, the Muslim League, and the Demand for Pakistan* (Cambridge, England: Cambridge University Press, 1994)

2. However, because of the Salman Rushdie fatwa, still fresh at the time, one of my committee members for the PhD dissertation at the University of Texas did caution me about the dangers of my research. He saw it in the transliterations/translations of Sufi poetry in my work. This poetry is continuously directed to the mullas, sheikhs, and imams making fun of their sole knowledge of the canon that is divorced from what is human, emotional, and truly intuitive. This argument is taken up in a discussion of Mansur Hallaj in this chapter.

3. I cite cases from Muslim states, although religio-political persecution is common to all states. Henry VIII's trial of Sir Thomas More (formerly lord chancellor of England) is well known. Today's Patriot Act is another instance.

4. For example, the compatibility of Islam with democracy based on the practices of the Pious Caliphs; see Anwar Syed, "Democracy and the Sharia," *Dawn*, May 10, 2009. http://archives.dawn.com/archives/30751.

5. For these Perso-Arabic terms I cite *Babylon, English Arabic Dictionary.* http://www.babylon.com/define/98/English-Arabic-Dictionary.htm.

6. Herbert Mason, *Al-Hallaj* (Surrey, England: Curzon Press, 1995), 51.

7. Ibid.

8. Arabic translation mine.

9. Mason, *Al-Hallaj*, 51.

10. Ibid., 52.

11. Ibid.

12. Ibid.

13. Muhammad's miʿraj is similar to Moses's encounter with the divine on Mount Sinai and the incident of the burning bush. In Muhammad's case, the divine is said to have revealed itself to him through removing the veil. In his nocturnal night journey Muhammad is said to have ridden on Buraq, a spiritual being with a woman's face and an animal's body; the journey started from what is now the Dome of the Rock. Hence in Islamic mystical poetry the divine veil carries an esoteric meaning: only through the spiritual inner world can this veil be removed to the true lover, as Muhammad's was or any other human being's can, from inner spiritual discipline. It was about such experiences that Hallaj spoke that brought the wrath of the ʿAbbasid court upon him. The state accused Hallaj of claiming divinity through *ilham*, spiritual insight. Many times he was accused of being a sorcerer and magician. Finally, he was tried for zandaqa, a Manichean heresy, and crucified.

14. Mason, *Al-Hallaj*.

15. G. F. Haddad, "Al-Hasan Al-Basri, d. 110" (Hijra), As-Sunnah Foundation of America, n.d. http://www.sunnah.org/history/Scholars/hasan_al_basri.htm.

16. Mason, *Al-Hallaj*, 5.

17. Tusalp.

18. The Zanj revolt involved close to 500,000 black slaves who were brought from Sudan and East Africa to work in the salt mines and perform other hard labor near Basra in Lower Mesopotamia. The revolt lasted for almost fifteen years, 869–883, and was led by

a Zaydi ʿAlid, a pretender who claimed descent from the fourth caliph, ʿAli. The Shiʿa propaganda about the gross mistreatment of the Zanj under the Sunni ʿAbbasid dynasty raised an outcry in the area where the administration claimed equality and human rights among all its members. However, the ʿAbbasids did historically create a program to make the state ethnically neutral, and through this they saved the state, especially as they gave significant positions to the *mawalis*, non-Arab Persians. Mahmood Ibrahim, "Religious Inquisition as Social Policy: The Persecution of the 'Zandiqi' in the Early ʿAbbasid Caliphate," *Arab Studies Quarterly* (Spring 1994). The ʿAbbasid dynasty was further continuously plagued with Shiʿa revolt such as that of the Qarmathians, who challenged ʿAbbasid authority. The Qarmathians hijacked the Black Stone of Kaʿaba and the Zam Zam Spring. They were an Ismaili Shiʿa sect. "Carmathians," *Babylon Dictionary*.

19. Massignon, *Hallaj: Mystic and Martyr*.

20. Manicheans were followers of Mani (d. 275), who claimed to be a follower of Zarathustra, Buddha, and Christ. His followers were persecuted for heresy. Shepard, 294.

21. Mahmood Ibrahim.

22. Ibid.

23. Ibid.

24. The Zanj revolt was one of the Shiʿa uprisings that the ʿAbbasids put down brutally but that led to the creation of an independent Shiʿa state in Egypt. It may be pointed out that although the ʿAbbasids came to power with support from the Shiʿa, the ʿAbbasids later persecuted the Shiʿa, against whom blasphemy laws were used. This is shown in figure 6.1, "Blasphemy Trajectories," a diagram in the next chapter.

25. Mason, *Al-Hallaj*, 26.

26. Ibid., 14.

27. See Shemeem Abbas, *Female Voice*.

28. In Massignon, *Hallaj: Mystic and Martyr*, 176.

29. Ibid.

30. Ibid.

31. Instances are available on international websites. The attorney's plea in such a matter is that his or her plaintiff is "insane." See news of the case against Anwar Kenneth in "Pakistani Christian Sentenced to Death," *BBC News, World Edition*, July 18, 2002. http://news.bbc.co.uk/2/hi/south_asia/2136291.stm.

32. Massignon, *Hallaj: Mystic and Martyr*, 175.

33. Ibid., 176.

34. Ibid.

35. Ibid., 163.

36. In India, some Muslim rulers sought counsel from Sufi authorities who further advised on political matters of the state. See Saiyid Athar Abbas Rizvi, *History of Sufism in India*, 2 vols. (New Delhi: Munshiram Manoharlal, 1978, 1983).

37. An example is the present-day frontier province of Pakhtunkhwa in northwestern Pakistan, where the secular Awami National Party was voted into power in the 2008 elections. The Islamic religious parties could not win the hearts and minds of the citizenry. See also the documentary *Dinner with the President*, filmed in Pakistan by Sabiha Sumar, a woman director and producer, and co-producer Sachithanandam Sathananthan (Vidhi Films, ZDF Arte, 2007). Citizens of Pakistan in the tribal areas of northern Pakistan speak up for a "modern" Islam and not one that is imprisoned in *riwaj* (tradition).

38. ʿAli Asani's work on this may be referenced. "Bridegroom Prophet in Medieval

Sindhi Poetry," in *Studies in South Asian Devotional Literature: Research Papers 1989–1991*, ed. F. Mallison and A. Erswistle (New Delhi: Manohar, 1994), 213–225.

39. Therefore, during a closed *sama*, a mystical song performance of the Chistiyya at Sufi shrines such as Data Ganj Baksh Hujweiri in Lahore or at Hazrat Mu'inuddin Chisti in Ajmer, only the select few who have been initiated into the ritual are permitted to attend. Mostly it is a male assembly. Until very recently, say, twenty years ago, Sufi performances were not for public consumption. However, with a newer, postcolonial order these are now available, such as qawwali performances in concert halls and the raqs of the Mevlevi Dervishes of Jalaluddin Rumi's shrine in Konya, Turkey. Performances are now arranged in concert halls for patrons in the native countries as well as international audiences globally. In some instances public performances of Sufi dance and music have become grossly commercialized, as in the case of Sain Pappu, a dhol (drum) player who performs on Thursday evenings at the shrine of Shah Jamal in Icchara, Lahore, in Pakistan. On political institutionalization of Syed families in Pakistan and their connections with Sufism and Sufi rituals see Sara F.D. Ansari, *Sufi Saints and State Power: The Pirs of Sind, 1843–1947* (Islamabad: Vanguard Books, 1992).

40. The West African Gnawa singers also bring the spiritual experience to the people through their music and song, in which they sometimes invoke Jewish spirits in their nocturnal rituals.

41. The latest trend in the spirituality of Sufism in Pakistan is Arif Lohar singing "jugni" on Coke Studio on YouTube. This melody is the latest among the younger generation of Pakistanis reacting to the orthodoxy.

42. The FM-radio mullas like Sufi Muhammad claim they are citizens, but one does not know who funds them and at what point they decided they would take on the state that initially birthed them through the Islamic parties. The histories and contexts are indeed bizarre: simply, these are many-headed monsters with many-headed histories.

43. A male colleague from my university in Islamabad confessed to me in early 2011 that the Swat Taliban had gotten hold of him around 2010 to slaughter him (*zibah*) for his outspoken speech in his village mosque, but his brothers arrived on the spot and saved him. My colleague said it was also because he had a modern crew cut and was clean-shaven that the Taliban targeted him.

44. And yet, a whole lineage of Hallajian mystics continued to spread his message and his *zikr*, the incantation "Anal-Haqq" (I am the divine truth). They perhaps continue to do it today also, secretly from the orthodoxy. Massignon's study *The Passion of al-Hallaj: Mystic and Martyr of Islam* (Princeton, NJ: Princeton University Press, 1982), volume 2, gives an extensive list of Hallajian mystics. It seems that the influence was strong east of the Persian Gulf right into Indonesia, and it is also possible that Massignon perhaps focused his study mainly in this region. His original Hallajian treatises are in French, which Herbert Mason has translated into English.

45. A Sudanese female colleague with me at the Girls College of Education reported that her father, a former vice chancellor of Khartoum University, witnessed the execution of a Saudi princess in Jeddah on which the 1980 drama-documentary *Death of a Princess* was based. This documentary cannot be bought anywhere now.

46. Massignon, *Hallaj: Mystic and Martyr*, 205.

47. Sura al-Ma'idah 5, 33; translation from 'Abdullah Yusuf 'Ali, 257.

48. Exile is not a part of Pakistan's postcolonial practices, and yet, on advice from Saudi intercessors, Nawaz Sharif, Pakistan's prime minister in 1999, agreed to go into ex-

ile. General Pervez Musharraf, then chief of army staff, charged Sharif with sedition when allegedly Nawaz Sharif ordered diverting Musharraf's plane from Sri Lanka to another airport. Nawaz Sharif in Musharraf's absence had appointed another army chief of his choice. Who was being seditious, Nawaz Sharif or Musharraf, no one knows. Fearful that he, too, might be executed like Zulfiqar 'Ali Bhutto was by General Zia-ul-Haq in the 1970s, Nawaz Sharif, his brother Shahbaz Sharif, and their families agreed to go into exile in Saudi Arabia, where Idi Amin likewise was living in exile. Nawaz Sharif and his family are now back in Pakistan.

49. Sura Ta Ha 20, 71, in 'Abdullah Yusuf 'Ali, 778.

50. Sura al-Shu'ara 26:49, in Abdullah Yusuf 'Ali, 914–915.

51. Sura al-Falaq 113, in Maududi, *Holy Qu'ran*, 1095.

52. Sura al-Nas 114, Maududi, *Holy Qur'an*, 1096. Maududi's translation is documented as one narrative, putting the footnotes into one text to make a continuum.

53. Aurengzeb's *Fatwa-e Alamgiri* is a text that I discuss with other literature on Hanafi Islam in this manuscript.

54. It is significant to note that although the British blasphemy law in India on whose template Zia-ul-Haq imposed his so-called Islamic blasphemy laws was in a penal code, it did not necessarily carry a corporal punishment. However, the general sneaked his criminal laws that carried corporal punishment under hadd (serious) crimes. Under his hadd offenses were blasphemy and zina, or fornication, crimes that carried physical punishment to the extreme. Zia-ul-Haq took these steps on advice from his Medinite Wahabi judicial adviser from Saudi Arabia. These laws had pharaonic punishments such as a death sentence with no provision for bail, as reported on the website of Women Living Under Islamic Laws (http://www.wluml.org/) as well as by 'Ali Eteraz in "Pakistan Is Already an Islamic State." Human rights groups in Pakistan have held many conferences and seminars on this issue, as it is a number one concern for the citizenry.

55. *Baghi* (rebel) is a term Tusalp also uses.

56. Bulle Shah learned music and dance while living with the "prostitutes," *kanjris*, in order to win back his mentor, Shah Inayat, who he knew loved dance and music. Abundant references to the "kanjri," the dance girl, were found in the oral singing culture of the qawwals at the shrine during my fieldwork in Kasur in 1993. It appears from the repeated references that Bulle Shah and his mentor revered the kanjri as an artist. I found the same reverence in my interview with Ustad Nusrat Fatch 'Ali Khan in 1992.

57. See Shemeem Abbas, "Risky Knowledge in Risky Times: Political Discourses of *Qawwali* and *Sufiana-kalam* in Pakistan-Indian Sufism," *Muslim World* 97, no. 4 (October 2007): 626–639. Abstract at http://onlinelibrary.wiley.com/doi/10.1111/j.1478-1913 .2007.00204.x/abstract.

58. Basically, Sufi poetry in Pakistan and India in the indigenous languages is sung in the voice of the woman, who is the devotee wooing the beloved.

59. Rizvi, *History of Sufism*.

CHAPTER 6

1. The exact Arabic name Ommayads is used here, as Moors were the North African Berber dynasties of the Maghreb and those on the peripheries of southern Spain.

2. Armstrong, 26.

3. Cheragh 'Ali, 13.

4. Ibid., 55. Here Cheragh 'Ali cites *Tanvir-ul Abshar*, which further cites the *Durr-ul Mukhtar, Kitab-ul Jihad* chapter "Murtad" (Apostate).

5. It was in the Battle of Karbala that Hussein, the Prophet Muhammad's grandson, and his followers were massacred by Yezid's army. Yezid was an Ommayad and a grandson of Muhammad's chief opponent, Abu Sufyan. Thus, the tribal battles between Muhammad's family (Hashemites) and the Ommayads (largely Sunnis) played well into the Shi'a-Sunni rift and the perpetration of blasphemy laws.

6. One of the twelve imams, spiritual leaders, who claimed spiritual insight from Muhammad's family. 'Ali, the Prophet's cousin and son-in-law, was the first of these twelve imams. Jafar al-Sadiq is reported to be the initiator of compiling the Shi'a fiqh, or jurisprudence.

7. Cheragh 'Ali.

8. Joseph F. O'Callaghan, *A History of Medieval Spain* (Ithaca, NY: Cornell University Press, 1975), 103.

9. The following are among online maps of Islamic Middle Eastern empires:

http://www.lib.utexas.edu/maps/historical/shepherd/califate_750.jpg

http://www.princeton.edu/~humcomp/map3.gif

http://www.princeton.edu/~humcomp/map4.gif

http://www.princeton.edu/~humcomp/mideastlate13.jpeg

http://www.princeton.edu/~humcomp/otto.jpeg

http://www.princeton.edu/~humcomp/ottosul.jpeg

10. Saint Stephen was the first Christian martyr, stoned to death in 34–35 CE in Jerusalem by an infuriated mob for accusing the Jews of persecuting the prophets who spoke out against their sins.

11. Daniel Baraz, *Medieval Cruelty: Changing Perceptions, Late Antiquity to the Early Modern Period* (Ithaca, NY: Cornell University Press, 2007), 53. Other sources are documented in O'Callaghan.

12. Andrew Wheatcroft, *Infidels: A History of the Conflict between Christendom and Islam* (New York: Random House, 2003).

13. The Prophet Muhammad did not advocate *malkiat*, monarchy, nor did he appoint a successor.

14. For background information see Wheatcroft, 73–88. Also view the DVD *Cities of Light: The Rise and Fall of Islamic Spain*.

15. This connects to Bishop Joseph's suicide in 1998 in Pakistan, where the bishop shot himself in a sessions court in Sahiwal over the death penalty of a Christian parishioner, as described in chapter 4.

16. See Cheragh 'Ali. He argues that Muslim common law is derived from the customary laws traced back to Christianity and Judaism that the Prophet Muhammad also applied at times. Otherwise, Muslim common law was based on the independent judgment, *ijtihad-e ra'y*, of the jurist. This, Cheragh 'Ali claims, is different from the revealed law of the Qur'an that is basically a moral code of ethics that dealt with correcting the ills of a tribal society of Arabia at the time.

17. The cases did not have the nuances that one finds in the Hallaj case in Iraq under the 'Abbasids and in the manner that the jurisconsults Ibn Dawud and Ibn Surayj took positions.

18. For details of Muslim jurists, historians, and intellectuals in al-Andalus see O'Callaghan, 91–162, 321; Olivia Remie Constable, ed., *Medieval Iberia: Readings from Chris-*

tian, Muslim, and Jewish Sources (Philadelphia: University of Pennsylvania Press, 1997), 77; Wael Hallaq, "Murder in Cordoba: Ijtihad, Ifta and the Evolution of Substantive Law in Medieval Islam" *Acta Orientalia* 1994, 55: 55–83.

19. Baraz, 55.

20. In Wheatcroft, 74.

21. Ibid.

22. Ibid.

23. The theory of oral culture and speech communication is one of the basic tropes that are followed in this book. Hence Wheatcroft's analysis converges with my speech communication theory starting from the Prophet Muhammad's education, or rather "oral literacy," that is the very rubric of the Qur'an. My analyses are based on Roman Jakobson, Goffman, Sacks and Schegloff, and others. More details are in the bibliography of Shemeem Abbas, *Female Voice in Sufi Ritual.*

24. Wheatcroft, in 366n52, writes: "The word 'dissemination' is a Derridean pun, filled with multiple connotations. It embodies the sexual act of in-semination, and no one can tell as a consequence how heritable qualities will change or transmute down the generations."

25. Ronald Segal, *Islam's Black Slaves* (New York: Atlantic Books, 2003).

26. Wheatcroft, 75.

27. Ibid., quoting Alvarus. Wheatcroft's information is based on Alvarus's main works, which were his letters (*Epistulae*), *Memoriale sanctorum*, *Vita Eulogii*, and *Liber apologeticus martyrum.*

28. Vaporis narrates three women Neomartyrs' stories. Nomikos Michael Vaporis, *Witnesses for Christ: Orthodox Christian Martyrs of the Ottoman Period 1437–1860* (New York: St Vladmir's Seminary Press, 2000), 179, 184, 230.

29. Besides Vaporis's narratives in *Witnesses for Christ,* also see Anton Minkov, *Conversion to Islam in the Balkans: Kisve Bahas Petitions and Ottoman Social Life 1670–1730,* Ottoman Empire and Its Heritage series (Leiden, Netherlands: Brill Academic, 2004), 82.

30. The Ottomans took over the region that was the eastern Byzantine territory where Orthodox Christianity was practiced. The Ottomans ruled from 1299 to 1922, and their territory spanned from southeastern Europe across western Asia and parts of North Africa. Greece and Crete together with the Balkans were also a part of the Ottoman Empire. The Ottomans made inroads into Hungary and Austria and continued to threaten the frontiers of European states. On the east they, like the 'Abbasids, fought the Persians. Their rule extended to the Levant: Syria, Iraq, Egypt, and the area along the Red Sea in the south that included the Muslim holy cities of Mecca and Medina.

31. Medieval European literature is replete with the figure of Muhammad as the anti-Christ.

32. Minkov, 83–84.

33. Minkov, 84.

34. Ibid.

35. Ibid. On the Ottoman fatwa collections also see Tusalp.

36. Minkov, 85–86.

37. H. Patrick Glenn, *Legal Traditions of the World: Substantive Diversity in Law* (New York: Oxford University Press, 2007), 80.

38. Tusalp, 17, citing Messick, Masud, and Powers, "Muftis, Fatwas, and Islamic Legal Interpretation," in *Islamic Legal Interpretation,* 4.

39. Minkov, 85–86. This may connect with similar situations during the Muslim sultanate period and thereafter in India when large numbers of Hindus, among them musicians, converted to Islam, (Rizvi, *History of Sufism*, vol. 1). As such the Sufi *qawwali-sema* devotional texts in Hindi of that period retained the Hindu names of mythical characters like Ram, Radha, and Krishna. I worked on a qawwali text of the Sabri brothers in which they sang of Mira Bai, a Hindu Rajput princess, for their expatriate Hindu, Sikh, and Muslim audiences in the United Kingdom in the 1980s. This was during the same period when the Salman Rushdie fatwa was launched at the behest of Muslim communities in the United Kingdom.

40. *Fetava-yi Efendi*, in Tusalp, 77.

41. Minkov, 85.

42. At a Catholic church service I attended in Austin, Texas, in 2009, one of the parishioners affirmed to me that she believed Islam to be a heresy. The remark struck me as one that in Pakistan could lead to a Christian's execution under the country's blasphemy laws.

43. Vaporis, 17.

44. Ibid., 175.

45. Ibid., 348.

46. Vaporis, 14, cites Maulana Muhammad 'Ali, *The Religion of Islam: A Comprehensive Discussion of the Sources* (Lahore, 1973), 438–439, as affirming that during the period of decline, Muslim sacred law (*sheriat*) was continuously transgressed by the Muslim judicial administration. Accordingly, death could be prescribed for sedition but not for apostasy.

47. This is my reading of Vaporis's study. Nomikos Michael Vaporis was dean at Hellenic College Holy Cross School of Theology in the United States from 1975 to 1985. He taught courses on Hellenic cultures, and these stories are derived from his collection *Lives*. Vaporis based his research on the lives of Neomartyrs that were written by anonymous authors. Many collections of such stories exist in the Greek Church, consolidated and printed by Stylianos N. Kementzetzis as *Synaxaristes Neomartyron* (Thessalonike, 1984). Vaporis's entire work is based on this collection.

48. Vaporis, 16. The Greek word "martyr" translates to "witness," and hence these martyrs were Jesus Christ's witnesses.

49. Glenn, 80.

50. In my email communications with Tusalp she affirmed that instances in her study are derived from many archival and scholarly sources.

51. Tusalp, 93–94. Also see table 6.1 in the present chapter.

52. See Siddiqui and Hayat and chapter 4 of this book.

53. For more on this rebellion see Fawzia Afzal-Khan, "Dispatches from the Frontlines of the Burqa Brigade: What Lies Beneath," *Counterpunch*, July 7–9, 2007, http://www.counterpunch.org/khan07072007.html.

54. *Fetava-yi Feyziye*, in Tusalp, 89–90.

55. *Fetava-yi Abdurrahim*, in Tusalp, 60.

56. Shemeem Abbas, *Female Voice in Sufi Ritual*.

57. The Mughals were an Islamic empire in India descended from Tamberlaine, Halagu Khan, and Changez Khan of Central Asia. Dara Shikoh was a scholar who translated the works of the Sufis into Persian, thus making them available to the west.

58. Tusalp, 76. Similar records are available on minority communities in both India and Pakistan. The *dalits*, "untouchables" and the lowest in the social ladder in India, fall

into such a category. The Pakistani census bureau keeps records of minorities including Christians, Hindus, and Parsis; such records are maintained in the electoral system as well.

59. Tusalp, 77, citing Develi, 69.

60. In Tusalp, 78, citing Robert Pattison from Gauri Viswanathan, "Blasphemy and Heresy: The Modernist Challenge," *Comparative Studies in Society and History* 37, no. 2 (April 1995): 407.

61. Afiya Begum (*alias*), personal communication, Austin, 2009.

62. Tusalp, 79–93.

63. Tamara Sonn, *A Brief History of Islam* (Wiley-Blackwell, 2004), 83–84.

64. Ibid.

65. Tusalp, 95–97, citing Madeline Zilfi's *Politics of Piety* (1988).

66. Ibid., 21. Here Zilfi calls the latter part of the seventeenth century and eighteenth century the *mollazade* period, when the leading members of the 'ulema dynasties such as Seyhulislam Feyzullah Efendi forced the hereditary tendencies in the system so as to make the *mesihat makami* an inherited post.

67. Sufi mentors did advise some Muslim monarchs in India; for example, Shaikh Saleem Chisti (1478–1572), a descendant of Hazrat Moinuddin Chisti, was Emperor Akbar's adviser. For more details also see Rizvi's two-volume *History of Sufism in India*.

68. Among the Sufi nomads and wandering minstrels discussed earlier was Shah Abdul Latif of Bhitai. The two works that enrich Shah Abdul Latif's poetry in the *Risalo* (Message) are the Qur'an and Jalaluddin Rumi's *Mathnawi*. Pakistani newspapers online report the rapidly expanding network of Wahabi madrassas (seminaries) in this land of Sufis in the Sind Province of Pakistan, (*Dawn*, July 9–10, 2009).

CONCLUSION

1. These are preserved in the *Tuhfat-ul Awam* (Gift to the People), which can be bought at any Shi'a *imambara*, a specialty bookstore that sells Islamic books.

2. Earlier, the Sassanids also had laws against *zindiqi* (magicians) that they particularly used against the Manicheans.

3. However, in Mughal India Sufis had been advisers to the monarchs, such as Akbar, who was a devotee of Shaikh Saleem Chisti.

4. See Ayesha Jalal, *Partisans of Allah: Jihad in South Asia*, 2008.

5. He was a follower of the intellectual school of Sayyid al-Qutb, a militant leader of the Egyptian Muslim Brotherhood who believed in armed jihad against colonial forces. Colonel Gamal Abdul Nasser had Sayyid al-Qutb executed in 1966 for sedition against the state for trying to assassinate Nasser. It was the same group that assassinated President Anwar Sadat in 1981 for the Egypt-Israel peace treaty.

6. At http://www.ashrafia.org.pk/Jamia_today.html. This seminary is named after Maulana Ashraf 'Ali Thanwi of the Deoband School.

7. At http://en.wikipedia.org/Darul_Uloom_Deoband.

8. Dars-e Nizami is named after Mullah Nizamuddin Sehalvi (d. 1748).

9. The term "Dar-ul-'uloom Islamiyya" is mine, as eventually the clerics were able to drive away most secular faculty, especially the women, from the campus around 1998. I may also mention that during this period I interviewed for the vice chancellorship of the Women's University in Rawalpindi, and although I was among the top three candidates who were short-listed, none of the three candidates was appointed. Another woman,

who was never a part of the selection process, was nominated vice chancellor through Islami connections of Abbaji (the Sharif brothers' father) of the Tablighi Jamaat, the proselytizing Islamic party. The Sharif brothers, Abbaji, and the rest of the family were granted asylum in Saudi Arabia when General Musharraf framed sedition charges against Nawaz Sharif for hijacking his plane from Colombo.

10. I am citing from a study on madrassa education in Bangladesh, Muzib Mehdy, *Madrassah Education: An Observation*, ed. Rokiya Kabir, trans. Nadia Shabnam (Bangladesh Nari Progati Sangha, September 2003). http://bnps.org/wp-content/uploads/2009/03/madrasah-education-an-observation.pdf.

11. Maulana Sufi Muhammad, an FM-radio mulla in Swat, asserted in 2009 that democracy is a kufr, or heresy.

12. A large number of children who were killed by Musharraf's forces in the Red Mosque madrassa fiasco were orphans from Swat and hence the vendetta of suicide bombings against the country's security forces.

13. See the DVDs of Robert Gardner's films *Islam: Empire of Faith* (2007) and *Cities of Light: The Rise and Fall of Islamic Spain* (2005).

14. In some African communities this is the worst insult women can inflict on the males in the society.

15. See the five-part documentary series *Women, War, and Peace* by PBS and WNET New York that premiered on PBS in October–November 2011.

16. Osama Siddiqui interview, part 1, *Harvard Law School Human Rights Journal*, November 11, 2011. http://harvardhrj.com/2011/11/osama-siddique-interview-part-i/.

17. Findings of the Human Rights Commission of Pakistan, *Dawn*, April 10, 1994, in Amritsari, *Blasphemy Law: From Ordinance to Murder*.

BIBLIOGRAPHY

PRIMARY SOURCES IN INTERVIEWS BY THE AUTHOR

Abdul Hai. Coordinator and field officer, Human Rights Commission of Pakistan. Karachi, June 2007.

Adam, Farooq. Chairman, National Accountability Bureau. Islamabad, 1999.

'Ali, Babar. Chief executive, Lahore University of Management Sciences and Babar 'Ali Industries. Personal communication, Kinnaird College for Women, Lahore, 1998.

Allana, Ghulam 'Ali. Chairman, Sind Language Authority. Hyderabad Sind, 1999.

Ara, Azra (alias). Female physician. Telephone interview, June 2009.

Awan, Mahmood (late). Attorney, Sessions Court, Panjab High Court, and Shari'at Courts. Islamabad-Rawalpindi, June–July 2008.

Ayub, Muhammad. Proprietor, director, Oriental Star Agencies Recording Company. Birmingham, England, December 20, 2005.

Aziz, Rashid. Attorney, Chief Justice (retired), Panjab High Court. Rawalpindi Cantonment, 1998.

Baloch, Amina (alias). Female Canadian citizen of Pakistani origin. Rawalpindi 1998 to date.

Begum, Afiya (alias). Housewife with significant military networks. Islamabad, 1998–1999.

Bordie, John. Ex-director, Center for Foreign Language Education; Professor Emeritus, Center for Asian Studies, University of Texas at Austin. 1999.

Brohi, Tahira. Editor, University Grants Commission. Islamabad, 1998–1999.

Burney, Muhammad Ilyas, Dr. Lieutenant General (late). Rawalpindi Cantonment, 1998.

Burqi, Javaid Iqbal. Human Rights Commission of Pakistan, Karachi, June 2007.

Cowasjee, Ardeshir. Journalist, *Dawn*. Karachi, June 2007.

Fernea, Elizabeth Wanrock (late). Professor of Comparative Literature and Middle Eastern Studies, University of Texas at Austin, 1999–2005.

Jones, Philip. Professor of Global Security and Intelligence Studies, Emery-Riddle Aeronautical University, Prescott, AZ, spring 2006.

Khan, Khalida Hanif (late). Housewife. Rawalpindi Cantonment, 1998–1999.

Lodhi, Ibadur Rehman. Attorney, Sessions Court, Panjab High Court, Federal High Court and Shar'iat Courts, Islamabad-Rawalpindi, 1998.

Mohan, Lal (alias). Member of Provincial Parliament. Christian Community. Human Rights Commission of Pakistan, Karachi, June 2007.

Muhammad Khan, Brigadier General (retired) (alias). Rawalpindi Cantonment, June 2008.

Naqvi, Jaleel. Professor of Persian (retired), M.A.O. College, Lahore, 1998–2008.

Naqvi, Khalida. Professor of English (retired), Wahdat College for Women, Lahore, 1998–2008.

Noorani, Kamran. Director, Pakistan Law House, Karachi, June 2007.

Rahim, Nahid. Program officer, Shirkat Gah (women's nongovernmental organization), Karachi, June 2007.

Rosser, Yvette. PhD student, University of Texas at Austin, 1998–1999.

Sahi, Muhammad Akrom, Brigadier General. Military secretary to Rafiq Tarar, president of Pakistan. Telephone and personal, president's house and Allama Iqbal Open University, Islamabad, 1998–1999.

Sardar, Badshah. Assistant professor of Pakistan Studies, Allama Iqbal Open University, Islamabad. Telephone communications, June 2009 to date.

Shafi, Surriya. Professor of English, Government College University, Lahore. Telephone and personal communication, 1998–1999.

Shah, Syed Ghaus ʿAli. Federal Minister for Education, Government of Pakistan. Islamabad, 1998.

Siddiqui, Anwar. Vice chancellor, Allama Iqbal Open University, currently president of International Islamic University, Islamabad, 1998–1999.

Siddiqui, Tariq ʿAli. Vice chancellor, Quaid-e Azam University, Islamabad, 1998–1999.

Tarannum Khan. Program officer, Human Rights Commission of Pakistan. Karachi, June 2007.

Wasim, Akmal. Attorney, Sind High Court, and faculty member, Hamdard University, Karachi, June–July 2007.

SECONDARY SOURCES

Abbas, Shemeem B. "Danish Cartoons." Discussant, panel, Manhattanville College, Purchase, April 3, 2006.

———. "Defending 'Dangerous' Ideas: Responding to Attacks on Intellectuals." Presentation at the University of Chicago Human Rights Program, October 7, 2004.

———. *The Female Voice in Sufi Ritual: Devotional Practices of Pakistan and India.* Austin: University of Texas Press, 2002.

———. "Human Rights, Women, Sufis, and the Islamic State." Presentation in Professor John Gitlitz's upper-division class, SUNY/Purchase College, October 18, 2005.

———. "Islamic Orthodoxy in South Asia." Class presentation, Emery-Riddle Aeronautical University, Prescott, AZ, March 13, 2006.

———. "Is This Islam? The Power of the Word." Public talk, Ban Righ Women's Center, Queen's University, Kingston, Canada, October 25, 2005.

———. "Islamic State, Heresy, and Freedom of Speech." Public talk for SUNY/Purchase College and Scholars at Risk, March 27, 2006.

———. "Law and Culture." Chair, session at the Association for the Study of Law Culture and Humanities 2005 Conference, University of Texas, Austin, March 11–12, 2005.

———. "Mosaics, the Clerics." Original poem read at Edinburgh Festival, Scotland, August 2005.

———. "Music, Sufism, and Islamic Orthodoxy." Presentation for "Spotlight on Our Liberal Arts and Sciences Faculty," SUNY/Purchase College Family Day, October 15, 2005.

———. "Musical Responses in Islam: Law, Culture, and Humanities." Presentation for the president's faculty colloquium, SUNY Purchase College, September 21, 2005.

———. "On the Margins, Pakistan's Blasphemy Laws." Presentation for South Asian forum, Columbia University, New York, April 10, 2006.

———. "Orthodoxy and Women's Human Rights Violation in Pakistani Universities." Presentation at annual fund-raising dinner, Institute of International Education, Chicago, October 7, 2004.

————. "Pakistan's Postcolonial Islamic Laws in the Era of Post-Cold War Politics." Paper presented at Beautiful Minds, Risky Times seminar at Duke University, September 23–24, 2004.

————. "The Power of English in Pakistan." (University of Illinois) *World Englishes* 12, no. 2 (1993): 147–156.

————. "Preparing for South Asian Diplomacy." Lecture at the George P. Schulz National Foreign Affairs Training Center, Washington, DC, March 19, 2004.

————. "Protest Elements in Sufi Songs." Paper presented at Pan Asian Music Festival, Stanford University, CA, February 10–12, 2006.

————. "Risky Knowledge: Postcolonial Laws in Islamic Societies." Paper presented at the Eighth Annual Conference of the Association for the Study of Law, Culture, and Humanities 2005 Conference, University of Texas, Austin, March 11–12, 2005.

————. "Risky Knowledge in Risky Times: Political Discourses of *Qawwali* and *Sufianakalam* in Pakistan-Indian Sufism." *Muslim World* 97, no. 4 (October 2007): 626–639. Abstract at http://onlinelibrary.wiley.com/doi/10.1111/j.1478-1913.2007.00204.x/abstract.

————. "Sakineh: The Narrator of Kerbala." In *The Women of Kerbala: Gender Dynamics of Ritual Performance and Symbolic Discourse of Modern Shiʿi Islam*, ed. Kamran Aghaie. Austin: University of Texas Press, 2005.

————. "Speech Play and Verbal Art in the Indo-Pakistani Oral Sufi Tradition." PhD diss., University of Texas at Austin, 1992. UMI 3523537, Ann Arbor, MI, 1993.

————. "Sufis, Performers, Orthodoxy." Public talk, Emery-Riddle Aeronautical University, Prescott, AZ, March 13, 2006.

————. "Threats to Intellectual Freedom in the Post–Cold War Era." Presentation at the Institute for International Education Scholars at Risk Fund, New York, March 15, 2004.

————. "When East Meets West: Law, Religion and Culture." Chair, session at the Association for the Study of Law, Culture, and Humanities 2005 Conference, University of Texas, Austin, March 11–12, 2005.

————. "Whose Islam Is It, the Clerics' or the Majority's?" Public talk, Queen's University, Kingston, Canada, October 26, 2005.

Abbasi, Wasim. "Fate of Teacher Accused of Blasphemy to Be Decided Today." *The Nation* (Pakistan). http://www.nation.com.pk/daily/today/national/isb6.htm.

Abd Rahman, Zainal Azam B. Senior Fellow/Director of the Center for Syariah, Law and Political Science, Institul Kafahaman Islam 1992–2009, Malaysia (IKIM). http://www.ikim.gov.my/v5/print.php?Grp=2&Key=769. Downloaded July 15, 2009.

Abu Zayd, Nasr Hamid. *Voice of an Exile: Reflections on Islam*. London: Praeger, 2004.

Afzal-Khan, Fawzia. "Dispatches from the Frontlines of the Burqa Brigade: What Lies Beneath." In *Counterpunch*. http://www.counterpunch.org/khan07072007.html.

————. *Lahore with Love: Growing Up with Girlfriends, Pakistani-Style*. Syracuse, NY: Syracuse University Press, 2010.

Aghaie, Kamran Scott. *The Martyrs of Karbala: Shiʿi Symbols and Rituals in Modern Iran*. Seattle & London: University of Washington Press, 2004.

Ahmad, Dohra, Iftikhar Ahmed, Zulfiqar Ahmed and Zia Mian, eds. *Eqbal Ahmad, Between Past & Future: Selected Essays on South Asia*. Karachi: Oxford University Press, 2004.

Ahmad, M. B. *The Administration of Justice in Medieval India*. Aligarh, India: Aligarh

University Publication, 1941. In *The Blasphemy Law: From Ordinance to Murder*, ed. Felix Qasir G.M. Amritsari. Karachi: Idara-e Amn-O Insaf, 1994.

Ahmad, Nazir. *Qur'anic and Non-Qur'anic Islam*. Islamabad: Vanguard Books, 1997.

Ahmed, Akbar S. "Pakistan's Blasphemy Law: Words Fail Me." *Washington Post*, May 19, 2002.

Ahmed, Asad 'Ali. "Specters of Macaulay: Blasphemy, the Indian Penal Code, and Pakistan's Postcolonial Predicament." In *Censorship in South Asia: Cultural Regulation from Sedition to Seduction*, ed. Raminder Kaur and William Mazzarella. Bloomington: Indiana University Press, 2009.

Ahmed, Salman, prod. *The Rock Star and the Mullahs*. Video. BBC, 2003.

Ahmed, Shahab. "Ibn Taymiyya and the Satanic Verses." *Studia Islamica* 87 (1998): 67–124.

Ahsan, Aitzaz. *The Indus Saga and the Making of Pakistan*. Karachi: Oxford University Press, 1996.

'Ali, 'Abdullah Yusuf, trans. *The Meaning of the Holy Qur'an*. 9th edition. Beltsville, MD: Amana, 1997.

'Ali, Asghar. "Fatwas, Their Acceptability, and Their Relevance." (Asian Human Rights Commission) *Religious Groups for Human Rights* 7, no. 37 (September 12, 2005). http://www.rghr.net/mainfile.php/0737/1000/.

'Ali, Ayaan Hirsi. *Infidel*. New York: Free Press, 2007.

———. *The Caged Virgin: An Emancipation Proclamation for Women and Islam*. New York: Free Press, 2006.

'Ali, Syed Amir. *The Spirit of Islam: A History of the Evolution and Ideals of Islam, with a Life of the Prophet*. New Delhi: Kitab Bhavan, 2000. Originally published 1922.

———. *A Short History of the Saracens: Being a Concise Account of the Rise and Decline of the Saracenic Power*. New Delhi: Kitab Bhavan, 2001. Originally published 1926.

'Ali, Tariq. *Bush in Babylon: The Recolonization of Iraq*. London: Verso, 2003.

———. *Can Pakistan Survive? The Death of a State*. Harmondsworth: Penguin Books, 1983.

———. *The Clash of Fundamentalisms: Crusades, Jihads, and Modernity*. London: Verso, 2002.

———. *The Duel: Pakistan on the Flight Path of American Power*. New York: Scribner, 2008.

'Ali, Tariq, and David Barsamian, *Speaking of Empire and Resistance: Conversations with Tariq 'Ali*. New York: New Press, 2005.

Aman, Mohammad. *Arabie Saoudite: La tradition du Hejaz*. CD. OCORA, Radio France. C560158 HM 79, 2001.

Amritsari, Felix Qasir G.M., ed. *The Blasphemy Law: From Commitment to Hara-Kiri*. Vol. 3. Karachi: Idara-e Amn-O Insaf, 1998.

———, ed. *The Blasphemy Law: From Ordinance to Murder*. Karachi: Idara-e Amn-O Insaf, 1994.

Andersen, Michael R. "Islamic Law and the Colonial Encounter in British India." In *Islamic Family Law*, eds. Chibli Mallat and Jane Connors. London: Graham, 1990.

Ansari, Sara F.D. *Sufi Saints and State Power: The Pirs of Sind, 1843–1947*. Islamabad: Vanguard Books, 1992.

Ariev, Hodri, Ratno Lukito, and C. Holland Taylor, principal authors. *Illusion of an Islamic State: How an Alliance of Moderates Launched a Successful Jihad Against Radi-*

calization and Terrorism in the World's Largest Muslim-Majority Country, ed. Abdurrahman Wahid. Winston-Salem, NC: LibForAll Foundation Press, 2011.

Arjomand, Said Amir. *Constitutional Politics in the Middle East with Special Reference to Turkey, Iraq, Iran, and Afghanistan.* Onati International Series in Law and Society, 2008.

———. *The Turban for the Crown: Islamic Revolution in Iran.* Studies in Middle Eastern History. Oxford University Press, 1990.

Armstrong, Karen. *Islam: A Short History.* New York: Modern Library, 2002.

Asad, Talal. *Formations of the Secular: Christianity, Islam, Modernity.* Stanford, CA: Stanford University Press, 2003.

Asani, 'Ali. "Bridegroom Prophet in Medieval Sindhi Poetry." In *Studies in South Asian Devotional Literature: Research Papers 1989–1991*, ed. F. Mallison and A. Erswistle. New Delhi: Manohar, 1994.

Aslan, Reza. *No God but God: The Origins, Evolution, and Future of Islam.* New York: Random House, 2006.

Ayoob, Muhammad, and Hasan Kosebalaban, eds. *Religion and Politics in Saudi Arabia: Wahabism and the State.* Boulder, CO: Lynne Rienner, 2009.

Baillie, Neil B.E. *Muhammadan Law*, Lahore: Premier Book House, 1965; originally published 1799–1883. In *The Blasphemy Law: From Ordinance to Murder*, ed. Felix Qasir G.M. Amritsari. Karachi: Idara-e Amn-O Insaf, 1994.

Bakhtin, M. M. *The Dialogic Imagination.* Austin: University of Texas Press, 1981.

Bannerji, A. C. *English Law in India.* New Delhi: Hans Raj Gupta and Sons, 1984.

Baraz, Daniel. *Medieval Cruelty: Changing Perceptions, Late Antiquity to the Early Modern Period.* Ithaca, NY: Cornell University Press, 2003.

BBC News. "Pakistani Christian Sentenced to Death." World Edition, July 18, 2002. http://news.bbc.co.uk/2/hi/south_asia/2136291.stm.

Begam, Jahan Ara. *Munis'ul Arwah.* Ed. Qamar Jahan Begam. Karachi. Library of Congress CC no. 91-931192, 1991.

———. *Sahibiyya.* Ed. Muhammad Ibrahim. (Ahmedabad) *Oriental College Magazine*, 1937, 1–19.

Begam, Qamar Jahan. *Princess Jahan Ara Begam: Her Life and Her Works.* Karachi. Library of Congress CC no. 91-931192, 1991.

Benton, Lauren. *Law and Colonial Cultures: Legal Regimes in World History; 1400–1900.* Cambridge, England: Cambridge University Press, 2002.

Bhutto, Benazir. *Daughter of Destiny: An Autobiography.* New York: Simon and Schuster, 1989.

———. *Reconciliation: Islam, Democracy, and the West.* New York: HarperCollins, 2008.

Cheragh 'Ali, Moulavi. *The Proposed Political, Legal, and Social Reforms under Moslem Rule.* Bombay: Education Society's Press, Byculla, 1883. Google Digitized Books Online, 2009.

Cole, J.R.I. "Popular Shi'ism." In *India's Islamic Traditions: 711–1750*, ed. Richard M. Eaton. New Delhi: Oxford University Press, 2003.

Collins, Joseph J. *Understanding War in Afghanistan.* Washington, DC: National Defense University Press, 2011. http://www.ndu.edu/press/lib/pdf/books/understanding -war-in-afghan.pdf.

Constable, Olivia Remie, ed. *Medieval Iberia: Readings from Christian, Muslim and Jewish Sources.* Philadelphia: University of Pennsylvania Press, 1997.

Corfis, Ivy, and Ray Harris-Northall, eds. *Medieval Iberia: Changing Societies and Cultures in Contact and Transition.* Woolbridge, England: Tamesis, 2007.

Crile, George. *Charlie Wilson's War.* New York: Grove Press, 2003.

Dawn. "Wahabi *Madrassas* in Sindh." (Karachi) *Dawn,* July 9–10, 2009.

DeLong-Bas, Natana J. "Wahabism and the Question of Religious Tolerance." In *Religion and Politics in Saudi Arabia: Wahabism and the State,* ed. Mohammad Ayoob and Hasan Kosebalaban. Boulder, CO: Lynne Rienner, 2009.

Digby, Simon. "The Sufi Shaikh as a Source of Authority in Medieval India." In *India's Islamic Traditions: 711–1750,* ed. Richard M. Eaton. New Delhi: Oxford University Press, 2003.

Eaton, Richard, ed. *India's Islamic Traditions, 711–1750.* New Delhi: Oxford University Press, 2003.

———. "The Political and Religious Authority of the Shrine of Baba Farid." In *India's Islamic Traditions: 711–1750,* ed. Richard Eaton.

Ebadi, Shirin. *Iran Awakening: A Memoir of Revolution and Hope.* New York: Random House, 2006.

El Fadl, Khaled Abou. *The Great Theft: Wrestling Islam from the Extremists.* New York: HarperCollins, 2007.

———. *Speaking in God's Name: Islamic Law, Authority, and Women.* Oxford, England: Oneworld, 2001.

Eltahawy, Mona. "Egypt's Sexist Divorce Laws Blamed Not on Islam, but on Men." *Guardian,* February 22, 2000. http://www.guardian.co.uk/world/2000/feb/23/4.

Ernst, Karl, and Bruce Lawrence. *Sufi Martyrs of Love: The Chisti Order in South Asia and Beyond.* New York: Palgrave Macmillan, 2002.

Eteraz, 'Ali. *Children of Dust: A Memoir of Pakistan.* New York: HarperOne, 2009.

———. "Pakistan Is Already an Islamic State." *Dissent,* April 30, 2009.

Foucault, Michel. *Discipline and Punish: The Birth of the Prison.* New York: Vintage Books, 1979.

———. "The Order of Discourse." In *Untying the Text: A Post-Structuralist Reader,* ed. Robert J.C. Young. London: Routledge and Kegan Paul, 1981.

Freedom House. *Saudi Publications on Hate Ideology Fill American Mosques.* Washington, DC: Center for Religious Freedom, 2005.

Friedman, Yohanan. "Islamic Thought in Relation to the Indian Context." In *India's Islamic Traditions: 711–1750.* New Delhi: Oxford University Press.

Galster, Steve. "Afghanistan: The Making of U.S. Policy, 1973–1990." In *The September 11th Sourcebooks.* Vol. 2, *Afghanistan: Lessons from the Last War.* National Security Archive Briefing Book no. 57, ed. John Prados and Svetlana Savranskaya. George Washington University, National Security Archive, October 9, 2001. Originally published March 1991. http://www.gwu.edu/~nsarchiv/NSAEBB/NSAEBB57/essay.html.

Gardner, Robert H., dir. *Cities of Light: The Rise and Fall of Islamic Spain.* DVD. 2007.

———, dir. *Islam: Empire of Faith.* DVD, 2005.

Gilmour, David. *The Ruling Caste: Imperial Lives in the Victorian Raj.* New York: Farrar, Straus, and Giroux, 2005.

Glenn, Patrick H. *Legal Traditions of the World: Substantive Diversity in Law.* New York: Oxford University Press, 2007.

Glubb, John Bagot. *Empire of the Arabs.* London: Hodder and Stoughton, 1963.

Gnawa Music. CD. Istikara, Rounder Records Corp 82161 5080 2 3, 2001.

Godfrey, Barry, and Graeme Dunstall. *Crime and Empire 1840–1940: Criminal Justice in Local and Global Context*. Portland, OR: Willan, 2005.

Guenther, Alan M. "Hanafi Fiqh in Mughal India: The Fatawa-e Alamgiri." In *India's Islamic Traditions: 711–1750*. New Delhi: Oxford University Press, 2003.

Haddad, G. F. "Al-Hasan Al-Basri (d. 110)" (Hijra). As-Sunnah Foundation of America, n.d. http://www.sunnah.org/history/Scholars/hasan_al_basri.htm.

Haeri, Shehla. *No Shame for the Sun: Lives of Professional Pakistani Women*. Syracuse, NY: Syracuse University Press, 2002.

Hallaq, Wael B., ed. *The Formation of Islamic Law*. Burlington, VT: Ashgate Variorum, 2004.

———. "From *Fatwas* to *Furu*: Growth and Change in Islamic Substantive Law." *Islamic Law and Society* 1, no. 1 (1994): 29–65.

———. "Murder in Cordoba: *Ijtihad*, *Ifta* and the Evolution of Substantive Law in Medieval Islam." *Acta Orientalia* (1994): 55–83.

———. *The Origins and Evolution of Islamic Law*. New York: Cambridge University Press, 2005.

———. "Was the Gate of *Ijtihad* Closed?" *International Journal of Middle Eastern Studies* 16, no. 1 (1984): 3–41.

Hallward, Peter. *Absolutely Postcolonial: Writing between the Singular and the Specific*. Manchester, England: Manchester University Press, 2001.

Halsall, Paul. "The Status of Muslims under Non-Muslim Rule." *Medieval Sourcebook: Pact of Umar, 7th Century?* In *Internet Medieval Sourcebook*. January 1996. http://www.fordham.edu/halsall/source/pact-umar.asp.

Haqqani, Hussain. *Pakistan between Mosque and Military*. Washington, DC: Carnegie Foundation for International Peace, 2005.

Hardt, Michael, and Antonio Negri. *Empire*. Cambridge: Harvard University Press, 2000.

Hasluck, F. W. *Christianity and Islam Under the Sultans*. Oxford, England: Clarendon Press, 2008. Originally published 1929.

Hatina, Meir. *Guardians of Faith in Modern Times: 'Ulema in the Middle East*. Social, Economic, and Political Studies of the Middle East and Asia. Leiden, Netherlands: Brill, 2008.

Hiro, Dilip. *War without End*. London: Routledge, 2002.

Hirschkind, Charles. "Heresy or Hermeneutics: The Case of Nasr Hamid Abu Zayd." *Stanford Humanities Review* 5, no. 1 (February 26, 1996), *Contested Politics*. http://www.stanford.edu/group/SHR/5-1/text/hirschkind.html.

Hoodbhoy, Pervez Amirali. "Towards Theocracy?" (India) *Frontline*, March 14–27, 2009. http://www.frontlineonnet.com/fl2606/stories/20090327260601600.htm.

Hufnail, Mark, dir. *Inside Islam Today*. DVD, History Channel, 2002.

Hussain, Neelam. "Women as Objects and Women as Subjects within Fundamentalist Discourse." In *Locating the Self: Perspectives on Women and Multiple Identities*, ed. Nighat Said Khan, Rubina Saigol, and Afiya Shehrbano Zia. Lahore: ASR Publications, 1994.

Ibrahim, Mahmood. "Religious Inquisition as Social Policy: The Persecution of the 'Zandiqi' in the Early 'Abbasid Caliphate." *Arab Studies Quarterly* (Spring 1994). http://www.findarticles.com/p/articles/mi_2501/is_nc_v16/ai_16502939/pg_5.

Iqbal, Muhammad. *Reconstruction of Religious Thought in Islam*. Lahore: Institute of Islamic Culture, 1986.

Jain, M. P. *Outline of Indian Legal History.* Bombay: N. M. Tripathi, 1966.

Jakobson, Roman. "Closing Statement: Linguistics and Poetics." In *Style in Language*, ed. T. A. Sebeok. Cambridge, MA: MIT Press, 1960.

Jalal, Ayesha. "The Convenience of Subservience: Women and the State in Pakistan." *Women, Islam, and the State in Pakistan*, ed. Deniz Kandioyoti. Philadelphia: Temple University Press, 1991.

———. *Partisans of Allah: Jihad in South Asia.* Cambridge, MA: Harvard University Press, 2008.

———. *The Sole Spokesman: Jinnah, the Muslim League, and the Demand for Pakistan.* Cambridge, England: Cambridge University Press, 1994.

Jamia Ashrafia. "Jamia Ashrafia Today." Ashrafia Islamic University Lahore, n.d. http://ashrafia.org.pk/jamia_today.html.

Jilani, Hina. "Law as an Instrument of Social Control." In *Locating the Self: Perspectives on Women and Multiple Identities*, ed. Nighat Said Khan, Rubina Saigol, and Afiya Shehrbano Zia. Lahore: ASR, 1994.

Kamali, Muhammad Hashim. *The Dignity of Man: An Islamic Perspective and Freedom of Expression in Islam.* Cambridge, England: Islamic Texts Society, 2002.

Kanhyalal, Hindi. *Tarikh-e Lahore.* Lahore: Majlis-e Tariqi-e Adab, 1977. Originally published 1884.

Khan, Nighat Said. "Reflections on the Question of Islam and Modernity." In *Locating the Self: Perspectives on Women and Multiple Identities*, ed. Nighat Said Khan, Rubina Saigol, and Afiya Shehrbano Zia. Lahore: ASR Publications, 1994.

Khan, Nighat Said, Rubina Saigol, and Afiya Shehrbano Zia, eds. *Locating the Self: Perspectives on Women and Multiple Identities.* Lahore: ASR Publications, 1994.

Khattak, Saba Gul. "A Reinterpretation of the State and Statist Discourse in Pakistan (1977–88)." In *Locating the Self: Perspectives on Women and Multiple Identities*, ed. Nighat Said Khan, Rubina Saigol, and Afiya Shehrbano Zia. Lahore: ASR Publications, 1994.

Khoury, George. "The Advent of Islam and Arab Christians." Catholic Information Network, January 17, 1997. http://www.cin.org/bushra/mag1196/0896khou.html.

King, Michael. *God's Law versus State Law: The Construction of an Islamic Identity in Western Europe.* London: Grey Seal, 1995.

Kirkpatrick, Joanna. "Peaceable Kingdoms, or, The Cosmic Waterhole: A Comparison of Popular Images from the USA, Pakistan, and Thailand." Revised and re-edited 2012 at http://www.artsricksha.com/readings/reading.asp?ID=47. Originally published in *Transports of Delight: The Ricksha Arts of Bangladesh*, Joanna Kirkpatrick. CD-ROM. Bloomington: Indiana University Press, 2003.

Koch, Ebba. *Mughal Art and Imperial Ideology: Collected Essays.* New Delhi: Oxford University Press, 2001.

Kugle, Scott. *Sufis and Saints' Bodies: Mysticism, Corporeality, and Sacred Power in Islam.* Chapel Hill: University of North Carolina Press, 2007.

Lamb, Christina. *The Sewing Circles of Herat: My Afghan Years.* London: HarperCollins, 2002.

———. *Waiting for Allah: Pakistan's Struggle for Democracy.* New York: Viking, 1991.

Liddle, Joanna, and Rama Joshi. *Daughters of Independence.* London: Zed, 1986.

Lorber, Judith. *Gender Inequality: Feminist Theories and Politics.* Los Angeles: Roxbury, 2005.

Madani, Mohammad Asrar. *Verdict of Islamic Law on Blasphemy and Apostasy.* Lahore: Idara-e Islamiat, 1994.

Mahmud, S. F. *A Short History of Islam.* Karachi: Oxford University Press, 1999.

Makhmalbaf. Mohsen, dir. *Kandahar.* DVD. 2001.

Malik, Iftikhar H. *Jihad, Hindutva, and the Taliban: South Asia at the Crossroads.* Karachi: Oxford University Press, 2005.

———. *State and Civil Society in Pakistan: Politics of Authority, Ideology, and Ethnicity.* New York: St. Martin's Press, 1997.

Malik, Jamal. *The Colonization of Islam: Dissolution of Traditional Institutions in Pakistan.* New Delhi: Manohar, 1996.

Marsh, Joss. *Word Crimes: Blasphemy, Culture, and Literature in Nineteenth Century England.* Chicago: University of Chicago Press, 1998.

Mason, Herbert. *Al-Hallaj.* Surrey, England: Curzon Press, 1995.

———. Foreword. *Hallaj: Mystic and Martyr.* Abridged edition of *The Passion of al-Hallaj: Mystic and Martyr of Islam,* by Louis Massignon, ed. and trans. Herbert Mason. Princeton, NJ: Princeton University Press, 1982.

Massignon, Louis. *Hallaj: Mystic and Martyr,* ed. and trans. Herbert Mason. Abridged edition of The *Passion of al-Hallaj: Mystic and Martyr of Islam.* Princeton, NJ: Princeton University Press, 1982.

———. *The Passion of al-Hallaj: Mystic and Martyr of Islam.* 4 vols. Trans. Herbert Mason. Princeton, NJ: Princeton University Press, 1982.

Masud, Muhammad Khalid. *Iqbal's Reconstruction of Ijtihad.* Lahore: Iqbal Academy, 1995.

Maududi, Syed Abul A'la, trans. *The Holy Qur'an.* Arabic and English. Lahore: Islamic Publications, 1981.

———. *A Short History of the Revivalist Movements in Islam.* Trans. Al-Ash'ari. Lahore: Islamic Publications, 1963.

Mehdy, Muzib. *Madrasah Education: An Observation.* Ed. Rokeya Kabir, trans. Nadia Shabnam. Bangladesh Nari Progati Sangha, September 2003. http://bnps.org/wp-content/uploads/2009/03/madrasah-education-an-observation.pdf.

Mernissi, Fatima. *Dreams of Trespass: Tales of a Harem Girlhood.* New York: Perseus Books, 1995.

———. *The Veil and the Male Elite: A Feminist Interpretation of Women's Rights in Islam.* New York: Perseus Books, 1992.

Metcalf, Barbara. *Islamic Revival in British India: Deoband, 1860–1900.* Princeton, NJ: Princeton University Press, 1982.

Minkov, Anton. *Conversion to Islam in the Balkans: Kisve Bahas Petitions and Ottoman Social Life 1670–1730.* Ottoman Empire and Its Heritage. Leiden, Netherlands: Brill Academic, 2004.

Moosa, Ibrahim. "History and Normativity in Traditional Indian Muslim Thought: Reading Shari'a in the Hermeneutics of Qari Muhammad Tayyab (d. 1883)." In *Rethinking Islamic Studies: From Orientalism to Cosmopolitanism,* ed. Carl Ernst and Richard Martin. Columbia: University of South Carolina Press, 2010.

More-Gilbert, Bart. *Postcolonial Theory: Contexts, Practices, Politics.* London: Verso Press, 1997.

Muhammadanism. "The Text of Pakistan's Blasphemy Laws." http://muhammadanism.org/Government/Government_Pakistan_Blasphemy.htm.

Mukto-mona. "Mukto-mona Special News." *Mukto-mona,* January 23, 2004. http://www .mukto-mona.com/news/shaikh_free.htm.

Mulla, Dinshah Fardunji. *Principles of Muhammedan Law.* Lahore: Mansoor Book House, 2007.

Mumtaz, Khawar, and Farida Shaheed, eds. *Women in Pakistan: Two Steps Forward, One Step Back?* London: Zed, 1987.

Musharraf, Pervez. *In the Line of Fire: A Memoir.* New York: Free Press, 2006.

Nasreen, Tasleema. *Lajja.* Kalakata: Ananada, 1993.

Noorani, A. G. "Pakistan's Blasphemy: Exploitation of Religion for Political Ends." (India) *Frontline,* July 28, 2003.

O'Callaghan, Joseph F. *A History of Medieval Spain.* Ithaca, NY: Cornell University Press, 1975.

O'Sullivan, Declan. "On the Anniversary of Ustadh Mahmoud's Execution (January 18, 1985). The Death Sentence for Mahmoud Muhammad Taha: Misuse of the Sudanese Legal System and Islamic *Shari'a* Law?" http://www.alfikra.org/.

Patel, Durab. "Blasphemy Law and Fundamental Rights II." HRCP (Human Rights Commission of Pakistan) Newsletter, *Frontier Post.* In *The Blasphemy Law: From Ordinance to Murder,* ed. Felix Qasir G.M. Amritsari. Karachi: Idara-e Amn-O Insaf, 1994.

———. *Testament of a Liberal.* Karachi: Oxford University Press, 2000.

Patel, Rashida. *Islamization of Laws in Pakistan.* Karachi: Faiza, 1986.

PBS and WNET New York. *Women, War, and Peace.* Five-part television series, October 11–November 8, 2011.

Pontecorvo, Gillo, dir. *The Battle of Algiers.* DVD. Criterion Collection, 2004. Original film 1967.

"Prison Guards Marry and Rape Virgins before Executions." Video. Uploaded to YouTube April 11, 2010, by MDSTVUSA. http://www.youtube.com/watch?v=w7D1hWvRGG8. Text attributed by *Fox News,* July 21, 2009, to *Jerusalem Post.*

Qadri, Shahid Hussain, and Ahsan Sohail Anjam. *Pakistan Penal Code (XLV 1860) with New Islamic Laws, 1979.* Lahore: Mansoor Book House, 2007.

Rahman, Fazlur. *Islam.* Chicago: University of Chicago Press, 2002.

Rahman, Mir Jamilur Rahman. "Mullahs and the Quaid." (Jang Group Online Editions) *International News.* http://www.jang.com.pk/thenews/sep2005-daily/03-09/oped /02.htm, accessed September 16, 2005.

Rahman, Tariq. "Pluralism and Intolerance in Pakistani Society: Attitudes of Pakistani Students towards the Religious 'Other.'" Paper. 2007. http://www.tariqrahman.net /language/Pluralism%20and%20Intolerance%20in%20Pakistani%20Society.htm.

Rashid, Ahmed. *Descent into Chaos: The U.S. and the Disaster in Pakistan, Afghanistan, and Central Asia.* New York: Penguin Books, 2009.

———. *Taliban: Islam, Oil, and the New Great Game in Central Asia.* London: Tauris, 2000.

———. *Taliban: Militant Islam, Oil, and Fundamentalism in Central Asia.* New Haven, CT: Yale University Press, 2001.

Rauf, Maulana Abdul, Abdul Wahedd Qasmi, and Mufti Khalid Mir. First Information Report (FIR): Case of Dr. Younus Shaikh. Islamabad, October 2, 2000. Posted by Rationalist International at http://www.rationalistinternational.net/Shaikh/fir_dr _shaikh.htm.

Reetz, Dietrich. *Islam in the Public Sphere: Religious Groups in India, 1900–1947.* Oxford, England: Oxford University Press, 2006.

Rich, George W., and S. Khan. "Bedford Painting in Pakistan: The Aesthetics and Organization of an Artisan Trade." *Journal of American Folklore* 93 (July–September 1980): 257–295.

Rizvi, Saiyid Athar Abbas. *History of Sufism in India.* 2 vols. New Delhi: Munshiram Manoharlal, 1978, 1983.

———. *Muslim Revivalist Movements in Northern India in the Sixteenth and Seventeenth Centuries.* New Delhi: Munshiram Manoharlal, 1995. Originally published 1965.

———. *Religious and Intellectual History of the Muslims in Akbar's Reign: 1556–1605.* New Delhi: Munshiram Manoharlal, 1975.

Rogerson, Barnaby. *Prophet Muhammad: A Biography.* London: Abacus, 2003.

Roy, Arudhatti. *The God of Small Things.* New York: Harper Perennial, 1997.

Said, Edward W. *Covering Islam: How the Media and the Experts Determine How We Should See the Rest of the World.* New York: Vintage Books, 1997.

———. *Culture and Imperialism.* New York: Knopf, 1993.

Schimmel, Annemarie. *And Muhammad Was His Messenger: The Veneration of the Prophet In Islamic Piety.* Chapel Hill: University of North Carolina Press, 1985.

Segal, Ronald. *Islam's Black Slaves.* New York: Atlantic Books, 2003.

Shah, Saira. *The Storyteller's Daughter: One Woman's Return to Her Lost Homeland.* New York, Anchor Books, 2004.

Shakir, Naeem. "Pakistan: The Blasphemy Law in Pakistan and Its Impact." (Asian Human Rights Commission) *Human Rights Solidarity* 9, no. 7 (July 1999). http://www.hrsolidarity.net/mainfile.php/1999vol09no07/1143/.

Shariati, 'Ali. *Fatima Is Fatima.* Tehran: Shariati Foundation, n.d. Trans. Laleh Bakhtiar, Tahrike Tarsile Quran, 1982. http://www.al-islam.org/fatimaisfatima/.

Shepard, William. *Introducing Islam.* New York: Routledge, 2009.

Siddiqa, Ayesha. "Many Readings of Shari'a." *Dawn,* April 3, 2009.

———. *Military Inc.: Inside Pakistan's Military Economy.* Karachi: Oxford University Press, 2007.

Siddiqui, Osama. Interview, part 1. *Harvard Law School Human Rights Journal,* November 11, 2011. http://harvardhrj.com/2011/11/osama-siddique-interview-part-i/.

Siddiqui, Osama, and Zahra Hayat. "Unholy Laws and Holy Speech: Blasphemy Laws in Pakistan—Controversial Origins, Design Defects, and Free Speech Implications." *Minnesota Journal of International Law* 17, no. 2 (Spring 2008): 303–385.

Sidhwa, Bapsi. *An American Brat.* New Delhi: Penguin Books, 1994.

Sikand, Yoginder. *Bastions of the Believers: Madrassas and Islamic Education in India.* New Delhi: Penguin India, 2005.

Singha, Radhika. *A Despotism of Law: Crime and Justice in Early Colonial India.* Delhi: Oxford University Press, 1998.

Smith, Martin, dir. *Return of the Taliban.* Video. (PBS) *Frontline,* 2005.

Sonn, Tamara. *A Brief History of Islam.* Oxford: Wiley-Blackwell, 2004.

Spellberg, Denis A. *Politics, Gender, and the Islamic Past: The Legacy of 'Aisha bint Abi Bakr.* New York: Columbia University Press, 1994.

Spivak, Gayatri. *A Critique of Postcolonial Reason.* Cambridge: Harvard University Press, 1999.

Stewart, Devin J. "The Ottoman Execution of Zayn al-Din Al-Amili." (Brill) *Dir Welt des Islam* 48 (2008): 289–347.

Stowasser, Barbara Freyer. *Women in the Qur'an, Traditions and Interpretation.* New York: Oxford University Press, 1994.

Sumar, Sabiha, dir. *Dinner with the President: A Nation's Journey.* Documentary film. Vidhi Films, ZDF Arte, 2007.

———, prod. *Khamoosh Pani: Silent Waters.* DVD. 2003.

Syed, Anwar. "Democracy and the Sharia." *Dawn,* May 10, 2009. http://archives.dawn.com/archives/30751.

Talbot, Cynthia. "Inscribing the Other, Inscribing the Self: Hindu-Muslim Identities in Pre-Colonial India." In *India's Islamic Traditions: 711–750,* ed. Richard M. Eaton. New Delhi: Oxford University Press, 2003.

Tareen, SherAli. "The Deoband Madrassa." *Oxford Bibliographies,* n.d. http://www.oxfordbibliographiesonline.com/.

Tarnoff, Curt. "Afghanistan: U.S. Foreign Assistance." U.S. Congressional Research Service, March 5, 2010. http://fpc.state.gov/documents/organization/139236.pdf.

Tayyab, Qari. "'Ulema-yi Deoband ke Dini Rukh aur Maslaki Mizaj." Deoband: India: Shu'ba-yi nashr wa isha't, n.d.

Tusalp, Emine Ekin. "Treating Outlaws and Registering Miscreants in Early Modern Ottoman Society: A Study on the Legal Diagnosis of Deviance in Seyhulislam Fatwas." Master's thesis, Sabanci University, Istanbul, 2005.

Ulfat, Ameena, and G. M. Chaudhry. *Women and Protection of Women's Rights.* Rawalpindi, Pakistan: Federal Law House, 2007.

U.S. Department of State. Office of the Spokesman. Summary of U.S. Assistance in Support of Afghanistan Compact. June 12, 2008. http://www.america.gov/st/texttrans-english/2008/June/20080612144851caifaso.632229.html.

U.S. House of Representatives. *Hearing before the Subcommittee on National Security and Foreign Affairs: Afghanistan and Pakistan, Oversight of U.S. Interagency Efforts.* Statement of Jacquelyn Williams-Bridgers, managing director, international affairs and trade, U.S. Government Accountability Office (GAO). Washington, DC: GAO, September 2000. http://www.gao.gov/new.items/d091015t.pdf.

Vaporis, Nomikos Michael. *Witnesses for Christ: Orthodox Christian Neomartyrs of the Ottoman Period 1437–1860.* New York: St. Vladimir's Seminary Press, 2000.

Verma, Babu Ram. *Muhammedan Law in India and Pakistan.* 4th edition. Allahabad: Law Publishers, 1968.

Warraq, Ibn. *The Origins of the Quran: Classic Essays on Islam's Holy Book.* New York: Prometheus Books, 1998.

Waseem, Shehzad. "Official Counterpoint: Politics of Fatwas." (Pakistan) *Daily Times,* August 6, 2004.

Watt, W. Montgomery. *Muhammad at Medina.* Karachi: Oxford University Press, 2006. Originally published 1956.

Wheatcroft, Andrew. *Infidels: A History of the Conflict between Christendom and Islam.* New York: Random House, 2003.

Wiederhold, Lutz. "Blasphemy against the Prophet Muhammad and His Companions (Sabb al-Rasul, Sabb al-Sahabah): The Introduction of the Topic into Shafi I Legal Literature and Its Relevance for Legal Practice under Mamluk Rule." *Journal of Semitic Studies* 42, no. 1 (Spring 1997): 39–69.

Wolpert, Stanley. *Jinnah of Pakistan*. New Delhi: Oxford University Press, 2005.

Women Living Under Muslim Laws. "Dhaka Court Bans Use of Religion in Politics." *Dawn* (by AFP), January 5, 2010, http://archives.dawn.com/archives/41393. Reprinted in (Shirkat Gah) *Newsheet* 22, no. 1 (March 2010): 1.

———. *Fatwas against Women in Bangladesh*. 1996. http://www.wluml.org/sites/wluml .org/files/import/english/pubs/pdf/misc/fatwa-bangladesh-eng.pdf.

Wright, Lydia. "Beyond the Mosque Walls: Legal Constructions 'Apostasy' and 'Blasphemy' in Egypt's Public Sphere." JSIS honors thesis, American University of Cairo, May 4, 2007. https://digital.lib.washington.edu/dspace/bitstream/handle/1773 /3106/Wright_project.pdf?sequence=1.

Young, Robert J.C. *Postcolonialism: An Historical Introduction*. Oxford: Blackwell, 2001.

Yousafzai, Kushal. "Pakistan: Music Has Died in the Swat Valley." *Freemuse*, April 23, 2009. http://www.freemuse.org/sw33496.asp.

Zaman, Muhammad Qasim. *The 'Ulama in Contemporary Islam: Custodians of Change*. Princeton, NJ: Princeton University Press, 2003.

Zilfi, Madeline. "The Kadizadelis: Discordant Revivalism in Seventeenth-Century Istanbul." *Journal of Near Eastern Studies* 45 (1986): 251–274.

———. *The Politics of Piety: The Ottoman Ulema in the Postclassical Age: 1600–1800*. Minneapolis: Bibliotheca Islamica, 1988.

Author's note: I have used Wikipedia, Google, Babylon Translation, BBC Urdu, Brill's *Encyclopedia of Islam*, and other Internet sources judiciously in this manuscript. Readers are encouraged to check the data for themselves.

INDEX

CPSIA information can be obtained
at www.ICGtesting.com
Printed in the USA
LVOW11s0845041116
511421LV00001B/58/P